"[AN] EVOCATIVE, INFORMATIVE, AND ACCESSIBLE BOOK."

—Publishers Weekly

"Weinstein has unearthed an amazing story of a language that helped to save a people. . . . [It is] full of fascinating characters and life-and-death causes. This story should interest anyone who wants to know how a culture can live in a climate of continuous adversity and still manage to thrive."

—The Cricket (Manchester, MA)

"Weinstein chronicles the history of Yiddish—a vessel brimming with stories, poetry, and music; she traces the twists and turns of its vibrant and remarkable path, which spans a millennium."

—The Jewish Journal

"Buoyed by amusing Yiddish proverbs and jokes, Weinstein provides a somewhat orderly outline to a nonorderly subject. . . . The central figures in Yiddish history play important roles."

—ANDREW DAMPF
Associated Press

"A warm, elegiac, and yet largely unsentimental history."

—Washington Jewish Week

"Recommended . . . Weinstein here makes the story of the Yiddish language accessible to the general reader. . . . Especially effective are biographical sketches of influential individuals such as playwright Sholom Aleichem and the Nobel Prize–winning writer Isaac Bashevis Singer."

—Library Journal

"Interesting and informative . . . Weinstein has written a riveting account of the rise and fall of Yiddish that is both readable and devoid of the jargon of [an] academic history."

—New Jersey Jewish News

YIDDISH

A NATION OF WORDS

Miriam Weinstein

BALLANTINE BOOKS • NEW YORK

A Ballantine Book
Published by The Ballantine Publishing Group

Copyright © 2001 by Miriam Weinstein

All rights reserved under International and Pan-American Copyright
Conventions. Published in the United States by The Ballantine Publishing
Group, a division of Random House, Inc., New York, and distributed in
Canada by Random House of Canada Limited, Toronto. Originally published
in slightly different form by Steerforth Press L.C., in 2001.

Ballantine and colophon are registered trademarks of Random House, Inc.

www.ballantinebooks.com

Library of Congress Control Number: 2002092340

ISBN 9780-345-44730-2

This edition published by arrangement with Steerforth Press L.C.

Cover illustration from the private collection of Gérard Silvain

145066704

For Peter, Eli, and Mirka —
my own personal golden chain.

און ווי דער אוראלטער קערנדל
וואס האט זיך פארוואנדלט אין זאנג-
וועלן די ווערטער אויך נעהרן,
וועלן די ווערטער געהערן
דעם פאלק, אין זײן אייביגן גאנג.

Un vi der uralter kerndel
Vos hot zikh farvandlt in zang —
Veln di verter oykh nern,
Veln di verter gehern
Dem folk, in zayn eybign gang.

And like the ancient kernel
that transformed itself in the stalk —
the words will also nourish,
the words which belong
to the people, on their eternal journey.

Abraham Sutzkever

Contents

Timeline

Cast of Characters

1040–1105   Rashi
1700–1760   Ba'al Shem Tov
1729–86   Moses Mendelssohn
1772–1811   Nakhman of Bratslav
1835–1917   Mendele Moykher Sforim
1851–1915   Yitzak Leib Peretz
1858–1922   Eliezer Ben Yehuda
1859–1916   Sholom Aleichem
1860–1951   Abraham Cahan
1860–1941   Simon Dubnow
1863–1928   Shimon An-ski
1864–1937   Nathan Birnbaum
1865–1943   Chaim Zhitlovski
1880–1943   Esther Frumkin
1893–1943   Israel Joshua Singer
1894–1969   Max Weinreich
1895–1952   Peretz Markish
1900–1944   Emanuel Ringelblum
1904–91   Isaac Bashevis Singer
1913–   Abraham Sutzkever
1955–   Aaron Lansky

A Note on Yiddish Spelling

The careful reader will find that on occasion the same Yiddish word may be spelled in more than one way. Wherever possible, I have transliterated and spelled Yiddish according to the YIVO standard, which is very clear and makes for easy pronunciation. (Just loosen up your throat and go for the guttural in the *kh*.)

When quoting material that was originally translated by others, however, I have retained earlier spelling. Just as we are aware of Shakespeare's spelling being different from our own, or the way we notice that our British contemporaries use "theatre" where we Americans write "theater," the varieties of Yiddish orthography have their own story to tell. I hope that readers will see this as part of the larger tale.

Yiddish Lands

Berlin

Antwerp

GERMANY

Frankfurt
•Worms

Troyes

FRANCE

Dachau
•Munich   Vienna•

Geneva

Limoges

Atlantic
Ocean

Baltic Sea

LITHUA

POLAND

Warsaw
Lodz   Lublin
•Keltz
Auschwitz
Prague   Cracow

CZECH REP.

SLOVAKIA

AUSTRIA   HUNGARY

Mediterranean

⌇⌇ Borders of the Pale of Settlement

0   100 km

0   600 miles

Chazaud

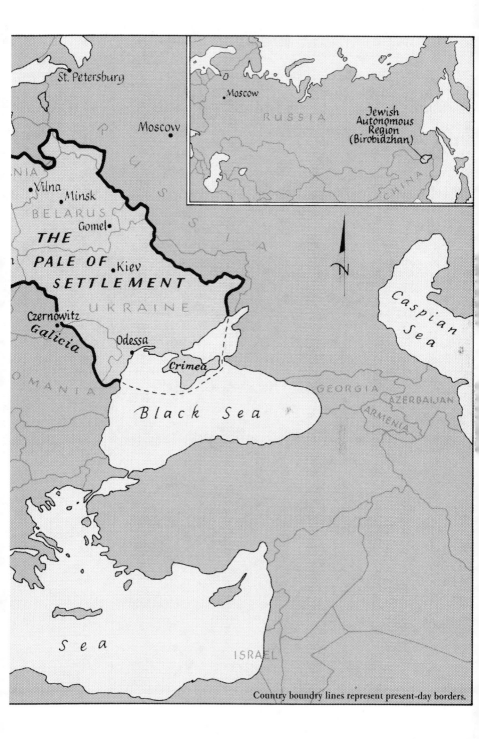

St. Petersburg

Moscow

Vilna

Minsk

BELARUS

Gomel

THE

PALE OF

SETTLEMENT

UKRAINE

Kiev

Czernowitz

Galicia

Odessa

Crimea

Black Sea

ROMANIA

Sea

ISRAEL

GEORGIA

ARMENIA

AZERBAIJAN

Caspian Sea

RUSSIA

Moscow

Jewish Autonomous Region (Birobidzhan)

CHINA

N

Country boundry lines represent present-day borders.

Talking Jewish

יאָ, גאָט, מיר זײַנען דײַן אויסדערוויילט פאָלק, אָבער פֿאַרוואָס האָסטו
אונדז געדאַרפֿט אויסוואַלן?

Yo, got, mir zinen dayn oysdervaylt folk, ober farvos
hostu undz gedarft oysvaln?

Yes, God, we are your chosen people. But why did you have
to choose us?

My parents loved to travel. They were not rich people, but in the
years after World War II they would leave our Bronx apartment and head off on vacations, first to Europe, and then little by
little to almost every continent. They visited big famous cities and
dusty crossroads towns. Often, they would return telling a variant
of a familiar tale: "There we were, in this little shop in . . ." (fill in
the blank: Dublin, Johannesburg, Tashkent). "I don't know; somehow I got the idea." (From what? A tilt of the head? A look in the
eyes?) "So I says to him, *'Vus makhst?'*" (what's doing). "And this
guy who, two minutes before, wouldn't give us the time of day
becomes all of a sudden our buddy, our friend. He invites us home,
shows us around the whole neighborhood, a regular *landsman*" (fellow countryman).

For a thousand years, this was the standard Jewish story. Yiddish
was the secret handshake, the golden key. It was the language that
defined a world and a people. *Yiddish* means "Jewish." Its words
were, simply, the sound of Jewish life.

Babies were born into rooms full of women crooning in Yiddish; corpses were washed and prepared to the sounds of Yiddish grief. For a people without a country, without a government, without protection of any dependable kind, language became a powerful glue. It connected European Jews to each other even as it separated them from their neighbors — people among whom they may have lived for hundreds of years. It also linked them to their past through their sacred language, Hebrew.

Because it was so easy for words and phrases from the Hebrew prayers they recited every day to slip into their ordinary Yiddish speech, their place in "Jewish time" was confirmed, from the beginning of the world until the coming of the Messiah and the End of Days. It allowed them to live outside Christian or secular history and keep their vision of peoplehood alive. In the meantime, when they wandered in the real, here-and-now world, it was their passport and amulet. It was their strength.

The tale my parents told on a dozen returns is hardly heard anymore. These days, unless your travels are circumscribed — retirement homes, Holocaust museums, Hasidic enclaves of Brooklyn or Jerusalem — you will not hear Yiddish in the shop or the street, the synagogue or the house. That is not to say that a few words of it aren't sprinkled through English, like raisins in rugelach. Politicians have chutzpah, TV personalities kibbitz, Americans of all ethnic backgrounds have learned to slap their hands on their hips and demand, singsong, "So what does that make me, chopped liver?" But as a living language, Yiddish barely qualifies. It is a speech system that is faltering, even on life support. (With one big exception: the ultra-Orthodox. Their astounding fecundity, history's latest surprise, may change the epilogue but does not alter the bulk of the tale.)

So how did it happen? How did a language that cursed and crooned for a thousand years fade in the course of one little lifetime? What could have happened to its self-contained world? (*Better a Jew without a beard than a beard without a Jew* would be the appropriate Yiddish proverb here.) And why was the tongue itself perhaps *einstik*, unique, in the history of languages? (Yes, I know that is an enormous claim.)

When my parents were born, in the early years of the twentieth century, something like eight million souls called Yiddish *mame loshn*, mother tongue. Their world was bursting with Yiddish schools offering competing political philosophies, newspapers on every side of every burning issue, plays that ranged from melodramas like Isaac Zolatorevsky's *Money, Love, and Shame* to significant dramatic works like Jacob Gordin's *Jewish King Lear* or Sholem Asch's *God of Vengeance*. It had journals of every stripe, thousands of book titles in print. Radio broadcasting and an international film industry developed as technologies grew.

By the time my parents died three-quarters of a century later, Yiddish books were being thrown out wholesale in trash cans and Dumpsters. New York's great newspaper the *Forverts (Daily Forward)*, which had outlived competitor after competitor, was reduced to a weekly written by people who, in more commodious times, would never have been caught dead sharing the same page. Not only did my parents' grandchildren not know the Yiddish language, but even the Hebrew they learned in Hebrew school had been systematically cleansed of the Yiddish pronunciation that had been ubiquitous in my parents' youth, and in mine.

But the object of this book is not breast-beating for the good old days of yore, when there was singing every *shabes*, Sabbath, chicken soup in every pot. The object, as any self-respecting *yid*, Jew, would know, is to strengthen the golden chain of continuity.

To that end, I have written history-as-story, filling the tale with flesh-and-blood people with obsessive humor, visionary courage, brilliant desperate causes, and glorious flaws. As will immediately be obvious, I am a journalist, not a historian, linguist, or any kind of scholar. I did my research — meeting mavens, experts; working my way through lights-on-timers library stacks — as a *yederer*, an everyman.

What I soon learned was that no language has been so adored, so despised, so ostentatiously ignored. Aaron Lansky, the book rescuer who invented the midnight Dumpster run, estimates that out of thirty-five thousand different Yiddish titles that have been published, only 0.5 percent have been translated into English. We won't even go into the number of folk tunes, music hall ditties, and poignant poems of labor or love that are known only to the Yiddish-speaking few.

So this is a story that begs to be told. The last book that chronicled the Yiddish language was a four-volume history written in Yiddish during and after World War II by the brilliant scholar Max Weinreich. Two volumes have been translated into English. They are heavy going. In the 1960s and 1970s Leo Rosten wrote marvelously funny books describing the way that Yiddish was used at the time, but they assumed some Yiddish or Jewish background or inclination.

This book requires nothing more than an open heart and a curious mind. Well, maybe also a certain flexibility with regard to spelling. Standardized Yiddish orthography was not even invented until 1936 and has been adopted, grudgingly, only in the last several years. Then there is the matter of standardized transliteration. (If you don't know what that means, don't worry, you'll learn.) Although I have tried to use it where possible, I have sometimes substituted more familiar versions, like the common rendition of Chanukah instead of the more correct *khanike*. I have tried to strike a middle ground between foreignness and flavor. Readers will learn how, for a language that has been roundly maligned and famously praised, even spelling proclaims a writer's political, religious, and cultural stance.

For me, this tale qualifies as a miracle. A language is born in shadow with the lowliest of aims — only for women, only for the untutored, only for ordinary, workaday use. Yet that very dailiness and lack of expectation allow it to grow. It expands, sweet and light as a New Year's honey cake, pulses with life for a thousand years. It links its people to their illustrious past. It has the world's best sense of humor, unable to resist the virtuoso joke even in the curse. *(May you turn into a blintz, and may your enemy turn into a cat, and may he eat you up and choke on you, so we can be rid of you both.)* It gets discovered by a generation of intellectuals and politicos. Time and again the highbrow thinks he will just use Yiddish to lure the uneducated masses to listen to him expound his brilliant ideas. And time and again it is he who does the listening and learning, in thrall to the language and to its folk.

Then, just when this poor no-account tongue goes into creative overdrive, winning a crumb of respect and even hope for a bit of glory, it all disappears. Holocaust, assimilation, executions, displacement, language police, and then, incredibly, stone silence. One brief moment of flame, *a pintele yid,* a spark of Jewishness, burns and then sputters. A few thousand folk songs, a few hundred ways of parsing the fine points of human behavior — *shnuk, shlemiel, shlimazl* — and those thirty-five thousand different books.

But even in dying, this most practical of tongues has a job to do: It allows Hebrew, the ancient, holy, pre-Yiddish tongue, to be reborn. Yiddish gives up its life for its parent/child. What could be more Jewish-motherish, more *hartsik,* caring, than that?

One staple Yiddish Hasidic tale concerns a poor bedraggled beggar who shows up in the snow of a cold Russian night while the family celebrates Chanukah warm and safe within. As the story unfolds, after the mendicant has come and gone, this *shnorer* turns out to have been, perhaps — it is never entirely clear — the Prophet Elijah, herald of *Moshiach,* the Messiah. Whatever he is, this ragged pauper, whether tattered or divine, has managed to bring at least the idea of the Beyond to this relentlessly commonplace earth.

The moral? Don't be so fast to dismiss the lowly. You never know who or what they truly are.

PART I

Birth and Growth

CHAPTER I

Long as the Jewish Exile

─────────

א איד האט ליב דעם געשמאק פון א אידיש ווארט אין זײַן מויל.

A yid hot lib dem geshmak fun a yidish vort in zayn moyl.

A Jew likes the taste of a Yiddish word in his mouth.

─────────

At the beginning of the High Holy Days that mark the Jewish New Year, Yiddish speakers often eat carrots. They eat them raw, they eat them cooked with other vegetables in sweet hearty stews. *Farvus,* you ask; why? Ah, let me tell you. They eat them because of their love not of vegetables but of puns. The Yiddish word *mern* has two meanings. As a noun it means "carrots." As a verb, it has a very different definition: "multiply." The carrots convey the hope for more years to come, making *mern* a two-fer; the tastiest kind of Yiddish word.

After Rosh Hashonah and its carrots, the Days of Awe unfold, a week of contrition and introspection. As these solemn days approach their finale, a bowl of cabbage soup often appears on the table. All right; cabbage. Lowly, penitential, no?

You should be so lucky, an explanation that plain. The Yiddish dish comes from the phrase that passed directly from German into Yiddish, *kohl mit vaser,* cabbage with water, the unadorned fact of cabbage soup. Much tastier, however, is the play on the Hebrew phrase *kol mevaser,* a voice proclaiming. It is a phrase that the carrot-eating soup slurpers will be hearing as part of the service that puts the final seal on that solemn time. Here is the classic Yiddish take on life: the voice of God translated into soup, soup transmogrified into the voice of God — and all in the form of offhanded punning culinary theology, learned around the supper table at home.

Thanks to their linguistic life story, Yiddish speakers have a full bag of multilingual tricks. A generation of Americans reared on tales of cowboys and Indians amused themselves by spinning elaborate jokes about Jeronowitz, Pocayenta, and their daughter Minnie Horowitz. Today, this same agile wordplay is skipping around the Internet: Recent Yiddish joke offerings included *goyfer,* a gentile messenger, and *blintzkreig,* a late-night refrigerator raid.

Yiddish began with the same impudent spirit, a hardy weed thrusting up between the cobblestones of the walled cities of medieval Europe. In our story, we will watch the scruffy language grow and branch out and blossom and bear fruit. Time and again we will see the heels of assault crush it down. And time and again we will watch it rise up, altered slightly but still itself, growing skyward once more. ("I rise once again and stride on" is the refrain of a Yiddish poem that, it should come as no surprise, became a popular song.)

We will use the language as a way to mark the meandering path of Jewish history. Then it will be time for a rest, maybe *a glezele tey, a shtikl broit, a shnapps* — a little glass of tea, a piece of bread, a drink of whiskey — in the shtetl, that archetypal Jewish town. We will track the language through the industrial and intellectual revolutions that swept Yiddish into the modern world. The language will blossom as its people, freed from the shackles of the past, stripped of the comforts of tradition, search for a future. Then we're going to talk some geopolitical specifics — what happened in Eastern Europe, Russia, Israel, and the United States. The Holocaust will shut the curtain on much of the world we have come to know. We will pause to mourn and to pay our respects. Then, like the Yiddish language and the people who speak it, we will gather our strength and our memories, pick ourselves up, and stride on.

Yiddish will teach us about the resilience of the self and the construction of boundaries against "otherness." It will show the deep satisfactions that come from community. We will learn how to make something from nothing, staring grim reality down the nose, one of the most popular subjects of Yiddish proverbs: *With weeping you pay no debts. Neither with cursing nor with laughter can one remake the world.* And one must always, in some way large or small, remake the world.

To understand how Yiddish arrived at its apparently weightless way of carrying such a heavy load is simple: We just have to start at the beginning of the world.

Jews measure time by cycles of exile and ingathering. They note episodes of destruction and, when they are lucky, rebirth. Mostly, though, it's been wandering. In the distant, sunny biblical past, Jews dwelt in their God-given land of milk and honey, Eretz Israel, the land of Israel. It was the home of the prophets, the Matriarchs, and the Patriarchs, anchored by the Holy of Holies, the Temple, in Jerusalem. The Jews who lived and worshiped there spoke Hebrew, the same language in which, according to rabbinic lore, God spoke to the angels before He created the world. For traditional Jews the language is that ageless, that intertwined with the Jewish soul.

If you like numbers, you will want to know that scholars locate the beginnings of Hebrew somewhere in the middle of the second millennium before the Christian, or common, era. The name Hebrew is the English version of the biblical *ivriim,* Hebrews. Referring to Abraham and his family or, as he is called in Yiddish, *Avrom aveynu,* Abraham our ancestor, it means "the people who crossed over." They were wanderers even then. It is not clear whether Abraham actually spoke Hebrew, but we know that Moses did, some four hundred years later on. The parting of the Red Sea, the giving of the Law at Sinai, the wandering in the desert — these core events of the Jewish ethos, to whatever extent they really took place, took place through real Hebrew words.

In the infancy of the common era a related language, Aramaic, gradually supplanted Hebrew in daily speech as well as in some

religious texts, such as the late-written Book of Daniel. We know
that the two languages lived together for several centuries because,
for example, of the practice of reciting certain prayers three times.
This comes from a period when they were read twice in Hebrew,
for tradition, and once in Aramaic, to make certain that everyone in
the congregation actually understood them. Even then, there were
a few whose Hebrew comprehension might have been a tad under
par. For the purposes of this story we will say "Hebrew" and mean
"Hebrew/Aramaic," giving ourselves the benefit of pretending that
history is simple. *If everyone pulled in one direction, the world would
keel over.*

Hebrew is written in an alphabet all its own, although many of its
letters make sounds that correspond to utterances in English. There
are letters for sounds we would recognize as *b,* for example, as well
as *t, m,* and *n.* But it is harder for non–Hebrew readers to pick out
the familiar sounds because, unlike European languages, Hebrew is
written from right to left. It does not distinguish between upper and
lower cases, and several letters take special forms when they appear
at the end of a word. Hebrew also has a different way of noting vowels: They are expressed as a system of dots and slashes that hover
around their consonants, moons to their suns. Many books, including the Bible, are written without any vowels at all.

This is how you would write this sentence in vowel-less Hebrew:

.rbh sl-lv n cntns sht trw dlw y h s sht

Even if two people speak the same language, if they write it differently the language is perceived in a slightly different way. If we
are literate, even as we speak words we have some mental sense of
the way they are written. The fact that Jews have written a great
variety of Jewish languages using the very same letters across continents and millennia is tremendously important. For Jews, the letters are in a sense alive. They have numerical equivalents suffused
with mystic significance. In Yiddish-speaking Europe, small boys

on their first day of *cheder,* school, would find the letters spelled out in honey, to let them know that learning was sweet. These delicious letters led the way back and forth, across oceans of exile, linking each child with that distant, golden land. *We Jews have many sicknesses, but amnesia is not one of them.*

When Jews recall their history, much of it is tragic. In ancient Israel, the Temple was destroyed twice. In Yiddish these cataclysms are referred to as *der ershter* and *der tsveyter khurbns,* the first and second destructions. The First Temple was destroyed in the sixth century B.C.E., before the common era, and signaled the beginning of the Babylonian Exile. The Temple was rebuilt, but this Second Temple was destroyed by the Romans in 70 C.E., after which the long exile began. Although Jews today commonly use the Greek word *diaspora* for "dispersion," the Yiddish term is *golus.* Of all the hundreds of thousands of words in the language, this one has gotten more than its share of use.

The stage for all this wandering was set in Hebrew. As Jews saw their Temple in ruins they cried in Hebrew, mourned in Hebrew, rent their biblical robes with Hebrew moans. The most primitive impulse of language, whether of a person or of a people, is often suffused with emotion. The baby's unmediated sound only little by little gets formed into words. For tiny individuals or mighty nations, language lets us know who we are. Hebrew was the first language in which people consciously defined themselves as Jews.

After these Jews had finished covering themselves in *efer,* Hebrew for "ashes," these cast-out Jews, without homes but with a clear sense of community, picked themselves up and moved on. They traveled on foot — entire families and clans. Often they ignored irony and seized oppportunity, making their living as traders in the wake of those same Roman armies that had destroyed the epicenter of their ritual cult and evicted them from their ancestral home. ("Choose life" is one of the all-time popular biblical quotes.) And so, in time, many Jews found themselves on the other side of the Mediterranean, in Southern Europe.

As the Jews walked farther and farther from Jerusalem, their holy city, the one thing they always carried with them was words. Words are infinitely light and can be fashioned into stories, songs, and prayers. Because Jews venerated them so, they wrote them in perfect Hebrew, without mistake. They rolled the heavy parchment into scrolls and carried these "books" of the Torah, the Jewish Bible, along with them. Even today, in synagogue services, as the scrolls make their way on a symbolic march around the congregation, people eagerly touch their prayerbooks to the Torah, then kiss the corners of their books. For a people without a homeland, without a centralized clergy, without any universally recognized authority on this earth, the words were all there were. *A Jewish thief steals only books.*

In time, the wandering Jews settled down. They put down their Torahs and their books, set up *yeshivas,* religious schools. They waited for the Messiah to come, praying, "Bring us safely from the corners of the earth, and lead us in dignity to our holy land." Every day they recited their Hebrew prayers, studied their Hebrew texts, spoke to each other in the Hebrew they remembered from the old land.

They also developed businesses, raised families, made homes. And because the territories they lived in were owned and ruled by Christians, they learned Christian languages. They had to. *Live among Jews, do business with goyim.* Sometimes Jews were forced to live in Jewish-only ghettos. More often they lived together by choice. Either way, Jews lived apart from their Christian neighbors. In addition to the obvious — separate religions — they had different holidays, different communal organizations, different social structures, different mother tongues. The Yiddish expression *di yidishe gas,* the Jewish street, doesn't refer just to the place where Jews work and dwell. It has a sense of comfort, of home.

On that street, language constantly shifted and grew. As Jews encountered new objects and ideas, they needed new names. Similarly, Jews might take a verb they had learned in one nation and conjugate it according to the rules of another. A noun they remembered from Hebrew might get spoken with a new accent or acquire a new way of becoming plural. Rules of this, dabs of that; syntax, vocabulary, and structure simmered in a new Jewish stew. Medieval Christians did not speak static languages either. When the Roman Empire with its official Latin disintegrated, hamlets and towns folded in on themselves. Dialects, accents, and vocabulary shifted dramatically by region. City boundaries, deep rivers, high mountains, all served to set one community's speech apart from another. Only centuries later would these narrow-band dialects coalesce into national tongues.

European Jews learned all the languages of their neighbors. They had to, if they wanted to make a living. Generally forbidden from owning land, severely limited in trades and professions, Jews became craftspeople, merchants, and traders.

They also became linguists. Jews created their own versions of more than a dozen European languages. They spoke Judeo-Greek, Judeo-Italian, Judeo-French, and the most widely used, Ladino, the Jewish language of the Iberian peninsula. They wrote all of these languages in the Hebrew alphabet, right to left.

While they were speaking these new tongues day to day, Jews continued to recite their Hebrew prayers. They also pursued their unique goal of having every man a scholar. Throughout what Christians call the Dark Ages, roughly from 500 to 1100, when reading and writing in the Christian world were reduced to the province of a few monks living in isolation, almost all Jewish men knew how to read — at the minimum the daily, Sabbath, and festival prayers. They could probably sound out a bit of rabbinic commentary as well.

So medieval Jews were almost always literate and at least bilingual: familiar with Hebrew and with a European tongue. They were also watchful, living with their bags packed. Because their Christian protectors could abruptly change their minds and cast them out, Jewish occupations were often portable. Jews lent money, and they traded in lightweight luxury goods — spices, silks, jewels, and fur. Fellow Jews provided ready-made trading contacts all through Europe and back toward the Middle East. They understood their far-flung cousins' precarious position in the world.

Throughout this time, anti-Jewish massacres broke out with the senseless repetitiveness of thunderstorms or earthquakes. When the Crusades raised much of Europe to a fever pitch in the defense of Christianity in 1096 and 1146, Jews were an obvious target for mob violence. But here is the striking thing: Although they were continually at risk, Jews felt secure in their peoplehood, creating a country of the mind through their books and their prayers.

As the years of dispersion stretched on into centuries, little by little Hebrew lost the elasticity of daily speech. Although it was still used for prayer, commentary, and legal contracts, as well as for an extremely basic form of communication (when in doubt, Jews could always trade biblical quotations to get their meaning across), the old language ceased to be anybody's first, native tongue.

It was after almost a millennium of exile, in the ninth century, that a population shift set the stage for a change in speech that marks the real beginning of our tale. Jews from what are now France and Italy began moving into a region of what is now western Germany, in the land bordering two rivers, the Rhine and the Main. These two groups of Jews spoke early Romance languages — one a medieval form of French, the other a medieval form of Italian. And, like Jews everywhere, they also (at least haltingly) read and spoke some Hebrew.

In the Germanic lands these new arrivals met not only each other but also the local Jews, who spoke a Jewish version of medieval German. And because conditions were relatively safe and stable over the course of several centuries, Jews from three different parts of Europe lived together in the German cities and towns. They did what people do all over the world. They raised children, earned their living, tried to make sense of their place in the world. Sometimes the things they saw or did or thought were new to them, so they labeled them with new words. These words came from the various languages the Jews had on the tips of their tongues. Sometimes they came out in new combinations, one sound from here bumping up against part of a meaning from there. Like *purim-shpil.*

The Jewish holiday of Purim celebrates the time, in ancient Persia, when the Jewish beauty Queen Esther helped her people to escape a death sentence at the hands of a wicked minister. Jews have come to celebrate this holiday with raucous good spirits. As they read the *megile,* the chronicle of the events, they are encouraged to drink so much that they cannot distinguish the name of the hero, Mordecai, from that of the villain, Haman. And since at least the fourteenth century, Jews have mounted elaborate, costumed plays, often using hyperbole, turning reality on its head, called *purim-shpiln.* The word comes from the Hebrew plural noun *purim,* meaning "lots," referring to the lots that were cast in ancient Persia to determine the fate of the Jews, and *spiel,* the German word for "recite" or "tell." The *-n* plural ending is typically Yiddish.

The components of the word once had separate, translatable meanings, but now they had melded into a Yiddish-only phenomenon. A new word had been born. Multiply that by thousands, and you have a new tongue. Hundreds of years later, only a Yiddish speaker would recognize a word like *purim-shpil.* Only someone immersed in the language would know that to call something a *purim-shpil* is to label it as being patently ridiculous. This is how languages work — layers of meaning accreting, giving rich meaning to human sounds.

We are lucky to have a real human being who can help lead us back to the first truly Yiddish sounds. Solomon ben Isaac, an eleventh-century wine merchant, led the kind of double life we often find among Jews. He lived in Troyes, in what is today northeastern France, quite near the German territories where Yiddish was forming. Ben Isaac spoke a Jewish version of Old French that scholars call Loez, from the Hebrew term for "foreign." But Ben Isaac was also known as the great commentator Rashi, from his Hebrew name, Rabbi Shlomo Itzhaki. As a scholar, he studied and commented on sacred Hebrew-language texts that were already hundreds of years old. This system of annotating, explaining, and adding to the ancient wisdom was one more way Jews maintained timeless, spaceless continuity and kept the "real," historical world at bay. Rashi, a leading guide to the great sea of Talmud, biblical commentary, is still routinely cited today.

Our interest in Rashi here is not because he was a humanistic sage who founded an important yeshiva and, with his thousands of glosses or explications, reinvigorated Torah. We are more concerned with what might be called his margin notes or jottings, because they are some of our first written hints about Yiddish.

Although Jews were only grudgingly given a place in medieval Christendom, within their own society great things were expected of them. By being able to read and recite prayers and follow the weekly Torah portion, all men, in some minimal way, assumed a place in the great transhistorical discourse. If they did not exactly write commentary, at least they knew that texts were being pondered and parsed by sages.

Theoretically, these texts were available to every Jewish man. It was Rashi's great genius to actually make difficult passages accessible. In a world where learning was a key to continuity, this was vitally important.

These texts themselves were critical. They described an intricate system of laws that regulated the minutiae of everyday behavior. They had to be understood in great detail. So Rashi sometimes used colloquial language — words that people of his time actually spoke. Commenting on a section of text that used the Hebrew concept of *kavod,* honor, he went into detail about what kind of clothing was honorable. In his description of appropriate attire, he used a word that a German or English speaker of today could recognize — *kniehoysen,* knee stockings. Another type of clothing was made from felt, or *feltrosh,* a word that was used by French speakers of his time. Rashi wrote these words, *kniehoysen* and *feltrosh,* in Hebrew letters.

These words tell us more than just their meanings. They let us know that, by the end of the first millennium of the common era,

Jews had formed a new amalgam, something quite different from both the Christian languages they heard around them and the Jewish version of any one of those tongues. Beginning somewhere between 900 and 1100 we are no longer talking, say, a Jewish dialect of Old French or Old Provençal. We are talking something new. We are talking Yiddish.

Of course, our understanding of these Yiddish beginnings is the stuff of scholarly sleuthing and leaps of faith. It's not as if someone sets out to construct a language from scratch and then, for the benefit of folks who may show up in a thousand years, leaves copious notes. Writing was vastly less common in the Middle Ages than it is today, and precious little of it has survived. All we have are scraps that scholars have found in a small number of letters and handwritten books. These are often tiny clues — scribblings in margins, groupings of words that are different from groupings that have shown up before. The number of written records of casual, informal daily speech that remain from the Middle Ages is, as you can imagine, minuscule. And even though we have some records of the words people wrote, we have no idea how they sounded. We know what language Rashi spoke only because he was, after all, the great Rashi. In the time before the printing press, few people left a written trail.

Let's take another example of how sounds and meanings shift and a new language is born. Yiddish-speakers have two ways to describe books. *Sefer* comes from Hebrew. At a time when books were limited to religious and moral documents, this word was sufficient to describe all books. But, during the Middle Ages, when a secular literature evolved, Jews distinguished these new books by calling them by a new name, *bikher,* a word that comes from German.

In such small ways, over the course of several hundred years, the Yiddish language grew. This early Yiddish included Hebrew words that moved into everyday speech, like *chaver,* friend, and *shabes,* Sabbath. It also had a sprinkling of words from the Romance languages the Jews had picked up across Europe. The Yiddish word *yenta,* a woman's name that has come to mean "busybody," is thought to come from the early French word *gentile,* gentle. But the great majority of its vocabulary and structure was Germanic (even today Germanic words account for three-quarters of Yiddish vocabulary). That close link between Yiddish and German would reverberate through the centuries. Jews who lived in the German lands took their informal name from the Hebrew word for Germany, *Ashkenaz.* The descendants of these early language makers are still called Ashkenazi Jews today.

The first sentence that scholars recognize as Yiddish comes from a book in the German city of Worms. It is a marginal jotting in a *mahzor,* or festival prayerbook. It is even dated, 1272. Someone, presumably the book's owner, a man who would have worn the special yellow badge or conical hat that medieval Christian law prescribed for Jews, wrote next to one of the Hebrew prayers, *Gut Tag, eem Btaga, S'vayr dis Mahzor in Bes Keneses traga.* A good day will happen to the person who brings this *mahzor* to the synagogue. And that is it — an almost-too-good first example of Yiddish. Written in Hebrew letters, next to a Hebrew prayer, this little note is directed to someone who recited the book's Hebrew benedictions but did not speak Hebrew day to day. In words that reflect their Germanic surroundings, the sentence reaches out to the next *mahzor* owner or at least *mahzor* carrier. Positive, upbeat, practical, deeply rooted in Jewish history. That's Yiddish.

By the time Jews were aware that they had created a new language, they were calling it *judenteutsh,* Jewish German; *ivri-teutsh,* Hebrew German; *loshn ashkenaz,* the language of Ashkenaz; or *zhargon,* the jargon. We can visualize how the language grew by looking at a word that is today pronounced "chunt," but that retains an earlier spelling, *cholent,* an infinitely variable and remarkably widespread dish based on beans that Jews make for *shabes* even today. (The nineteenth-century German poet Heine called it "the heavenly food that our dear Lord God himself once taught Moses to cook on Mount Sinai.") Because work was forbidden on *shabes,* Jews were not allowed to make fires. So housewives would leave the pot in a slow oven where the ingredients — a bit of meat, a mixture of grains, as well as the beans — melded over time. *Cholent* is said to have come from the Latin *calere,* to heat, which later turned into the French word *chaud,* warm. (The English word *chowder* is said to come from the same French root, although it followed a different culinary branch.)

So Yiddish simmered slowly, like *cholent.* Some Hebrew spellings changed. Vowels were added, making the spelling more phonetic. Other languages, English included, have also been formed by the accreting and shifting of source words over time. But Yiddish speakers tend to be aware of the components that shaped their language and can sometimes skew their speech in the direction of one or another of the tongues in its blend. This self-conscious language is full of sayings about itself: *Hebrew one learns; Yiddish comes naturally.*

For centuries after their new language began, Jews continued to live in the German lands. They sometimes called the language that they spoke Jewish, or, in its own language, *Yidish.* (The first recorded use of this term comes from 1597.) The word itself is related to *judisch,* the German word for "Jewish." Just as, for a German speaker, a Jew is *ein Jude,* Yiddish speakers refer to a Jew as a *yid.* Yiddish speakers will often say *yid* or *goy* instead of "man," thus clarifying whether the subject is Jewish or not.

Calling their language Jewish made sense. It was both a prism and a skin, a way to see out and a way to stay in. In a world of earthly wandering, "Jewish" was a people's linguistic home.

At the same time, Yiddish also helped its speakers "understand" Hebrew. By letting words and phrases slip from the prayers of the older language into the younger, it kept the sacred tongue available to people who did not speak it every day. Truth be told, although all Jewish men have long been expected to be literate in Hebrew, this has not always been possible. Still, "importing" blocks of Hebrew phrases or proverbs kept the language, if not alive, then at least accessible, a ready source of quotations, examples, and turns of phrase. Yiddish is acutely aware of human limitations. *If you sit in a hot bath, you think the whole town is warm.*

By the thirteenth century Yiddish had become widespread among Western European Jews. It had made such inroads in replacing Hebrew and the local Christian languages that writers began to translate parts of the Bible into Yiddish. But because of the great respect that Jews had for their ancient language, whose texts they continued to study, the newer, more workaday tongue was held in low regard. When books began to be written in Yiddish, they almost always started with disclaimers. These books were for women, the authors said. They were for the uneducated. This prejudice was to dog Yiddish throughout its long life. In a culture that valued learning, no one wanted to admit to ignorance.

But this younger-sibling quality had benefits as well. It allowed Yiddish to maintain a particularly female association. Although Jewish women were not generally educated in Hebrew, they did have some Hebrew prayers of their own; lighting the candles that ushered in the Sabbath was their responsibility and joy. They performed rituals at times of menstruation, pregnancy, birth, illness, and death. Each significant act, from discarding a no-longer-kosher pot to keeping the angel of death from an ailing child, had its requisite Hebrew mantra or prayer.

But Yiddish became truly theirs. One of the few women to emerge from the anonymous Middle Ages is known as Dulcie of Worms. She was remembered by a contemporary rabbi because of her outstanding talents. She lived in the late twelfth and early thirteenth centuries with her husband and two children in the same city and at about the same time as the *mahzor* owner. She belonged to a special group of educated women called *firzogerins,* reciters. In the women's section of the synagogue, these women translated the Hebrew prayers, often explaining or embellishing as they went.

The best of them helped women create their own prayers, which focused on family and community, and which were in Yiddish. Where traditional Hebrew prayers focused on the Patriarchs — Abraham, Isaac, and Jacob — the women addressed themselves to the Matriarchs — Sarah, Rachel, Rebecca, and Leah. Dulcie, who was murdered by Crusaders in 1213 and was publicly mourned as a martyr, was remembered as "a singer of hymns and prayers, a speaker of supplications." She was a translator and creator.

Translation is rarely a simple matter; our words shape who we are. Language is not just a passive reflection of how we think; it forms and focuses thought. Once we label something, we perceive it differently from the way we experience an unnamed event. A person can be aware of something vague, but feelings are sharpened when that miasma gets a name: Homesickness. Chicken pox. Anticipation. Love. It is commonly said that the Jews don't keep Sabbath; Sabbath keeps the Jews. Likewise, European Jews didn't just invent Yiddish; Yiddish helped them invent themselves.

Medieval women began to create Yiddish prayers called *tekhines,* which were more personal than men's. Here Sarah Bat Tovim, who lived somewhat later, in the early seventeenth century, in what is now Ukraine, asks for God's help: "God should have great compassion for me and for all Israel. I should not be homeless for long. . . . The fact that I am homeless should be a sacrifice for my sins. God Almighty, blessed be He, should forgive me for talking in the synagogue during services in my youth." Some things never change.

One Yiddish book of Bible commentary and tales was so popular it has been in print continually since the early seventeenth century — more than 350 editions. The *Tsenerene,* named for its opening line, "Go out and see," is still used by the ultra-Orthodox today. If a Yiddish speaker wants to describe a rare occurrence, he can say, *"Vi a yidene on a tsenerene,"* like a Jewish woman without a *Tsenerene.*

With the invention of the printing press, Yiddish even got its own typeface, called *vaybertaytsh,* women's interpretation. Slightly different from the font typically used for Hebrew, it made it easy to distinguish the languages in books that contained both. (Sometimes Hebrew and Yiddish texts were printed side by side.)

Still, we must not think that Yiddish was only a women's language. All Jews spoke it every day. *Shpielmener,* literally "talking men," the Jewish equivalents of medieval troubadors, regaled audiences at fairs with Yiddish versions of tales that were similar to the French romances and the Arthurian quests. One series that was written down was called the *Buovo bukh* because of its wonder hero, Buovo. In time his name was confused with the Yiddish word for "grandmother," *bube.* Even now, any outrageous tale is called a *bube meyse,* a grandmother's tale.

Along with the Yiddish books that survived, an accident of history preserved a sack of poignantly undelivered Yiddish letters that had been sent from Prague to Vienna in 1619, in the middle of the Thirty Years War. Sarel Gutman wrote her husband in a letter he never received, "I have been ever grieved because I have not heard a word from you for seven weeks, where you are in the world, especially in such a situation as that which we have now. May the Lord, be He praised, turn everything to good soon."

A woman named Henele wrote, "My lovely dear sister and brother, I have been told that the duke of Bavaria has captured Nordlingen. I should like to know whether this is true. I had no letters from our sister Gutle, may she live. I should like to hear and see much good for good, therefore write me often, please, so that each may at least know of the other's health, particularly in these days when sinful man has so much trouble again."

Yiddish speakers would see many more days in which sinful man made no end of trouble. But their language would become one of their comforts and strengths. In time, they would weave it into one of the most beloved cultures of the world.

CHAPTER 2

Poland: Rest Here

פאלשע פרידן איז בעסער ווי א ריכטיגע קריג.

Falshe fridn iz beser vi a rikhtige krig.

A bad peace is better than a good war.

True to the habits of the wandering Jews, almost as soon as
Yiddish coalesced into a separate language, some of its speakers
began to move. In the eleventh and twelfth centuries, small numbers of Yiddish-speaking Jews left the German lands and started
walking east. The move picked up momentum when, over the
course of the fifteenth century, a series of expulsions drove Jews
from several German and Italian territories.

In Poland a sizable population of Jews from the west met a much
smaller group who had arrived via the east. Hundreds of years
before, these eastern Jews had walked from Israel by way of
Byzantium. By this time they spoke some form of Slavic. And
because their numbers were much smaller than the Ashkenazi
Jews, they largely disappeared into their ranks. But they brought
one more strand to be woven in.

The Polish kings were happy to have the Jewish merchants,
traders, and bankers. They treated their minorities relatively well
— no ghettos, hats, crusades, or sudden expulsions. They did it
because they understood that they could use the Jews to their
advantage. These ultimate outsiders had no ties to the Polish political system and so could be played as political pawns. Jews inhabited

25

a separate social space, somewhere between the Polish landowners and peasants, a situation that was to have disastrous consequences later on. For the time being, though, it worked for all concerned.

The Jews were happy not to be persecuted. The Poles profited from the Jews' trading contacts. Poland was just beginning to exploit its vast natural resources, and the Jews, thanks again to their wanderings and to their carefully maintained culture, religion, and language (the universal Hebrew and the increasingly widespread Yiddish), easily took to being middlemen, merchants, and financiers. At home, the nobles often hired Jews to manage their estates and businesses. They valued their dedication and industry as well as their trading connections. These Jews also deflected the peasants' ire. Sometimes as buying agents for the nobility and sometimes on their own, Jews occupied a central position in producing and distributing such staples as wheat, wine, sugar, lumber, and fur. The Polish landowners gave them exclusive rights to distill grain, make and sell liquor, and keep inns.

A succession of kings granted them semi-autonomous status. A Jewish council represented them at court while, within their own communities, they were left on their own. For once, the answer to the question that Jews ask reflexively, is it good for the Jews, was yes. For the first time in centuries, they had a measure of real stability. They told themselves that "*Poylin*," the Yiddish pronunciation of the name of the country, was the same as the Hebrew word that meant "a rest in exile." A few even have said, *An hour in the Garden of Eden is also good,* although no one would have confused Poylin with Eden.

Every Jewish village or Jewish portion of a town or city was organized as a *kehile,* community, that in effect governed itself. Each Jew was included, no matter how pious or nonobservant, how rich or poor. The *kehile* funded the rabbinic-based legal system, supported a religious-run educational system, and built an extensive social service network that followed Jewish law and tradition.

Every aspect of life was accounted for. The community provided dowries for poor girls. Special societies looked after orphans and buried the dead. Craft unions maintained their own study groups. An oft-repeated Talmudic tale describes a man who bores a hole in a boat full of people. When the others object, he says that he is only boring it under his own seat. His fellow travelers reply that, although he may be literally correct, they are all in the boat together, and together will all drown.

European Jews were all too aware that they could find themselves without warning on the brink of drowning. Their only sure protection was maintaining the communal boat. The Yiddish language became the caulk that kept the water out and the passengers dry. *Whatever happens to the people Israel also happens to Mr. Israel* means that the individual Jew is inseparable from the Jewish community. In its Eastern European home, Yiddish helped the Jewish community construct its distinctive way of life.

We can get a glimpse of the way that community fit into the larger social framework courtesy of the Yiddish theorist Chaim Zhitlovski. He grew up in the nineteenth century, when much of Polish Jewry was under Russian control, but the dynamic he describes between Russians and Jews was similar to what existed between Poles and Jews. Each group had its clearly defined sphere: "My uncle Michal in Ushach distilled vodka for the Russian people and made a fortune on the liquor tax. My cousin sold the vodka to the peasants. The whole town lived off the Russian peasants. My father hired them to cut down Russian woods which he bought from the greatest exploiter of the Russian peasant, the Russian landowner. The lumber was shipped abroad, while the Russian villages were full of rotting, dilapidated huts, covered with rotting straw-thatched roofs."

The Zhitlovskis lived under Russian control because in the sixteenth century many Polish subjects, Christians as well as Jews, had settled the eastern lands they called the Ukraine. (The name means "frontier.") Once there, Jews again established their own separate communities. They organized schools for their sons, where they studied Hebrew texts but discussed them in Yiddish. By this time, even a speaker of medieval German, had he magically survived, would have had difficulty understanding Yiddish. Pronounciation had changed, and the language functioned in a different culture. How, for example, would a Christian German have understood a phrase like *a ganz yor shiker, purim nikhter,* "drunk the whole year but sober at Purim"? He could have parsed some words; understand *ganz* as "all" and *yor* as "year." But the context was a Jewish one — the upside-down celebration of a holiday that would have meant little beyond the Jewish world.

Jews even had separate Yiddish names for their cities and towns. They spoke not of Vilnius but of Vilna. The small town that was known as Miedzyrzec to the Polish authorities was Mezritsh to the Jews who lived there. Even the town that we have come to know by its German name, Auschwitz, had a Polish title of Oswiecim and a Yiddish moniker of Oshpitizin. Walking into such a town any time over the course of hundreds of years, a visitor would have seen shop signs in Yiddish, still written in the right-to-left Hebrew alphabet. He would have heard Yiddish spoken all around him. Even the *yeshive bukhers,* the religious school students, arguing some abstruse point of Talmudic law would have been doing so in their singsong style and, to be sure, with a great deal of "leakage" of the original Hebrew, in normal, everyday, down-to-earth *mame loshn.*

This Yiddish, in its Eastern European home, became even more distinct. Some of the Germanic and Romance elements were replaced by vocabulary and structure that seeped into the language courtesy of the Jews' new Slavic neighbors. By the seventeenth and eighteenth centuries, the Yiddish language had taken on the form and content that was to sustain it through its period of extraordinary growth: between 10 and 20 percent Hebrew, a few percentage points of Romance words, a good three-quarters Germanic vocabulary, and the rest Slavic words and structure. Although words that had come from Hebrew normally retained their Hebrew spelling (no vowels) and plural forms (adding -*im* or -*es* to the end), most spelling, syntax, and usage were more Germanic or Slavic. Yiddish had coalesced into a geographically dispersed but coherent tongue. *If you don't know Hebrew, you're an ignoramus. If you don't know Yiddish, you're a gentile.*

Pronunciation varied by region, and the language could tilt toward its neighbors — more Germanic borrowings in the German territories, more Slavic farther east. Although spelling and usage varied by region and personal preference, Yiddish speakers had no problem understanding each other. The difference in pronunciation between *git* and *gut* could be negotiated and laughed over.

The written language changed slightly. Although its new vowels made it more phonetic than Hebrew, it retained the separate forms of certain end-of-word letters.

This is what this sentence would look like in Yiddish:

.hsidy ni kil kol dluw cnetnes siht tahw si siht

After centuries of stasis, a change in politics in the last quarter of the eighteenth century was to alter the destinies of Yiddish speakers. The kingdom of Poland, which at its height had extended all the way from the Baltic Sea in the north almost down to the Black Sea, lost its power and was partitioned. In three stages, this once-great nation was gobbled up by its more powerful neighbors. So the Jews, without moving, found themselves living in new lands. The Hapsburgs, who took over a section of southern Poland renamed it Galicia, were accustomed to having Jewish subjects, but the Romanov tsars, who now controlled the bulk of Poland, including Ukraine, were not. The Russian situation was complicated by the fact that much of the actual land still belonged to Polish noblemen. Many were absentee landlords who continued to employ Jews as estate managers. The tsars, finding themselves on top of this already complicated arrangement, were at a loss as to how to act toward the million and a half Jews now under their control. In the coming years they would try, in no particular order, and with even less success, isolation, subjugation, conversion, neglect, and destruction. Many years later, Albert Einstein would write that each nation, like each tree, is born with its own shadow. He called anti-Semitism the shadow of the Russians.

For over a century, one of the few constants in Russian policy toward the Jews was the Pale of Settlement. Covering parts of several provinces, it was the only area within which Jews were allowed to live. (A pale is a stake stuck in the ground to make a fence, the mark of a boundary one may not cross.) Even within it, Jews needed special permission to live in large cities. They were often forbidden from owning land, were limited in their occupations, and were excluded from the professions and from government service. They were forced to pay special punitive taxes, and the army was used as an instrument of terror. Jewish boys as young as eight were routinely conscripted into the Russian-language tsarist army for an astonishing twenty-five years, by which time few could remember anything about their former lives. A Yiddish song advised, with mordant humor, *"Beser tsu lernen khumesh mit Rashi / Eder tsu esn di soldatske kashe."* Better to learn sacred books with Rashi than to eat the soldiers' *kashe,* cereal.

In addition, Jewish living under the tsars always had to be prepared for the occasional wild-card pogrom (the word comes from the Russian term meaning "destruction"), which could range from random to state-supported violence.

What is remarkable is the extent to which, even under these harsh conditions, the Yiddish speakers thrived. By the end of the nineteenth century, the Russian Jewish population had grown to five million. Historians cite early marriage, a high birthrate, and relatively good health, owing in part to Jews' concerns with ritual cleanliness, as reasons for this tremendous jump at a time when the Russian Christian population showed only modest gains.

Virtually every one of these five million Jews spoke Yiddish. For many, especially among the poor, it was their only language.

Russian, Polish, or Ukrainian was picked up as needed to speak to customers in the market or to deal with government officials. Virtually all the men knew at least some Hebrew; they certainly knew enough to read and recite a succession of prayers. But Yiddish was truly *mame loshn*. It was the first language that Jews learned. It linked Jews across a wide expanse of Europe, from France in the west to deep into the Russian hinterlands. A fully formed and functional language, it had, by this time, served its people for something like seven or eight hundred years.

CHAPTER 3

Shtetl: A Separate World

צווישן יידן איז מען קיינמאָל ניט פֿאַרלוירן.

Tsvishn yidn iz men keynmol nit farloyrn.

Among Jews one is never lost.

One Yiddish word that has moved into English untranslated and seemingly untranslatable is *shtetl*. For most English speakers, the word evokes a sort of Neverneverland-on-the-Vistula, a charming little town where bearded Jews in long coats happily dance and devoutly pray. A buxom mother holds aloft a plate of steaming *latkes*, pancakes; her poor but happy children await with bright eyes. Tevye the dairyman is forever arguing with God; the snows may be deep but the welcome is warm.

The funny thing is how much of this was, in a deep sense, true. If you put aside for a moment the superficialities — the centuries of bone-wearying poverty (most Jews were not estate managers or international traders), the abysmal standard of living, the wave after wave of vicious pogroms, the absolute dearth of any status or power in the "real" world — these self-contained communities functioned extraordinarily well. The Yiddish language and culture, intertwined with the Hebrew language and religion, acted like amniotic fluid. They bathed Jews in a soft warmth, cushioning them from the onslaughts of an uncaring world. In Yiddish, Jews expressed their understanding of what it took to create their community. *One log alone doesn't warm the fireplace.*

From the fifteenth through the nineteenth centuries, almost all Eastern European Jews lived in small- to medium-size towns that came under a succession of monarchs, none of whom was ever Jewish. Sometimes these communities were composed only or mostly of Jews; sometimes Jews and gentiles lived separate lives in the same towns. All shtetl-dwelling Jews spoke Yiddish, although some also knew the language of their Christian neighbors. Those neighbors, for their part, rarely learned Yiddish; and those who did were a continual source of wonder.

Like our glimpse of the beggar-as-Prophet-Elijah, the shtetls were infinitely more than their physical selves — ramshackle collections of wooden houses, shops, and communal buildings connected by icy, dusty, or muddy streets. They formed a brilliant if schizophrenic response to an often hostile world. By creating a separate reality that was rooted in language, the shtetls allowed a people to prosper in its own terms. Then, when a shift in history allowed the shtetl dwellers a bit of breathing room, they could burst out on the world's stage ready to shine.

The word *shtetl* is deceptively simple; it means nothing but "town." It is the diminutive of *shtot,* city, whose plural is *shtet.* (There are two ways of forming the plural of *shtetl: shtetleh* and *shtetls.* We will go with the simpler.) The warmth and evocativeness of the term come not from its literal meaning but from a whole web of associations. That is how language works.

So let's get ourselves a shtetl guide; better yet, let's get two. Like so many other Jews born in Eastern Europe, the Singer brothers, Israel Joshua and Isaac, had their first sights and smells, their first boyhood adventures and pranks in shtetls, although different ones, as it happens. (Israel Joshua, born in 1893, was eleven years older than his brother, Isaac. When the younger sibling began writing, he took the name of Bashevis so as to distance himself from his already well-known brother. Yiddish writers of their time often used just the first initial of their given name, so, by the time that Isaac began publishing, he was aware that the world did not need a second

I. Singer, author.) Their father, a Hasidic rabbi, was pious and poor, but their maternal grandfather, although also a rabbi, managed to maintain a substantial home. The boys spent a lot of time there, and it was from this grandfather's yard that the young Isaac Bashevis looked around and described his world:

> In Grandfather's yard there was a spot shielded by a wall on one side, a Sukkoth booth on another, and the dog catcher's potato field on the third. At a fence there, under an apple tree, I studied an eighty-year-old physics textbook. Although concealed, I could see the synagogue, the house of prayer, the bath, and the vast fields that extended toward the forest — the sky was as blue as the curtain before the Holy Ark on the days between Rosh Hashanah and Yom Kippur.

The boy saw the world — vast fields, forest, blue sky. But he did not see the natural world in the same way that the gentile potato field owner might have. (Keep this in mind later on when we hear the argument that Yiddish has few words to describe nature; it names relatively few varieties of flowers, for example, but it is rich in descriptions of human character.) Young Isaac looked out and saw Jewish communal institutions, Jewish holidays, Jewish learning. His language reflected his worldview. The English expression "small world" has a Yiddish equivalent — *velt mit veltlech,* a world with small worlds. Yiddish speakers knew that very different people could live side by side.

Much later, when Isaac Bashevis was an old man, he described the Yiddish take on life: "Yiddish had a Weltanschauung of its own. It was saying, one cannot go through life straight and directly, one can only sneak by, smuggle one's way through it. The leitmotif of Yiddish was, that if a day passes without a misfortune it is a miracle from heaven." For a time in the Jewish history of wandering, the shtetl provided the soil where, God willing, that miracle might happen.

The most respected people in the shtetl were rabbis and scholars.

(*Rabbi* means "teacher." Jews do not have a hierarchical clergy.) A wealthy man's greatest status symbol was a son-in-law who was a scholar. The Yiddish word *ķest,* which does not have an equivalent in non-Jewish languages, refers to the practice of a man's supporting his new son-in-law for a year or two of study. This focus on learning was a powerful cultural response to a worldly situation that, century after weary century, held out so little hope. Although some Jews became relatively well-to-do, their economic status was always precarious, beyond their control. So, although they appreciated worldly goods, riches were never the ultimate test. Jews could control their own behavior within their own code of values, little more. (A Yiddish speaker might say, raising his eyebrows, *"vi a tsadik af der velt,"* like a saint in this world.)

When a young American woman, Grace Goldman, visited her relatives in the Polish shtetl of Bransk in the summer of 1932, she was struck by the spiritual heft of that world. Although the family lived in "little more than a two-room shack . . . in the most inconceivable and primitive surroundings imaginable," without even a regular outhouse, "my uncle's house was sanctified — a holy tabernacle. They were learned people. The days were filled with a succession of prayers. . . . On a Sabbath, the mean houses and streets took on a still, ethereal light, a strange silence, as though holy."

Each small act of daily living was bound up in ritual, linking every aspect of mundane life to the divine. This was a people that was capable of calling what we refer to as toilet paper *asher yotser papir,* a phrase that shows us Yiddish at its most flexible, joining the Germanic word for "paper" with the Yiddish pronunciation of the Hebrew words *asher yotser.* Translated as "who has fashioned," it is a phrase from the blessing recited after what English speakers euphemistically refer to as using the bathroom. So the shorthand joined a functional paper with a particular prayer. In this seamless world the holy and the profane were linked, not opposed. Where Christians separated their priests from the world, Jews enthusiastically immersed their rabbis in the minutiae of everyday life. Yiddish, a musical string that vibrates to the sounds and meanings of transcendent Hebrew as well as to the here and now of daily life, was often the link.

One Yiddish joke describes all the women of the town lined up to use the *mikve,* the ritual bath, as a custom on the eve of the Sabbath. The *rebetsin,* the rabbi's wife, elbows her way to the front of the line.

"It's important for me to get ready," she announces. "I have to please the rabbi." (It is a *mitzve,* a good deed, to make love on *shabes.*) The women allow her to pass. But then another woman elbows her way past them all, past even the *rebetsin.* It is none other than the town whore.

"I deserve a place in front," she announces. "I have to please half the town."

Although Jewish women often fared better than their non-Jewish neighbors in terms of both status and learning, we should not delude ourselves with feminist revisionism. They were always far more likely to be literate than were non-Jewish women, but even in a culture that placed tremendous value on knowledge, women were not encouraged to learn. It was not unusual for women to run the house and earn the family's livelihood, allowing their husbands the luxury of religious study. In synagogue they sat separately, following the service as best they could with the help of the *firzogerin,* as well as special Hebrew prayerbooks with Yiddish translations.

Women's status came from their role as guardians of the home and family — no small jobs in a culture with no hope of worldly success. In time, a mainstay of Jewish movies and plays would be a scene of *shabes licht,* Sabbath candle lighting, with the mother of the household lit by the candles' glow. Of all the pet names that Yiddish has picked up over the centuries, its most enduring is *mame loshn.* Hebrew might be *loshn koydesh,* the holy language, but in human experience, *mame* comes first.

In Isaac Bashevis Singer's childhood, the Jewish context defined everything. Even sitting outdoors reading physics, he wrote, "Sometimes, out of habit, I chanted a Talmud melody as I studied."

That mental habit is telling. For boys who, from the age of three on, spent eight to ten hours a day, six days a week, in their school or *cheder* (the word means "room"), memorizing, chanting, studying Hebrew texts, these words became second nature. Yet these Hebrew texts were discussed in Yiddish. Back and forth, back and forth went the arguments, the phrases, the words.

When a Yiddish-speaking man wanted to make a point, dozens of biblical or rabbinic examples, which he had learned in Hebrew, were always on the tip of his tongue. How easy for the words or phrases to slip out; for his wife then to use them in turn; for Hebrew to entwine itself with Yiddish speech.

When a bully in school punched young Isaac Singer, he said, "I called him an Esau and predicted that his hereafter would be spent on a bed of nails." When he made a new friend, he described him as "a fine, decent person without social ambitions. We studied from the same Pentateuch [the first five books of the Bible], walked with our arms about each other, and learned to write Yiddish. Others, jealous, intrigued against us, but our friendship remained constant. We were like David and Jonathan." Young Isaac might have lived in twentieth-century Poland, but in his mind he lived in the world of David and Jonathan, in the overarching biblical past.

Meanwhile, his older brother, Israel Joshua, gave us a description of what was, for shtetl dwellers, the all-too-real here and now. In his description of the seasonal markets and fairs that were a mainstay of shtetl life, we can see something of the relations between gentiles and Jews. Here is Israel Joshua's picture of market day:

> The Jews came to sell, the gentiles to buy. . . . Shoemakers and hatters, capmakers and tailors, cattle dealers and horse dealers, butchers, tanners, and bristle merchants; young men, old men, Jews in long beards, and journeymen in modern dress; women, girls, and children all poured in in wagons and carts to set up booths and stands in the marketplace, squabbling and bickering over space, over boundaries, over everything under the sun. . . .

> Each time a fight broke out, the Jewish merchants started to tie up their bundles, fearful that "it" was starting at last. ["It" was anti-Jewish violence. Singer's audience would have known very well what "it" referred to.] But soon they unpacked again and resumed trading.

Everywhere, Singer saw signs of the differences between non-Jews and Jews:

> The gentile pig-butcher, it seems, was an object of particular disdain, not only because Jews were not allowed to eat pig, but because of the unnecessary cruelty of his slaughter.
>
> My father walked around ashen-faced, his heart filled with compassion for the anguished beasts that, even though they were impure, were still creatures of God.
>
> "Almighty God, will we ever be redeemed from these heathens?" he cried out as the shrieks of the tortured animals and the coarse voices of drunken peasants filled the air.

The elder Singer lamented in Yiddish, but his references were pure Hebrew. When he used phrases like "creatures of God," or "will we ever be redeemed," these would have been Hebrew words. And Singer could expect that his readers would understand the references, feel the linguistic shifts.

We can understand the shift when we consider the Yiddish translation of "guest." A Yiddish speaker has two choices — the German-derived *gast* or the Hebrew-derived *oyrech*. The second word is used most often as part of the phrase *oyrech auf shabes,* guest for the Sabbath, which has a very particular meaning. *Shabes,* the day of rest, study, prayer, and spending time with the family, was (and still is) the height of the Jewish week, the day when every man was a king. Because travel was not permitted on Sabbath, a person far from home would find himself some local family's Sabbath guest. In addition to being a treat for the guest, this was seen as a pleasure for the host, because it was a chance to do a *mitzve* (the Hebrew-derived word has connotations of commandment, good deed, and pleasure). One Yiddish joke tells of a host who, at the end of the Sabbath, presents his *shabes oyrech* with a bill for his hospitality. The guest, flabbergasted by such an unheard-of turn of events, refuses to pay, and agrees to bring the matter before the town rabbi. When the rabbi sides with the host, saying that the guest should indeed pay for his welcome, the guest is beside himself, because such a decision runs counter to the very core of Judaism.

Finally, the host breaks into a grin. "I never really meant you to pay," he explains. "I just wanted you to understand what a *shlemiel* our rabbi is."

That working definition of the word for "guest" also gives you as a bonus an implicit definition of *shlemiel*. If you add to this sort of culturally informed description a slew of ritual folk phrases and proverbs, you will have some sense of how Yiddish functioned as keeper of a distinct and viable world. It kept outsiders out; it solidified the group within; it formed a protective layer around holy Hebrew, its core.

Scholars call this condition "internal bilingualism," which means that every Jew knew at least aspects of two languages. Yiddish and Hebrew, although distinct and separate, are inextricably linked. The fact that virtually all Jewish males and even some females knew Hebrew but did not use it every day kept it accessible but apart. It did not have to change to meet the needs of daily life, yet it was never removed from the people. It never became remote, like Latin. This linguistic intertwining, unique in the history of languages, has been expressed in many ways. Yiddish has been called the handmaiden of Hebrew. Hebrew has been termed the library of Yiddish. The combination has been called one literature in two languages. *God speaks Yiddish during the week and Hebrew on the Sabbath.*

In addition to this Hebrew/Yiddish braid, Yiddish had another strand — what scholars call "external bilingualism" — knowing a second language that is not your own. Because there was no

"Yiddishland," no state that had Yiddish as its official tongue, Yiddish speakers always lived as boarders in somebody else's home. More often than not, because of her breadwinner's role, it was the woman of the family (the *balebuste,* housewife) who could speak at least some German, Polish, Russian, Ukrainian, Hungarian, or Czech. The Singer brothers' mother, Batsheba, sold yeast cakes, a line of work that was often reserved for the *rebetsin.* It was a typically Yiddish linking of the secular and the sacred, as well as a characteristically practical approach to life: Give the rabbi's wife a job so her husband can spend more time on his — and the community's — spiritual well-being. *A peeled egg doesn't leap into the mouth by itself.*

Yiddish has always been open to neighboring tongues, its speakers aware of how languages bend and shift, as we saw in the *gast/oyrech* tale. A pious man like the elder Singer would have spoken a Yiddish more richly Hebrew; his more worldly sons would have peppered their speech with more Polish words.

But the linguistic raw material was always transformed in a Yiddish context. For example, the names of many of the days of the week came directly from German, which makes it easy for us, as English speakers, to recognize them, because they come from common roots. *Zuntik, montik, dienstik, mitvoch,* and *donershtik* are the days of the week beginning with Sunday. But the Yiddish expression *ale montik un donershtik,* every Monday and Thursday, would be meaningless to an outsider, even if he could recognize the words, without knowing that Mondays and Thursdays are the weekdays when the Torah is read in synagogue. Another example is the expression *reyn vi erev Pesach.* One can translate that sentence literally, "clean as the night before the holiday of Passover," but that would mean nothing without knowing that, before Passover, Jews clean their houses meticulously so as not to leave even a crumb of leavened bread, the final ritual check carried out by the light of a candle and with the dusting of a feather. So the most commonplace expressions placed the speaker in the context of Jewish history and theology.

This was the genius of the culture. Nothing was excluded. Although all human societies have to, in some way, provide for a range of human needs, the Yiddish-speaking shtetl world relished the breadth of that range. Because there was nowhere else for Jews to go, the Jewish community, *kehile,* had to include everyone. Just as the traditional method of study that held pride of place in this community was *pilpul,* a back-and-forth, question-and-answer form of discourse, it was the dialectic that made this culture go. Nothing was off bounds. Intellectualism, base earthiness, selfishness, generosity; each human impulse was acknowledged. *If God lived on earth, people would break His windows.*

This rounded sense of humanity is one reason that the shtetls have resonated so deeply with Jews and non-Jews alike. Here is a memory from the *yizker bukh,* remembrance book, for the town of Jadow, that gives us the texture of a small-town fair. "A variety of jugglers, organ grinders, and 'magicians' would also come and they were a special attraction for children. As part of their trade all these tricksters would wear Turkish hats, speak various languages, and grow hoarse from screaming 'hocus pocus.' When it was time for *minkhe* |afternoon prayer| all these 'Turks' would go to the synagogue. It turned out that they really were Jews."

Throughout their long history of exile, Jews were great masters of what might be called the Turkish hat trick. Although they became whatever they had to be, they never lost track of who they were. They lived in a stateless reality, yet refused to define themselves in anybody else's terms. For a thousand years, many of the functions that in other developed societies were backed up by governments or armies existed only in Yiddish words.

That is why, in the stage and film versions of *Fiddler on the Roof* — a modern musical adaptation of the Yiddish tales written by Sholom Aleichem, whom we will meet later on — when Tevye leaves his shtetl, audiences throughout the world break down in tears. Even if they have never heard of Hebrew or Yiddish, even if they know nothing about the millennia of exile, they feel some loss of that nourishing home. That Yiddish could have been one of the linchpins of such a world is one measure of its strength.

CHAPTER 4

Enlightenment and Hasidism: The Head and the Heart

פֿון דײַן מויל צו גאָטס אויער.

Fun dayn moyl tsu gots oyer.

From your mouth to God's ear.

In the eighteenth century two massive social movements swept through the Jewish world and changed Yiddish forever. For the *Haskalah,* the Jewish version of the European Enlightenment, Yiddish represented every loathsome thing the modernists wanted to expunge. For members of the Hasidic movement, self-described pious people whose favored mode was mystic joy, the language signfied the celebration of Jewish spiritual life. The tongue that, until this point, had remained hidden in plain sight now came into full view. Yiddish became both savior and villain. After this, both those who loved it and those who derided it did so confident in the knowledge that history was on their side.

By the early eighteenth century, it had been three hundred years since the majority of Jews had moved from the German lands eastward to Poland. Those who had left and those who had stayed behind now spoke slightly different languages. And their lives had definitely diverged. The German Jews were less separated, physically and culturally, from the German Christians. They dressed and acted much like their non-Jewish neighbors. As well, because the Yiddish spoken in what became Germany had not picked up the additional layer of Slavisms, the language remained closer to its earlier base.

For example, two of the most characteristic Yiddish words, *zeyde,* grandfather, and the all-purpose *take,* pronounced "*TAH-keh,*" used almost as an accent, something like "so," were Slavic additions. German Jews most often called their language, which they wrote in Hebrew characters, either *yidishtaytsh,* Judeo-German, or just *zhargon,* jargon.

The term *jargon* was known in many European languages and had the same demeaning connotations in all. (In its original Spanish, it had meant "the twittering of birds.") Christian scholars of the period searched for what they called "pure" languages, hunting them like prize mushrooms or truffles. The greatest catch was the occasional "wild child" who, by some grim accident, had been reared apart from human contact. Researchers were desperate to discover what language these unsocialized children would speak "naturally." (Latin was a leading contender.) We now know that most languages are far from pure, and that to develop language, children need human socialization. Because Jewish society was nothing if not sociable, Yiddish can be described as one of the most richly human of tongues.

We will remember that Yiddish had been born in the fertile soil of the German river valleys, that much of its vocabulary had come from local German dialects, and that it had retained many of these words and formats when its speakers had moved east. In some instances, Yiddish had kept medieval forms of words while "mainstream" German had moved on. There was also the question of context, the way that a Germanic word would take on a different meaning when it was used by Jews. *Mentsh* is a wonderful example. In German it means simply "man," while for Yiddish speakers it conjures up a whole set of moral and ethical expectations.

So Yiddish both was and was not German — was, because it shared a core vocabulary; was not, because about a quarter of its words never had been German. Many of its grammatical forms came from other languages, and the pronunciation and meaning of words that had begun as German had shifted dramatically. Perhaps most importantly, it functioned in a very different world.

But the closeness still rankled. We are more easily offended by people who are like us than by those with whom we have little in common. It may be useful to think of Yiddish and German as the siblings from hell.

At this point, some seven or eight centuries after Yiddish had broken from its Germanic base and become Yiddish, many of its speakers, depending on where they lived and what they heard from the Christians around them, could not speak or understand German. And because of the separate alphabet, far fewer could read German. As might be expected, this was most obviously a problem for Jews who lived in German-speaking territories.

In many ways, these Jews were more integrated into the dominant culture than were their cousins in the Polish kingdom. They were clean-shaven bankers and secular philosophers. A few were even welcomed at court. So when the fresh breeze of the Enlightenment swept through Western Europe, German Jews were invigorated by it as well. Christians and Jews alike were ready to shed what they saw as dark medieval superstitions and emerge into a new era of logic and clear thought. For Jews, the Enlightenment or *Haskalah* (the term comes from the Hebrew word for "reason" or "understanding") meant broadening the definition of knowledge beyond the world of the rabbis and sages. But only a Jew who had been raised in that tradition was capable of leading them out.

Moses Mendelssohn (1729–86), a linguist and philosopher from Desau, had a hunchback and a stammer, but rose through the ranks of Berlin society because of his capacious intellect, as well as his charm, humanity, and willingness to tackle publicly the difficult issues of his day. In a period of public debate of religion and philosophy, Jews and Germans alike were open to change. And Mendelssohn, the most visible and respected Jew of his time, wanted to take full advantage of this opportunity.

Eager to lay down what he saw as the burden of his Jewishness, Mendelssohn peered into the future and imagined Judaism and Christianity merging in a cloud of rationality. Although the *Ostjuden,* eastern Jews — the German Jews' name for their relatives who lived in Eastern Europe — were not particularly interested in becoming like their Polish neighbors, many Western European Jews, or *kulturjuden,* were only too happy to have the chance to blend in. As one of the most "acceptable" Jews of his time, Mendelssohn the *maskil,* the enlightener, took it upon himself to help "normalize" his fellow Jews.

First they would have to drop their low-status Yiddish. As we have seen, language is both a way into and a way out of a culture. Speak my language and you have more of a chance of getting to know me. If you don't speak it, there is no chance at all. If Jews wanted to mingle with Christians, they would have to perfect their German. More than that, Yiddish would have to go.

Mendelssohn translated the Pentateuch, the first five books of the Old Testament, into German, although he wrote it out in Hebrew letters so his fellow Jews could at least sound it out if they were not adept at German. Then he proceeded to go on an absolute tear against Yiddish, which he called "Jargon." In 1782 he wrote, "I am afraid that this Jargon has contributed not a little to the rudeness of the common man, and I anticipate good results from the growing usage of the pure German vernacular among my brethren."

For Jews to make the switch from being a separate people to becoming Germans of the Hebrew persuasion, they would have to shrink Judaism down from an all-encompassing system of living to a mere religion. Hebrew might still play a role in their prayers; indeed, as a "classical" language, Hebrew had some prestige among educated Europeans. In their public lives, however, Jews would be Germans pure and simple. And because national identity was coming to mean having a common national language instead of speaking a hodgepodge of local dialects, it became essential for Jews, if they wanted to be considered German, to speak the German language. That might sound like a fairly simple shift. But it cut deep into the self-image of a people.

In what looks to our eyes like self-loathing, German Jews began to say terrible things about Yiddish. Although many of them had spoken nothing but from birth until death, they somehow considered it to be less than a real language. From our current point of view, that is impossible. Present-day linguistic theory holds that we humans are, in a sense, programmed for language; the words we place together follow patterns that are fairly consistent across cultures and times. Languages may be more or less elaborate, but there is no question that eighteenth-century Yiddish, whether in the German lands or farther east in Poland, was a complete and rich tongue.

Linguists are reluctant to pin down word counts and thus rank languages in terms of comprehensiveness, because no standards of inclusion exist. For example, respected Shakespeare scholars have counted up the Bard's vocabulary and have come up with totals that range from sixteen thousand to thirty thousand — a difference of almost 100 percent in a finite body of work. Imagine the room for disagreement if you try to pin down an entire language! To give some sense of the range, however, estimates for the number of words in major modern European languages fall in the hundreds of thousands.

Here is how the Yiddish scholar Joshua Fishman approaches the issue: "It took four volumes of Yudl Mark's Great Dictionary of the Yiddish Language (1961–1975) just to accommodate the words beginning with aleph." The first letter of the Yiddish alphabet takes up so much dictionary space because nearly all Yiddish prefixes begin with it. "Those four volumes contain 80,000 words. He estimated that he had twice as many more words in his card-catalog for all the other letters."

So we are definitely in the hundreds of thousands range. The Yiddish speakers in Mendelssohn's Germany might not have availed themselves of every one of the words Mark found almost two centuries later, but they certainly had enough to lead full, rich Yiddish-only lives.

To give the *maskilim* like Mendelssohn their due, however, it must be admitted that at this point Yiddish was still used primarily as a folk language, more spoken than written. Its literature had certainly not kept pace with that of other European tongues. The Yiddish equivalents of Cervantes or Molière had not yet been born, one of the reasons being that the rise of European literature was linked to the growth of national identities. Since there was no Yiddishland, it stood to reason that a Yiddish literature would be slower to come. Besides, the Jews had invested their intellectual energies in their religion. Their secular literature was stalled at the level of the retelling of popular tales. But the language was there, available, waiting to be used.

Much has been made of the poor showing of Yiddish in the natural arena, its scanty listing of words for different varieties of animals, birds, trees, flowers, or fruits. The Yiddish speaker can differentiate between a *margeritke,* daisy, a *bez,* lilac, and a *roiz,* rose, for example, but would not have the dozens of distinctive floral names available to the English speaker with a horticultural or naturalistic bent. This makes sense when you consider how rarely Jews were permitted to own land or even to work on it. But the Yiddish vocabulary is spendthrift in personal relations, which also makes sense when you take into account the preoccupation of the Yiddish world with community, its obvious pleasure in the variety, extent, and subtlety of human relations.

Isaac Bashevis Singer listed some of the ways that the concept of a poor man could be expressed in Yiddish: "You can say a poor man, a pauper, a beggar, a mendicant, a panhandler. . . . But in Yiddish you can say: a poor *shlemiel,* a begging *shlimazl,* a pauper with dimples, a *shnorer* multiplied by eight; a *shlepper* by the grace of God, an alms collector with a mission, a delegate from the Holy Land dressed in seven coats of poverty, a crumb catcher, a bone picker, a plate licker, a daily observer of the Yom Kippur fast and more and more."

But eighteenth-century German Jews could not afford to appreciate these delicacies of their native tongue. Faced with the first-ever opportunity to leave the confines of their Jewish-identified world and move into the wider society, they perceived the old Jewish language as holding them back. To let go of it, they had to convince themselves that it was less than a "real" language. One of Mendelssohn's followers, David Friedlander, while acknowledging the place of Hebrew as the language of the traditional prayers, continued to push for German and against Yiddish. He wrote, in 1798:

> The Judeo-German current among us, a language without rules, mutilated and unintelligible without our circle, must be completely abandoned; and both the Hebrew language as well as our German mother tongue must be studied in methodical fashion from childhood on. . . . If — as everyone will admit — the child fails to receive in the so-called Judeo-German language proper conceptions about anything whatsoever in the world, how can the person later, in his more mature years, deport himself in accordance with correct principles?

From our current multicultural perspective, this linguistic abandonment reeks of self-hatred. How could a language that expressed the daily needs and transcendent visions of an entire society be "without rules, mutilated"? And isn't any language unintelligible outside its circle? It was a measure of the Jews' lack of confidence that they spoke as if the language they used every day did not really exist.

Language lies at the very core of human identity. Just beyond the glow of the mother's smile, the feel of the father's large arms, words tell us who we are. The Yiddish baby is *tsatskele, bubele, tayer kind,* a Jewish child born into a Yiddish world. One of the recurring contradictions of Yiddish is this: The language's very same cozy, in-group insulating comfort also shut its speakers off from the wider world. When the non-Jewish world was a threatening, hostile place, the balance tipped. Jews took comfort in their homogeneous group with its own separate tongue, and Yiddish rose in stature. But when the tides of history shifted and the outside world opened up, when the world beyond *di yidishe gas,* the Jewish street, offered something positive without extracting too high a price in return, then the opposite happened. Jews could go off to seek their fortunes in the wide world, and their mother tongue looked like a liability.

The us/them maneuver is always delicate for Jews. A Yiddish proverb expresses this dilemma with precision: *A maskil meg zein a yid, ober zein kind?* The enlightener can be a Jew, but can his child? Here is one case where a proverb has an objective correlative: Out of Moses Mendelssohn's six children, four converted to Christianity. But even though his descendants did their best to free themselves from what they considered the limitations of their Jewishness, German society long continued to see them as Jews. Mendelssohn's Christian grandson, the great composer Felix, was plagued by anti-Semitism throughout his life, and, indeed, long after his death. Yiddish folk wisdom got this one exactly right. The *maskilim* squandered their *yerushe,* their heritage. But they made their choice. From this point onward, Yiddish atrophied in German-speaking lands.

As often happens in history, however, the opposite impulse was gaining ground at much the same time, a period of great transformation. While the *maskilim* were promoting a more rational form of Judaism in hopes of more easily fitting into the non-Jewish world, charismatic wonder-working rabbis were mining the rich mystical heritage of Judaism and making it accessible to the masses. Just when Mendelssohn's children were feeling the cool drops of baptismal water on their foreheads, another school of Jews was becoming more Jewish, not less. *Yeder rebe hot zein derech un yeder derech hot zein rebe.* Every *rebe* has his way, and every way has its *rebe.*

Israel ben Eliezer (1700–1760), known as the Ba'al Shem Tov, master of the good name, or Besht, was the center of this revival. Born in a shtetl in what is now Ukraine, he immersed himself in the Kabbalah, the mystical works that, at the time, were studied only by a privileged few. It was his genius to transform the ascetic discipline into a joyous and populist way of seeing the world. In a society that had long valued intellectual study, he elevated the use of fervent, direct prayer. Where traditional rabbis rarely preached, mostly occupying themselves with matters of law, the new *rebes,* the Hasidic version of rabbis, were charismatic and available. They closely advised their devoted followers, who were called Hasidim, pious people.

Whether this was a reaction to the rationalism sweeping in from the west or a vital homegrown movement is open to debate. There is no question that Hasidism flourished. People flocked to the mystic *rebes* who taught their followers through parables and apocryphal tales. The men sang and danced together — ecstatic songs and wordless, hypnotic incantations called *nigunim;* circles and chains of explosive, rhythmic motion.

These new *rebes* were totally unlike their highly intellectual counterparts, who carefully backed up their authority with centuries of law and commentary. Instead of citing authorities like Rashi, now six hundred years dead, they focused on making the language of prayer available to all. Rashi might have translated individual words. The Hasidim effected an entire linguistic shift. As the Besht himself said, "I let the mouth speak what it wants to say."

For the mass of Eastern European Jews, that mouth wanted to say its piece in Yiddish. The Hasidic *rebes* made a point of preaching in Yiddish, of translating Hebrew texts into Yiddish, often printing the two versions side by side. No more disparaging introductions to bilingual books with disclaimers about having been written for women or the uneducated. They acknowledged what Yiddish had always been — the vibrant speech of the millions, the voice of a people.

The Hasidim may be best known for their rich vocabulary of wonder tales — nine hundred angels descending to earth to help a poor Jewish water carrier, a man mysteriously appearing as a horse, endless sightings of the Prophet Elijah. Here is a typical tale:

When a rabbi ate with a rich man, he was dismayed to see the rich man eat only bread, and advised him to eat meat and drink wine. But the rich man replied that he was simple in his tastes, a response that obviously displeased the rabbi. When later one of this rabbi's followers asked him why he had advised the rich man to consume lavishly, he replied, "If he eats meat, then he will realize that the poor man at least needs bread. If he himself eats bread, he will think the poor man can live on stones."

These tales were wildly popular, but in typically iconoclastic Yiddish fashion, the anti-Hasidic story evolved just as quickly and spread just as far. One goes like this: A pious Hasid was telling a friend about all the miracles his *rebe* had performed. One of these involved his *rebe* out walking with one of his followers on Yom Kippur, a day when Jews are supposed to fast. They saw a Jew brazenly standing against a wall eating a piece of herring and a slice of bread.

The follower was aghast and hoped that the wall would fall down on the shameless Jew and break his bones.

But the *rebe* disagreed. "Perhaps he has a good reason for committing this sin," he said. "Instead of cursing him I will bless him, and pray that the wall does not fall and crush him."

"And what do you think happened?" the Hasid announced, glowing. "The sinner was not struck dead! The wall did not fall down!"

If not all Jews were swept up in the swirling Hasidic dance, these intense, ecstatic, tight-knit groups exerted tremendous cultural influence; they were the shtetl Jews distilled to their archetypal form. A popular Yiddish song describes how, when the *rebe* dances, all the Hasidim follow his lead and dance; when the *rebe* sings, they all raise their voices; when he sneezes, they sneeze; when he sleeps, they all lay down their bearded heads. But if it was tempting to parody these leaders and followers, we will also see successive generations of non-Hasidic Jews returning to the wellspring of their proverbs, myths, songs, and allegorical tales.

For our purposes, it is important to note that these songs were sung, these miracles celebrated, in Yiddish. The great eighteenth-century leader Nakhman of Bratslav wrote about the Hasid, "In the sacred tongue [Hebrew] it will be difficult for him to say everything that he wishes and he will not be able to be as sincere since we do not speak the sacred tongue. . . . In Yiddish, it is possible to pour out your words, speaking everything that is in your heart before the Lord." Perhaps most tellingly, he explained, "In Yiddish, it is easier to break one's heart."

Hasidism never really took hold in Germany, but it blazed a broad trail across Eastern Europe. Henceforth every shtetl, every family, would have its Hasidic side. At its height, close to half the Jews of Eastern Europe might have been Hasidim. When in the nineteenth century the camera entered the shtetl, its unblinking eye revealed the variety of Jewish life. Jews in the long beards and floor-length coats (different styles of coat, belt, or hat echoed the dress of particular *rebes*) mingled freely and constantly with more worldly Jews who followed the latest Western fashions. Communities are never monolithic, Jewish communities least of all. *Two Jews, three opinions.*

In the great divide of enlighteners and pietists, both sides had something important in common. They were beginning to respond to the question that would present itself with increasing urgency in the coming century: How much were Jews to be part of the wider world, and how much were they to be separate from it? This philosophic query more or less defines the Yiddish language, a tongue that borrows liberally from the surrounding culture even while its main function is to unite its speakers and distinguish them from their non-Jewish neighbors.

This round of rationalism versus emotionalism also accomplished something beyond even the great movements of religious ferment and cultural change. It made Jews aware of the language they were speaking. Their words made it obvious if they were leaning toward assimilation or separation, focusing on the "them" or the "us" of the eternal Jewish continuum.

By the end of the eighteenth century, Yiddish had become an audible part of group definition. It had been used in the service of causes, getting bound up in them along the way. As succeeding generations became aware of each historical crossroad, they could look back to this primary schism.

For those who had chosen German, Yiddish would dog them with continuing embarrassment and worse. It was a symbol of where they had come from, of what they once had been. Even our term Eastern European Jews comes from *Ostjuden,* the German Jews' term for their eastern cousins, and that came to have a derogatory connotation.

Those who had chosen Yiddish could understand how effectively the Hasidim had taken what they saw as their birthright and used it to energize their communal life. The Yiddish language, an agent of fame or of shame, had lost any remnant of neutrality. From this point forward, whether they embraced it or fled from it, it would continue to be a conscious part of the identity of European Jews.

PART 2

The Modern Era

CHAPTER 5

Eastern Europe:
Opening the Gates

נייע נעסטן, נייע פייגל
וועלן נייע לידער זינגען

Naye nestn, naye feygl
Veln naye lider zingen.

New nests, new birds / Will sing new songs

Y. L. Peretz

Just as the aftershocks of the Enlightenment and the spread of Hasidism subsided, a new wave of social, political, and economic change swept the Yiddish world. In Russia the serfs were freed in 1861, and two years later in Poland the nobility was stripped of its power. At the same time, the mid–nineteenth century, the industrial revolution was arriving in Eastern Europe — a full hundred years later than it had come to the west.

The new machines brought the modern world into small towns whose rhythms had not changed since the Middle Ages. Railroads replaced wagons, transforming business and personal boundaries. Sewing machines made old crafts redundant, and new, urban factories lured Jews away from the small towns. As the weekly markets and seasonal fairs lost their critical role in the regional economy, the shtetls went into free fall. A complete social structure that had evolved over centuries was now quickly forced to respond to changes in every area of life.

The advent of first the telegraph and later the mass newspaper put local storytellers out of business and gave even the *rebes* real competition. Now, if a Jew wanted to make sense of a puzzling question — say, how to project himself into a Jewish *and* a European future — he could consult not only his local rabbi but also the authors he could read in the new Yiddish newspapers. (Popular writers sold their services internationally, through the Jewish Telegraphic Agency.) A Jew could see traveling productions of Yiddish plays like Abraham Goldfaden's *Capricious Bride* or translations of *Romeo and Juliet,* listen on the new phonograph to Yiddish songs like the frankly sentimental "Belz" or "Oyfn pripetshik," or dance to klezmer music influenced by musicians thousands of miles away.

This dislocation spawned both uncertainty and opportunity. The Yiddish world responded with an immense outpouring of creative energy. Yiddish-speaking theoreticians invented a dazzling rainbow of "isms." Yiddish writers created new genres, which in turn encouraged new markets. What had been largely a folk language was transformed into an instrument of politics, science, literature, and art. This abundant flowering transformed a people.

Literature was the focused beam of light that both lit up and reflected the Yiddish world, and ushered in the golden age of Yiddish literature. This was largely the work of three writers — Mendele, Y. L. Peretz, and Sholom Aleichem — who worked at the top of their genres without sacrificing popular appeal. In typically Yiddish fashion, they are referred to as family. First comes the *zeyde*, grandfather, known to posterity as Mendele.

Sholem Yankev Abramovitsch was born around 1835 in a shtetl that, for the half century since the division of Poland, had been under Russian rule. But although he might have been Russian by birth, he would never have been categorized as a Russian writer. Such a classification would have meant little to the Russians or to his Yiddish readers. We must keep this in mind as we come to know our modern Yiddish cast of characters. Although they were separated by political boundaries, the Yiddish culture within which they worked existed in a realm of its own.

Like other intellectuals of his time, Abramovitsch wrote in respectable Hebrew — translations of European scientific texts, as well as essays and stories. Yiddish, as he later recalled,

> in my time was an empty vessel, filled only with ridicule, nonsense, and the twaddle of fools. . . . The women and the commonest people read this stuff, without understanding what it was they read. Other people, though they knew no other language, were ashamed to read Yiddish, not wanting to show their backwardness. . . . This was my dilemma, for if I started writing in this "unworthy" language my honor would be besmirched. . . . But my concern for utility conquered my vanity and I decided, come what may, I would have pity for Yiddish, that rejected daughter, for it was time to do something for our people.

What began as a matter of duty soon became a labor of love. Abramovitsch discovered the language he had known since birth. Although he continued to revere Hebrew — he said that speaking only Yiddish or only Hebrew was like breathing through only one nostril — he threw his fortunes in with those of Yiddish: "I fell in love with Yiddish and wedded her forever."

Abramovitsch took the pen name of Mendele Moykher Sforim, Mendele the Bookseller (pen names were ubiquitous among Yiddish writers in this era), and created the persona of an unsophisticated but decent man. Readers were delighted to find a recognizably modern character at the center of Mendele's tales, and ever afterward the author was confused with his fictional self. Although no one would count Mendele as a great writer, his stories, deeply rooted in the folk tradition, created a new genre and legitimatized the language.

Just as important, Mendele began writing at a time when it was possible for him to reach an audience. His debut coincided with the introduction of new technology, as well as with a window of political liberalism. The year after Tsar Alexander II freed the serfs, a weekly Hebrew newspaper in Odessa, *Ha-melitz,* published a Yiddish supplement, *Kol mevaser* (Voice of the People). It was 1862, just when Mendele was beginning to write.

A young fan of Mendele's, Simon Dubnow, gives us a glimpse of him at work, lifting himself out of the Hebrew tradition and creating something new. Dubnow reports that, when he came upon Mendele at his desk, the author insisted that he was not writing but only driving away flies. According to him, Mendele said, "When I write Hebrew, all the prophets fall upon me: Isaiah, Jeremiah, the writers of the Song of Songs and Psalms, and each one of them proposes that I take a ready-made verse or an established phrase from him alone, for this expression. In order not to write in ready-made clichés, I first have to drive away all those flies."

That is a wonderfully apt explanation of the difference between the Hebrew and the Yiddish of the time. Hebrew was a dowager with a stiff, beaded wardrobe, Yiddish a scrappy street kid with a certain panache. Hebrew bore the weight of ages; Yiddish was malleable and loose. Because it was culled from half a dozen languages and was considered insignificant enough that no one looked after its interests, Mendele and his fellow writers could rework it as necessary, creating their own style.

Mendele's mantle was carried by Yitzhak Leib Peretz, his literary son. The younger man (1851–1915) interpreted Yiddish folk materials and themes through a modern European lens. To his eye, the Hasidim were already picturesque, their clothing old fashioned, their wonder tales quaint. An attorney who lived in Warsaw and who spoke Russian and Polish with his family even as he made his home a headquarters for Yiddish writers, Peretz favored a smorgasbord approach to culture, dipping into the traditional world on an as-needed basis. What the two men had in common was the way their work was immediately taken up by a Yiddish-reading public that had been vastly underserved. As newspapers became commonplace and cheap, their writers became household names. In no time, they were being cited as authorities.

As might be expected, the rabbis and religious teachers were not about to let themselves be pushed aside by tale spinners. Even worse, from their point of view, Yiddish speakers could begin to read authors who weren't even Jewish. The last third of the nineteenth century saw the translation into Yiddish of the modern European canon. Shakespeare, Dickens, Baudelaire, Dostoyevsky, and Mann appeared. Jews could read Jack London and Jules Verne, as well as locally produced Yiddish pulp fiction. The Jewish religious and educational establishment railed against the new wave of books. But Yiddish had taken on a new job. In addition to being a shutter that could be closed against non-Jews, it had become a window that opened out on the wider world.

One young woman described the way this transformation played out in her little town. Dvoyre Kutnik of Luninyets recalled her father's opening a lending library:

> He was undaunted by the great difficulty presented both by the Tsarist regime, which did not give its permission, and by the religious Jews, who were afraid that "Avrom Hershl will be trafficking in forbidden books." . . .
>
> Bit by bit my father inculcated in people an appreciation of the Yiddish classics. Every Friday afternoon our house was visited by seamstresses, serving girls, salesgirls, and also working men, tailors and shoemakers, who remembered to stop off at Avrom Hershl Melamed's house on their way back from the bathhouse. The books were mostly hidden in the dresser, while revolutionary pamphlets were kept under the straw mattress on my mother's bed.
>
> The library had a powerful influence on the readers. The small-town inhabitants acquainted themselves with the wider

world. Their eyes were opened, and they began to understand that there was a world full of problems beyond Luninyets, and even beyond Pinsk.

No longer limited to religious teaching and a spotty folk litera- ture, Yiddish readers and writers began to imagine radically dif- ferent alternatives to their lives. As well, they started to become conscious of their background in historical time. In the 1880s Alfred Landau, a German Jew, studied Yiddish as if it were a real language, not just a corrupt form of German. He concluded that it had come from medieval German — a thought that, at the time, was totally new.

Yiddish was accruing a consciousness of its past and a mission for its future, but it still needed a great artist, preferably someone who could use the virtuosity of the language to engage the audience and give it a new sense of itself. Yiddish found that and more in the youngest of the trio of *di classikers,* the classic Yiddish writers — Sholom Aleichem.

Sholom Aleichem was the man who first called Mendele *zeyde.* With his playfulness, suppleness, and mix of styles, accents, and allusions high and low, he wrote work that was Yiddish in both content and form. The writer who had no problem referring to himself, tongue firmly planted in his cheek, as the Great Writer Mr. Sholom Aleichem also, by the very fact of his oeuvre, made the case for Yiddish. Any language that could win the devotion of a writer of such invention and versatility was worthy of respect. As well, his life's path echoed the journeys of both his characters and his readers.

Born Solomon Rabinovitch in 1859 in a small shtetl under tsarist rule in what is today Ukraine, he came from a well-to-do Hasidic family. Rabinovitch described the way his father "acted as agent for land-lease properties, supplied sugar mills with beets, ran the rural post office, traded in wheat, handled freight on barges on the Dnieper River, cut lumber, fattened oxen for the market." His family was central to the community. "Saturday nights we had open house for the entire town for the observance of the Departure of the Sabbath. On the eve of every holy day, the people of Woronko came first to us for the blessing consecrating the festival. All the news of the world reached us first and spread to the rest of the town from our house. For a bit of socializing over a glass of wine, they came to us. For stories about the Rabbi [Hasidic], to our house. For political discussions, to our house."

But this center of influence was not to last. When Solomon was twelve, his father lost all his money and the family was forced to move to a new town, where they ran an inn. The next year his mother died and was replaced by a stepmother who seems to have been especially cruel.

The boy was bright, however, and with a traditional Jewish and a Russian education, as well as strong writing skills, he was able to secure a good job. When he was eighteen, he became the tutor to the children of one of those rare creatures — a wealthy Jewish landowner. He promptly fell in love with the man's eldest daughter. When his employer realized what was happening, he sent the poor young teacher packing. But finally, six years after he had first met her, he and his beloved Olga eloped.

Rabinovitch's new father-in-law, in an about-face, welcomed him with open arms. Then, when the older man died soon afterward, the former tutor gained control over a sizable fortune. Unfortunately, when the Kiev stock market crashed in 1890, the fortune was lost. By age thirty-one Rabinovitch had known wealth and poverty, life in the country, the large city, and the small Jewish town. He had also known a succession of losses, which may have helped to prepare him for his later role as chronicler of the demise of the archetypal Yiddish home.

First in Kiev, then in Odessa, the Rabinovitches established an upper-middle-class Russian-speaking domicile. Olga became a dentist. Their growing family had servants and a summerhouse. Rabinovitch managed money and wrote tales for Hebrew journals.

But, as his daughter Marie Waife-Goldberg later described it, "He was struck by the realization that Hebrew, with its difficult vocabulary, its flowery style, and the scholarship needed for its mastery, was serving only the special few. . . . Besides, a Jewish author *thought* in Yiddish even if he wrote in Hebrew, so why not write directly in the language of his thinking? Why not write in Yiddish?"

Status, was one obvious answer. Rabinovitch was an ambitious young man. But he was also mischievous, warm, creative, and deeply tied to the common folk. It was the latter side of him that won out. In 1883 young Rabinovitch submitted a Yiddish story to *Ha-melitz*, the same journal that had published Mendele. He took as a pseudonym Sholom Aleichem, a standard Yiddish greeting that comes from the Hebrew and means literally "Peace, friend," and began his Yiddish career to immediate acclaim. Like Mendele, the man became twined with his persona. Unlike Mendele, however, Sholom Aleichem was a writer with universal appeal.

His instant popularity propelled him to a perch as the Jewish Mark Twain. (Twain, for his part, had the wit to call himself the American Sholom Aleichem.) Sprightly and fun, his stories were meant to be read aloud. They were full of asides — "What do you think of such talk?" "Doesn't he deserve to be cursed with the deadliest of curses?" — that speak to a modern, self-conscious sensibility. They were sold as cheap pamphlets or printed in the mass-market Yiddish newspapers that grew with the same speed as Sholom Aleichem's career.

As his daughter described it, "On a Friday morning in almost any sizable Jewish community, one could see a woman carrying a basket of food for the Sabbath, fish, *challah* |ritual bread|, vegetables, etc., with a story of my father's on top of the heap. The story was meant for family reading, the man of the house reading it aloud to his wife and children after the meal as part of *Oneg Shabbat*, Delight in the Sabbath."

Sholom Aleichem was the first person to earn a living as a Yiddish author even though, despite tremendous popularity, his financial position was never secure. In addition to his own writing and lecturing, he worked on behalf of Yiddish literature, publishing an anthology called *Di yidishe folks bibliotek* (The Jewish Folk Library).

The social climate throughout the era was precarious at best. The tsarist regime, although sporadically benign, also backed a succession of campaigns against Yiddish publications, constantly changing the rules about what could or could not be printed. Socialist publications like *Der yidisher arbeter* (The Jewish Worker) and *Arbeter-shtime* (Workers' Voice) were forced to circulate underground. The more mainstream journals and papers were sometimes outlawed, sometimes allowed. But whenever they appeared, they flourished. The five million Yiddish-speaking Jews who lived in Russia at the turn of the twentieth century were eager for stories that spoke to their lives.

But the market for Yiddish publications regularly transcended international borders. *Der hoyzfraynd* (The Home Companion) was published in Warsaw. *Der yid* (The Jew) was a biweekly in Cracow; *Di velt* (The World), a weekly in Vienna. All were circulated internationally. Although Yiddish dailies began publication in New York in the 1880s, because of a much more fragile political climate, the first Yiddish daily did not emerge in Russia until 1903 — the St. Petersburg–based *Der fraynd* (The Friend).

In this time of extraordinarily fast and wide-reaching change, Sholom Aleichem helped Jews become conscious of their shtetl-based world just as many of them were leaving it behind. The compacted time frame of appreciation and loss ratchets up the emotional intensity of his work.

To a story called "The Merrymakers," Sholom Aleichem added the subtitle, "Sketches of Disappearing Types": "Obviously the 'Merry Crew' is getting smaller, is shrinking from year to year. Many of the revelers have died out and those who are left will soon go too. And so I hasten to set down their names and to describe each one separately with all his quirks and oddities. Let there be a memorial

no matter how small, let there be a record of how Jews used to celebrate and make merry in their exile when *Simchas Torah* came."

As much as he loved the people, so much did he revel in their
language. Although he referred to it as "the poor Jargon," he adored
the flexibility and vitality of Yiddish. He is a translator's nightmare,
writing the Yiddish that his characters spoke, rich in the nuances
of region and class, sometimes Germanized or Russified, mock-
scholarly or down-to-earth. Mirroring Yiddish speech, he embed-
ded whole blocks of Hebrew in his tales. These included quotations
from the Bible or from the daily or holiday prayers. Sometimes
these chunks of Hebrew are correct; sometimes they are semicor-
rect; sometimes they are purposefully misstated or misinterpreted,
depending on the speaker's personality or level of education.

For example, Shimon-Eli, the plodding central character in "The
Haunted Tailor," has the same tendency toward mangling biblical
references as does Sholom Aleichem's most famous character, Tevye
der milkhiger, Tevye the dairyman. "The Haunted Tailor" is laid
out as a scriptural tale, each section beginning with a Hebrew phrase
introducing us to the mundane events of Shimon-Eli's life, the sort
of structural joke any Yiddish speaker would appreciate. When his
overbearing wife Tsippa-Beila-Reiza demands a goat for the family,
Shimon-Eli replies, "You're right, no doubt. . . . There is a saying,
Every Jew should have a goat. As it is written." Yiddish readers
would have recognized the phrase "As it is written," a formula
included in many Hebrew prayers, and would have known as well
that nowhere in any holy book was it written that every Jew should
have a goat. "Tsippa-Beila-Reiza shrieked, 'I say a goat and he gives
me a quotation. I'll give you quotations. . . . I'll quotation your eyes!
He feeds me quotations. My fine breadwinner, my *schlimazel.* I'll
give you the entire Torah for a cream borscht.'" Nothing could be
more distinctly Yiddish than this borrowing of Hebrew, this
Talmudic taking of logic to its extreme.

But the real genius of Sholom Aleichem was the intimate, just-
between-us-Jews way he helped his readers get some perspective on

their worldly situation — which was, after a brief interval of liberality, swiftly going downhill. The last two decades of the nineteenth century saw the deepening of the world crisis that would lead to world war and revolution. Sholom Aleichem helped his readers to laugh, but it was the nervous chuckle of a person who hurries along a dark street. He looks anxiously over his shoulder while hoping against hope that something better awaits up ahead.

In "The Tenth Man," one of Sholom Aleichem's *Railroad Stories,* the plot revolves around the need of the nine Jewish men in the car to find a tenth so they can pray. One of the nine in particular needs to mark the anniversary of the death of his only son. There is a tenth man in the car, but he gives no sign of being Jewish, and he ignores the father as he relates his sad tale. "It had been a struggle, the boy's father told us, just to get the body returned by the prison so that it could be brought to a Jewish grave — and the youngster, he swore, was perfectly innocent, he had been railroaded at his trial. Not that he hadn't been in thick with the other revolutionaries, but that was still no reason to hang him."

Then all of a sudden the tenth man announces, in Yiddish, "Count me out!" He says he does not believe in such things, and he doesn't bother to specify whether by that he means God, prayer, community, or the interweaving of all three.

The others are horrified, but the bereaved father tells the young nonbelieving Jew he deserves a gold medal and says that, if he agrees to make a tenth, then he, the father, will tell him a tale to explain his opinion. The prayers that ensue are heartfelt, "like balm to one's weary bones." The father then launches an account that turns into three tales in one, including a Jew who saves a group of fellow Jews, a gentile who saves a townful of Jews, and a Jewish boy who gains exemption from the hated Russian draft when a running sore is discovered on his head. Then the father concludes: "And now tell me, my dear young friend, do you understand your true worth? You were born a Jew, you'll soon be a goy, and you're quite a running sore already."

In real life, the man who became Sholom Aleichem felt the cer-
tainties of the old familiar world drop out from under his feet. The
shtetls of his youth were dying, and his upper-middle-class urban
existence gave out as well. His family was trapped by the vicious
pogroms that erupted in Russia in 1905. They managed to escape to
Western Europe, where, unfortunately, the Dreyfus affair in
France had recently demonstrated once again the chimera of safety
for European Jews.

Suffering from tuberculosis and diabetes, Solomon Rabinovich,
aka Sholom Aleichem, aka Mr. Sholom Aleichem the famous
author, made the anxious rounds of European spas and sanatoriums.
The outbreak of World War 1 found him and his family at a
German spa. As Russian citizens they were deported, finding temporary refuge in Denmark. But Sholom Aleichem, now in precarious financial straits as well as poor health, felt he would do better in
America, where he had once had a successful lecture tour. In a
move that showed the breadth of his popularity, the editors of all
the New York Yiddish newspapers joined together and found a
wealthy Jew who advanced first-class fare for the Rabinovich family. In 1915 they arrived in New York.

With war engulfing Europe, Sholom Aleichem, ailing and
strapped for cash, wrote as much as he could. In fiction he returned to
his ersatz hometown. His story, "Progress in Kasrielevke" describes
how much he yearned for the past and how clearly he understood that
it was gone: "Where did the famous little people with their little ideas
disappear to? Where were all those know-it-all, bearded Jews who
poked fun at everything? Where were those young people with canes
who used to wander around the marketplace looking for business in
vain, who out of depths of despair ribbed one another and then the
whole world?" Not only the people, but also their archetypal
Yiddish communal institutions were gone:

> As I walked through the village, I looked for at least one of
> the old clubs. I remember there used to be clubs to the point

of excess here. And I'm not talking about the Psalms and Mishna Clubs. I mean societies like the Free-Loan, the Free-Kitchen, the Visit-the Sick, the Clothe-the-Poor, the Help-the-Needy, the Medical-Aid, the Relieve-the-Oppressed. It seemed that all these groups had gone the way of their founders. They passed on like most of the little people, like lonely old Rabbi Yozifl, may the fruits of Paradise be his. Thinking of him brought tears to my eyes.

Sholom Aleichem revised one of his stories of Tevye the dairy-man, a series he had been working on for twenty years, the story of a man who, in trying to marry off his daughters, is in a sense trying to find a future. Where in an earlier version Tevye had been able to deflect a crowd of peasants bent on violence, Sholom Aleichem now saw that it was too late for the Tevyes of the world. In the new version, the poor innocent who chatted with God, who railed at God, who mangled every Hebrew quote he could half-remember, was driven from his village and his home.

Sholom Aleichem continued to write short stories and in June 1915 started publishing his autobiography. It ran in weekly install-ments in the New York Yiddish newspaper *Der tog* (The Day). His work was also introduced to the English-speaking public. In January 1916 the *World*, New York's largest English-language paper, began to run his series *Motel, Son of Paysie the Cantor.* It was syndicated in newspapers across the United States, with a combined circulation of five million.

But Sholom Aleichem was not able to enjoy his American suc-cess. A year after he arrived in the United States, his health gave out. In May 1916 he died in his apartment on Kelly Street in the Bronx.

His funeral was called the event of the decade by Jews and non-Jews alike. His will was entered into the *U.S. Congressional Record.* A portion of it reads, "Wherever I die I should be laid to rest not among the aristocrats, the elite, the rich, but rather among the plain people, the toilers, the common folk, so that the tombstone that will be placed on my grave will grace the simple graves about me, and the simple graves will adorn my tombstone, even as the plain people have, during my life, beatified their folk writer."

A guard of Yiddish writers stood watch while some fifteen thousand mourners trooped up the apartment house stairs to pay their last respects. Newspapers estimated the crowd watching the funeral procession variously as one hundred thousand and two hundred thousand. His daughter wrote that the people who lined the route from the Bronx through Manhattan out to the cemetery in Brooklyn were "weeping bitterly as if the deceased was a close member of their own family, a father, a brother."

Sholom Aleichem helped Yiddish speakers become publicly aware of the sheltering world they had created for themselves just as it was being swept from them. He and his readers ran a race against time. The flowering of Yiddish literature coincided with the scattering of the Yiddish world.

CHAPTER 6

The Road to Czernowitz:
The Politics of Language

אין אלגעמיין, קען געזאָגט װערן אז יידן האָבן זיך ניט געמישט און זיך
ניט אינטערעסירט אין פּאָליטיק. אָבער געליטן פֿון פּאָליטיק האָבן זײ
גענוג אין אַלע צײיטן.

In algemeyn, ken gezogt vern az yidn hobn zikh
nit gemisht un zikh nit interesirt in politik. Ober gelitn
fun politik hobn zey genug in ale tseytn.

Generally, one can say that Jews didn't mix in and weren't
interested in politics. But miseries from politics they had
enough of in all times.

Bransk Yizker book

As Yiddish writers worked to make sense of the changes in the
world around them, the pace of those changes kept gathering
speed. One new development was both cause and effect. Until this
point, Yiddish-speaking Jews had largely distanced themselves
from politics. Now they rushed in, eager to remake their world.

In the last quarter of the nineteenth century and the first quarter
of the twentieth, the traditional Jewish society splintered and then
split tantalizingly, frighteningly wide open. Jews could choose —
indeed, had to choose — which parts of their religious and cultural
past would most effectively lead them forward. To their surprise,
intellectuals, politicians, and linguists discovered that one of the

71

answers — sometimes The Answer — was Yiddish. The thousand-year-old folk language became a vehicle of transformation. It was also itself reborn.

The birth, however, was not an easy one. As the old shtetl organizations broke down, Jews brought their manifold organizing and community-building skills, along with centuries of unfulfilled yearnings, to the construction of new ideologies, visions, and movements. Every group seemed to have a different plan for the future, and the "isms" (*izmes* in Yiddish) multiplied like mice. Should Jews throw in their lot with the great working class? Would they always be separate because they were Jews? Should they stay in Eastern Europe or try their luck in England, South America, or that great magnet, the United States? Would they be better off building their own homeland, or should they just hunker down in the lands where they were?

And always, always, the question: What language should they speak? How would their words shape and define who they were and who they would become? What would those words say about their link to each other and to the great past? The choice of whether to speak Yiddish, the language of the Jewish folk; some form of Hebrew, which would need a major infusion of life; or whether to speak another, non-Jewish European language, was heavily weighted with the baggage of history and self-esteem.

In 1887 one Yiddish speaker, acutely aware of the way language could bring people together or keep them apart, even invented an international language from scratch. Ludwig Lazarus Zamenhoff, an optometrist from Bialystok, an area that bounced back and forth between Poland and Russia, came up with a language he called Esperanto. But a Jewish joke describes an Esperanto conference in which the delegates speak the *real* international language — Yiddish.

In this time of social upheaval, however, Jews looked for answers everywhere. *Every man has his own mishegas*, his own craziness, the Yiddish proverb says, and this period of aestheticists, anarchists, assimilationists, Bundists, folkists, Golus Nationalists, Hebraists, Marxists, nihilists, socialists, territorialists, Yiddishists, Zionists, and Labor Zionists seemed to bear it out.

The year 1897 saw the birth of two world movements — Bundism and Zionism — that took very different paths. Both played important roles in the destiny of Yiddish. The first organization to be founded was the Bund, the General Jewish Workers' Union, in Lithuania, Poland, and Russia. (*Bund* means "union.") It was begun in Vilna (now Vilnius, Lithuania) by left-leaning middle-class Jews. It focused on the here-and-now problems of the Jewish proletariat, a population that was growing exponentially as Jews moved to the cities. These new urban dwellers felt the frustration of being exposed to new ideas even as their few political options shrank. The Bundists decided to work to improve the situation of European Jews.

A Bundist leader, Vladimir Medem, recalled how he had come to this way of thinking, as opposed to Zionism, which to him meant spinning dreams of some mythic return to faraway Palestine, a land Jews had not seen in almost two thousand years: "I remember one evening when we went walking together through the Jewish quarter, in the outlying poor little streets with their poor little houses. It was Friday night; the streets were quiet and empty; the Sabbath candles burned in the little houses. . . . I was strongly impressed by that unique charm of the peaceful Friday nights and felt a romantic association with the Jewish past, a warm, intimate closeness." This closeness, however, did not lead him away from the European environment he had always known. "My sentiment for Jewry was always, as a Zionist might express it, a *galut* |exile| feeling. The palm trees and the vineyards of Palestine were alien to me. I think this is an indication that my Jewishness was really an ingrained living Jewishness, not a literary fancy."

After all, the Jews had lived in Europe for almost two millennia. Any decent, caring person would work to improve their future right there. Bundists drew strength from their class consciousness and from their folk culture. Both of these came from, and were expressed through, Yiddish, the language of the common people. One of the Bund's first publications was a Yiddish translation of the *Communist Manifesto* with an introduction by the young leftist Chaim Zhitlovsky, whom we have met before. Called "Yiddish — Why?," the introduction linked the language with left-wing thought in a way that would endure for decades to come.

The year 1897 also saw the birth of a very different organization. In that year the Zionists held their first international congress in Basle, Switzerland. Led by Theodore Herzl, they chose for the name of their organization the Jerusalem hill Mount Zion, on which the city of David had been built — the place where Jews prayed that they might someday return.

Their goal was quite different from that of the Eurocentric Bundists; they wanted a homeland controlled by Jews. The location of this new land, however, was not at all fixed. Some Zionists were in favor of Eretz Israel, now known as Palestine. (Later on in our story we will meet the slightly mad shtetl-born Eliezer Perlman, who was, at the time, almost single-handedly trying to stake out a Jewish future in Jerusalem.) Proposals were floated for various more or less practical sites, including Cyprus, the Dakotas, and Uganda, the last of which was actually under serious consideration for several years, rejected only in 1905.

The Zionists met yearly, wrote voluminously, and kept careful notes. Naturally they needed an official language, something that could be spoken by most of the movement. For many decades, the obvious choice was Yiddish. When Herzl translated his German-language Zionist Congress brochure into Hebrew, it sold only two thousand copies. When Sholom Aleichem translated it into Yiddish, it sold twenty-five thousand. In a low moment, Herzl used classic Yiddish slang, albeit with Germanic spelling, when he complained in his diary, "Fact is — which I conceal from everyone — that I have only an army of *Schnorrers* [beggars]. I am in command only of boys, beggars and *Schmocken* [pricks]."

The writer Maurice Samuel made this jibe about Zionists trying to speak Hebrew: "To speak Hebrew is like riding on a noble horse; at first exhilarating, then rather uncomfortable, and finally a torture. Dropping into Yiddish is like getting off the horse onto your own two feet. What a *mekhae!*" (Yiddish for "pleasure.")

The secretary general of the first Zionist conference was to play a critical cameo role in the history of Yiddish. Nathan Birnbaum (1864–1937) was a brilliant but dour man, a nonpracticing Viennese attorney and freelance intellectual. His parents were Hasidim from Galicia, which was then a province of the Austro-Hungarian Empire. (Its territory falls in what is today Poland and Ukraine.)

Growing up in Vienna, Birnbaum had gotten the kind of secular education unknown in the provinces at the time. As a modern worldly Jew, he shied away from both the Yiddish of his parents, as well as from *judeln,* the local Jewish German dialect that had survived, despite the influence of the *maskilim.* Still, a century after the *Haskalah,* a Jew in the Germanic lands knew that if he wanted to get ahead in the world, he had better take pains to speak a German that was beyond reproach.

Unfortunately, Birnbaum's face belied his refined speech. His long, gaunt, dark visage, which fit the German stereotype of what a Jew looked like, prevented him from building any reasonable kind of legal career. He was thrown back into the arms of his people, whether he wanted to be there or not.

While still a student, in 1882 he founded an organization with the Hebrew name of Kadimah, with the dual meaning of "eastward" and "forward." He then established a journal called *Selbst-emancipation!* (Self-Emancipation) and even coined the term Zionism. When Herzl planned the first-ever Zionist Congress, Birnbaum was an obvious choice for the organizing committee. Unfortunately, the two men clashed badly. Herzl was narcissistic and controlling, Birnbaum shrill and easily angered. Where Herzl could be charismatic and charming when necessary, even Birnbaum's admirers admitted that he was a difficult character. Herzl, a better politician than Birnbaum could ever hope to becoming, froze the dour attorney out. Although the Zionists met every year, Birnbaum never attended another congress.

It is impossible to know how much of Birnbaum's subsequent theoretical shift was a result of this personal tiff. In short order he abandoned Zionism and threw himself into an alternate plan, which he called Golus Nationalism. It had some similarities to Bundism but championed Jewish nationalism in place of the left-wing organization's class consciousness. Birnbaum argued that, rather than focus on some more or less unattainable extraterritorial homeland, Jews should work to create a haven — even a real country — where they already lived, in Europe. This was even becoming a reasonable idea, given the European national and ethnic groundswell. Other ethnic groups — Poles, Ukrainians, Finns — were making nationalistic demands. Why not the Jews?

One answer was immediate — language. European national movements were based on national languages. If the Jews wanted to become a nation among nations, they would have to establish an official, spoken, common tongue. The obvious candidate was Yiddish. And even though Birnbaum called it "that hoarse child of the ghetto, that miscarriage of the diaspora," he began to study it.

Soon Birnbaum, like so many others before him, succumbed to its charms. The ascetic intellectual fell in love. Always a man in search of a mission, Birnbaum began to see Yiddish as being worthy of his considerable devotion — the true national language of European Jews. He took on both the language and the idea of the language as a calling.

Birnbaum was hardly alone in his understanding that Yiddish, which by that time had between eight and nine million speakers worldwide, could become a rallying point for Jewish identity. In 1905 the writer Abraham Reisen had written in the journal he published in Warsaw, *Dos yidishe vort* (The Yiddish Word), "Yiddish is not just a means to educate the masses but a goal in its own right. It will serve the Jewish intelligentsia and will thus reflect all the trends and tendencies of the great world, so that the Jewish intellectual interested in higher questions will not have to resort to other literatures in other languages, a move that alienates him from the Jewish people." Where the Bundists had seen language as a unifying force in the service of politics, Reisen saw it as an intellectual quest. At the same time, for Birnbaum, the language became an obsession.

The first validation of Birnbaum's idea of promoting Yiddish as an agent of Jewish advancement came from the other end of the globe. In 1906 South Africa, its population swelling with Russian Jews escaping from waves of government-sanctioned anti-Semitism, placed Yiddish on the list of European languages that immigrants could use to fulfill their literacy requirements. This meant that if the only language a person could read and write was Yiddish — even with its Hebrew characters, its fusion vocabulary, its areas of linguistic poverty and richness — that person could be judged to be literate. This was a breakthrough — the first time anywhere in the world that Yiddish had received official government recognition. It was a landmark for the language and its people.

Another tantalizing possibility soon followed. The Austro-Hungarian Empire offered ethnic groups or nationalities the possibility of becoming autonomous regions under the Hapsburg umbrella. (Like most countries of the time, the empire was multilingual.) A variety of peoples — Ukrainians, Serbs, Croatians, and "Czechoslavs," as well as Jews — envisioned the benefits of becoming nations within the empire. They would be able to take control of state-sponsored courts and schools. They could receive state subsidies in theater, literature, journalism, and art. And, of course, the psychological boost would be immeasurable. To establish a Jewish nation, even if it wasn't in the ancestral homeland, even if it remained a province of a foreign empire, would still be a tremendous step forward.

But first the Golus Nationalists would have to win at least shared control of a province. Galicia, where Birnbaum's parents had been born, was an obvious choice. A million Jews lived there, and a million more could influence events from the neighboring province of Bukovina.

But Yiddish speakers would have to mobilize themselves to demonstrate their political strength. For Jews who had spent the past two millennia ignoring their status in the Christian world, this represented about as big a change as could be conceived. And the Polish- and German-speaking Christians who controlled these eastern outposts of the Hapsburg Empire were not about to relinquish any of their power. The stakes were high, and both sides knew it. The 1906 census contained only two choices for native languages — German or Polish. For the first time ever, Jews staged a write-in campaign for Yiddish.

The Christians were in control, however, and Jews who declared for Yiddish were jailed for their efforts. Recognition would not come easily. But the Jews, becoming aware of just how much they had missed during their centuries of disenfranchisement, were not about to give up.

The very next year, hopes were again raised when the empire granted universal suffrage for the parliamentary election. If Jews could vote, they could elect a Jewish delegate. Birnbaum decided to run for a seat from Galicia. Many of the Ukrainians who lived there supported him. They saw the Jews as natural allies in their goal of establishing their own national state. But many Galician Jews feared anti-Semitic outbreaks more than they believed in the possibility of change.

Sadly, their fears were justified. On election day, imperial troops sealed off the provincial capital. The only people who voted were those on the government payroll. Birnbaum was defeated; no surprise. But he was resilient and soon set his sights on the next opportunity, the census scheduled for 1910. If he could get Yiddish recognized as a native language, it would have the potential of becoming a national language. If Austro-Hungarian Jews could demonstrate that they had a national language, they would be that much closer to becoming a nation. Birnbaum was committed. He was willing to try.

But first the matter of bread and butter intervened. Unable to practice his profession, and with a wife and three children to support, this man who spawned a succession of brilliant, utopian dreams was always casting about for ways to earn a living. In 1908 he embarked on a lecture tour of the United States. As more and more Jews fled the anti-Semitism that was endemic in Eastern Europe, New York was rapidly becoming the world's largest Jewish city. During this trip Birnbaum began to promote his latest plan — an international conference on Yiddish.

This startling idea had been hatched entirely in Birnbaum's active mind. Although at this point Yiddish had already been spoken for almost a thousand years, it had no written history, no standards of spelling, grammar, or usage. There had never been any gathering of any sort devoted to the theory, practice, or study of Yiddish.

Birnbaum found two allies in New York — the novelist and dramatist David Pinski, and Chaim Zhitlovski, the cerebral left-wing theorist who described shtetl Jews and translated Marx. In Pinski's Bronx apartment and in lower East Side "evenings," this trio presented their plan to the public. They believed that as religion declined in the modern world, the Yiddish language would fill in the gap, functioning as the glue that would hold the Jewish people together.

One small problem was that Birnbaum the lecturer could barely stumble along in Yiddish. Although he had studied it, he still could not comfortably speak the language onto which he was now pinning the hopes of an entire nation. This irony was not lost on his audiences. Years later, he would recall, "The humorous papers, in particular, set upon me with a vengeance. But to tell the truth, I played right into their hands in that I held my lectures in German."

Undaunted by the mixed reception he received in the United States, Birnbaum stepped up plans for the conference. The agenda was incredibly ambitious, covering ten different topics, including spelling, grammar, and foreign and new words, as well as such problems as the economic situation of the Yiddish writer. Of course there was no funding or sponsorship of any kind. In the beginning of summer 1908, the three men sent an invitation to several Yiddish organizations whose addresses they had on hand. The invitation was also published in the American and European Yiddish press. As well, they sent copies to the most important Yiddish authors of the day.

The invitation first described the progress of Yiddish: "Its literature has achieved a level of which no one had imagined it capable. Yiddish newspapers are distributed in hundreds of thousands of copies daily and weekly. Yiddish poets write songs which are sung by the people, stories which are read by the people, plays which the people eagerly flock to see." Still, for all of that, the language was not cherished:

> Where older languages were "guarded as a precious child," Yiddish was allowed to roam about freely and wildly in the linguistic world to attract all sorts of diseases and perhaps even death. . . . Thousands of Yiddish words are replaced by German, Russian and English words which are completely unnecessary. The live rules of the language which are born and develop with it in the mouths of the people go unrecorded and it appears not to possess any such rules. Each person writes it in another way with his own spelling because no standard authoritative Yiddish orthography has thus far been established. . . .
>
> True, the disgrace attached to Yiddish in the past has diminished. People are less and less ashamed of the contemporary language of our people. . . . But it is still an object of ridicule and contempt.

The invitation called for "some sort of protection for our precious mother-tongue" and offered voting status at the conference to all who agreed with the organizers' aims.

The five-day conference was called for August 1908 in Czernowitz, a middle-size city in the Austro-Hungarian province of Bukovina. (Today it is in Ukraine.) It was chosen because it was home to many Vienna University students who had been influenced by Birnbaum's writings and lectures (they would be able to do the grunt work for the event) and because it was a centrally located, multicultural, multiethnic city in which Jews felt relatively at ease. Even so, the leader of the *kehile,* the local Jewish community, would not let the student organizers use its meeting space because he feared anti-Semitic reprisals.

The conference planners were abundantly endowed with idealism but woefully short on organization. Nobody seems to have taken notes. The agenda was immediately scuttled. Decorum was thrown out the window. The left-wing Bundists, who had recently adopted Yiddish as "the language of the Jewish proletariat and of the intellectuals that serve and lead the proletariat," had their own political agenda, as did the right-wing Zionists, who did not have the faintest interest in the class struggle at home. Participants faced off: champions of Yiddish against proponents of a revival of Hebrew, left against right. There was also plenty of posturing, confrontations, walk-outs, and tears.

The conference floundered on what was paradoxically both the smallest and largest detail: the difference between "a" and "the." Birnbaum, giving his first-ever speech in Yiddish, called for the elevation of Yiddish to the status of *the* national Jewish language. Those who supported this position felt that, if the conference could agree on that description, the Hapsburgs might be more inclined to give Yiddish its official due.

But that would mean setting aside the claim of Hebrew to being a national Jewish language. It had been two thousand years since *loshn koydesh,* the holy language, had been the universal Jewish spoken tongue. It had been a thousand years since it had been much used in daily speech. Even though a few obsessed and scattered souls were, at the time, working to modernize it in the Holy Land, few sane people thought they would succeed. But still, *koydesh* was *koydesh,* and the thought of having lowly Yiddish elbow out the respected, revered tongue, even if it was only in the political arena, was wrenching.

Even the beloved Yiddish writer and conference participant Y. L. Peretz could not bring himself to do it, in the end. He started off boldly enough, ready, it seemed, to elevate Yiddish, proclaiming, "Let the state no longer falsify the cultures of peoples. . . . We proclaim to the world: we are a Jewish people and Yiddish is our language. In our language we want to live our lives, create our cultural treasures, and no longer sacrifice them to the false interests of the state which is only the protector of ruling, dominating peoples and the blood-sucker of the weak." But he could not, when push came to shove (and it almost did come to blows), pit Yiddish directly against Hebrew. By the end of the conference he was backtracking: "The Conference only has the right to undertake to help the folk language [Yiddish] to rise to the level of a national language."

He would support "a." He would not support "the." And there it stood. Yiddish might be half of one's breath, as Mendele had said. But the conference was not prepared to stop breathing through the other nostril, to set Hebrew aside.

In the end, the conference issued a compromise proposal, recognizing Yiddish as a national language and demanding for it "political, communal, and cultural equality." It also noted that "each participant in the Conference, as well as each member of the future organization, retains the freedom to relate to the Hebrew language according to his personal convictions."

Except that there were no future organizations, conferences, committees, books, or reports. The disorganized undertaking soon petered out. Then came the next blow. The year after Czernowitz, the Imperial Court in Vienna handed down the verdict that Jews in Galicia and Bukovina were not an ethnic group but a religious community, and thus Yiddish would not appear with the eight other language choices on the upcoming 1910 census.

This was crushing. But for the first time, Jews in Galicia and Bukovina were so incensed they were ready for action. They held rallies and mass meetings; they organized a write-in campaign to place Yiddish on the census forms. Birnbaum himself led a rally of three thousand people in Czernowitz — this in the city whose Jewish community, two years before, could not commit itself to housing the Yiddish conference. The local newspaper of the Jewish Social Democratic Party cried, "Citizens! Workers: we call on you to make a strong protest. We call you into struggle! In the Jewish streets, in the name of the organized Jewish proletariat we raise the slogan: in the census questionnaire state that your language is Yiddish!"

Unfortunately, on census day it all came to naught. When the forms were handed in, government functionaries simply erased the word "Yiddish" and, depending on geography, replaced it with either "Polish" or "German," never minding the fact that the people being counted may not have understood a word of German or Polish and may not have spoken anything but Yiddish from birth until death.

It was a hard blow, but almost a decade after the conference, after the carnage of World War 1, there were in fact two direct results of what champions of Yiddish took to calling "Holy Czernowitz." In 1917 the United States followed the lead of South Africa and approved Yiddish as meeting the literacy requirements of immigrants. And in 1918 the Treaty of Versailles, which marked the end of World War 1, recognized the language rights of several European minorities, including Jews. It did not specify what Jewish language or languages were meant, but it was still a historic step. Jews in the newly established Polish Republic gained the right to control state-funded elementary education in their own language. For the first time in human history, an international treaty protected the linguistic rights of the Jews.

CHAPTER 7

Russia: Kissed by a Thief

נאָך אַ קיש פֿון אַ גנב, צייל איבער דײַנע צײן.

Nokh a kish fun a ganef, tzeyl iber dayne tzeyn.

If you're kissed by a thief, count your teeth.

By the early twentieth century Yiddish was a modern international language, its story unfolding concurrently in many
locales — good for Yiddish, but bad for us who must keep track of
its interweaving strands. Characters we meet in Russia show up
later, still arguing in Yiddish, in the cafeterias of New York. An
idea hatched on one side of the Atlantic or the Mediterranean
comes to fruition across the sea. Although this chapter, like each of
the chapters that follow, focuses on events in one country, we should
remember that we're looking at a language that can't be confined by
national boundaries. Our best hope, then, is to take a lesson from
the Jewish Turk at the shtetl fair and try to keep several balls up in
the air.

Along the twisted roads of Russian history the phrase "the Jewish
Problem" appears again and again. It is never explained, always a
given, understood from its context to imply that Jews are like food
poisoning or dysentery in the body politic — something to be lived
with intimately and interminably. No matter what the Russians
tried, it was impossible for them to ignore the Jews, impossible to
digest them, impossible to disgorge them.

Because virtually all Russian Jews spoke Yiddish, while only a minority of them were fluent in Russian, the language was often the stand-in for the people. In Mother Russia and in its successor the Union of Soviet Socialist Republics, Yiddish was demeaned, extolled, and exploited — all with the abrupt and seemingly irrational policy shifts that have been the hallmark of the country. As one writer, Pinkhos Kaganovich, known as Der Nister, the Hidden One, described one of the low moments of this relationship, "We have been left with nothing. . . . we have no God and no Torah. All we have are the letters of the Yiddish alphabet."

We will begin our Russian tale at the end of the nineteenth century with a woman, Esther Frumkin, who played a central role in the turbulent transition from monarchy to state socialism. She was one of the most powerful Jews, and most powerful women, of her day. A solid person with a broad face and hair severely parted in the middle, she wore an expression as weighty as that of any of her male colleagues. This demonic worker and inspirational speaker was a champion of the Jewish laboring class. Because the mark of proletarian Jews was their language, Yiddish became the arena of her work.

Frumkin was born Malka Lifshitz in 1880 in Minsk, a large Russian city with a population that was more than half Jewish. Her grandfather was a rabbi, but her father, a well-to-do merchant, was a man with more liberal ideas. He educated his daughters in Russian and the emerging modern Hebrew, as well as in Yiddish. Like a small number of other bourgeois Jewish women, she attended a Russian *gymnasium,* or elevated high school. Given the Jewish value on education and the tradition of women making their way in the world while their husbands studied, it is not surprising that by the end of the nineteenth century, Jewish girls were three times as likely to be able to read and write Russian as their Christian counterparts, even though for the Jewish girls Russian was a second language. Still, Yiddish was omnipresent among Jews. When the first-ever census was taken in tsarist Russia in 1897, almost 98 percent of Jews listed Yiddish as their native tongue.

But change was sweeping the Romanov Empire. And much of it, in the short term, did not help the Jews. The urban factories that tempted them from their shtetls only served up a different sort of poverty — rootless and anonymous, without the stability and support of the small-town *kehiles*. One 1903 observer noted that "fully 80 percent of the Jewish population of Vilna do not know in the evening where they will obtain food the next morning." Although non-Jewish citizens were not well off either, Jews suffered from additonal burdens of discriminatory taxation as well as exclusion from the more lucrative trades and professions.

Luckily for Frumkin, her family was secure. From her comfortable home, she must have been familiar with the traditional Yiddish patterns of taking responsibility — housewives handing out *shalach-mones,* Purim baskets, to the poor, or feeding the indigent as part of wedding celebrations. But in the newly industrialized society, this sort of piecemeal *tsdoke,* charity, was doing a poor job of insulating Jewish workers from the worst excesses of the new capitalism.

Soon, the determined young woman was caught up in the left-wing revolutionary fervor of the age, setting her goal as nothing less than a fundamental restructuring of society. By age seventeen she was teaching Jewish working women at secret "workers' circles." Basic education came first: math, geography, Russian. But right behind were the latest socialist ideas. Frumkin later recalled:

> We would sit until one in the morning in a stuffy room, with only a little gas lamp burning. Often, little children would be sleeping in the same room and the woman of the house would walk around listening for the police. The girls would listen to the leader's talk and would ask questions, completely forgetting the dangers, forgetting that it would take three quarters of an hour to get home, wrapped in the cold torn remnant of a coat and through deep snow. . . . With what rapt attention they listened to the talks on cultural history, on surplus value, commodity, wages, life in other lands. How many questions

they would ask! What joy would light their eyes after the circle leaders produced a new number of *Yidisher arbeter* [Jewish Worker, a socialist newspaper]. Or even a brochure!

Frumkin saw firsthand the importance of writing, the power of words. She went on to the university in St. Petersburg, where she studied education and philology, the study of language. Back home again in Minsk, she became active in the Bund, the left-wing champion of the Jewish proletariat. She soon became its only female decision maker.

Idealistic middle-class Jews like Frumkin were often caught between conflicting loyalties. Although they had been brought up to value the great Russian culture to which they were just gaining some access, their sympathies lay with the poor Jews who mistrusted the Russians and their language. Athough some Jewish intellectuals like Lev Trotsky, born Leon Bronshtein, identified with the Russian left, those like Frumkin who joined the Bund soon realized how central Yiddish was to Jewish proletarian life.

Those young reformers who had abandoned it for Russian took it up again. Full of visionary zeal and romantic intentions, many found in Yiddish the qualities that had attracted them to the working people who spoke it. They were entranced by its rhythms, smitten by the earthiness of its proverbs. It is easy to imagine their appreciating a saying like, *if you could pay people to die for you, the poor would make a good living.* As they championed the simple poor, they also worked to raise the status of what they saw as a vibrant, honest tongue.

Even more: They saw that Yiddish could be the medium in which workers and intellectuals together created their new vision of the Jews. Cleansed of its biblical references, it could become an indigenous rallying point. It would unite Jews without resorting to rabbis, holidays, synagogues, or other reminders of a theocratic past. Improving the status of Yiddish, the language of the disenfranchised, the language of women and of the poor, early on became a structural plank in the Bundist platform.

Frumkin, from her female perspective, understood the strength of the home-based Jewish women's religious traditions — the Friday-night candle lighting, the Passover seders, the special holiday foods rich with meaning. For example, the *challah,* the special bread that graced the Sabbath meal, was lovingly braided by the women who baked it. But on Rosh Hashonah, the New Year, it was formed into a circle, to remind those about to consume it of the cycle of the year. Or it might be shaped like a bird, a *faigele challah,* to evoke the sins of the past year that would, they hoped, fly away. Frumkin the educator appreciated the power of intimate lessons, of *heymish,* homespun, symbols, something at which Yiddish culture excelled. She was one of the people who worked to imbue the old religious rituals with new political meaning, transforming them into Bundist rites.

The Bund grew quickly. In the first two decades of the twentieth century, it became a counterculture, an alternate universe. It also became Frumkin's home. She traveled to Western Europe, learning about the new Montessori system of education. She wrote for the Bundist press. She helped to organize a system of secular Yiddish schools for children, as well as societies for literature, music, and drama for adults. The Bundist *folkshuls* and the *cheder metukan,* improved schools, used modern pedagogic techniques and taught worldly subjects. With branches for children and adults, they were Frumkin's old women's workers' circles on a larger scale.

Like many Yiddish writers, Frumkin adopted a pen name, Esther Frumkin or sometimes just Esther, after the Jewish queen of Purim fame. (Frumkin's given name, Malke, means "queen.") Her goal was to replace what she saw as the old superstitions that had weighed heavily on women with a new consciousness of family and class. Women, the natural leaders, would model a home-based morality that would be an example to all the laboring masses.

Not surprisingly, all this political activism caught the attention of the tsarist government. For her political work, Frumkin was arrested three times. For a while, she was also deported from Russia.

Although we have records of long disputatious political debates, we know little about Frumkin's personal life. We do know that she was married briefly three times, once to a fellow Bundist, Boris Frumkin. One source has him dying of the tuberculosis he contracted in prison soon after Frumkin had given birth to their child; another has him alive on the eve of World War II. Another of her husbands was a rabbi named Wichmann; indeed, a different source names him, not the Bundist, as the father of her daughter. This rabbinical connection is intriguing, the lack of information frustrating given Frumkin's antirabbinical work in later years.

We know one more personal detail: Frumkin remained a responsible family woman, caring for her child, the child of her wet nurse, and, after her sister's death, her two nieces as well.

Frumkin's life was ruled by ideology and punctuated by high drama. At the 1908 Czernowitz conference, when some of the participants were temporarily excluded from the event's formal banquet because they were not wearing proper evening clothes, she registered an objection. But even after the policy had been changed and the ill-clad delegates admitted, she was not pacified. She made an angry speech and stormed out of the hall.

But Frumkin at Czernowitz also took a broader view. And because she was the Bundist delegate as well as the correspondent for the Vilna Bundist newspaper, her opinion carried a lot of weight. Frumkin, more than anyone, pressed the conference on the question of recognizing Yiddish as being the only Jewish national language, thus stalling consideration of other items on the agenda. Some have argued that she was the person most responsible for the conference's lack of results.

When Peretz proposed establishing an international system of Yiddish schools, libraries, theaters, and cultural institutions, Frumkin put her considerable strength into opposing the idea. This seems bizarre, given her commitment to Yiddish and to the Jewish working classes, who would only have benefited from the plan. Evidently Frumkin was afraid that, if Yiddish became identified with all the world's Jews, it would dilute its meaning for Russian Jews. She saw Yiddish as being the rallying point for Jews under tsarist oppression, and she did not want its potency diminished by its use throughout the diaspora. Frumkin felt so strongly about this that she resigned from the conference in protest. If this all sounds convoluted and excessive, we should keep in mind the widespread expectation of ideological purity. Ideas, positions, and arguments were all these people had.

But conference histrionics must have looked like child's play when, soon afterward, war and revolution shook the world. The trauma and destruction of World War 1 were compounded by the equally devastating upheaval of the revolution and civil war. The Russian economy was devastated, and it was only too easy to blame the Jews. At least a hundred thousand were killed in pogroms. Entire shtetls were destroyed, and thousands of Jewish orphans haunted cities and towns.

In the province of Ukraine, for example, while the population as a whole increased by 36 percent between 1897 and 1926, the number of Jews declined by 5 percent. Thousands more would have perished were it not for the charity that regularly arrived from Jews who had emigrated to the United States.

When the Russian Revolution broke out, it was widely welcomed by Jews who had no love for the Romanovs and felt that conditions for them could only improve. The March 20, 1917, issue of the New York Yiddish newspaper the *Forward* proclaimed, in a banner headline, "Jewish troubles are at an end."

But when the Bolsheviks consolidated power in postrevolutionary Russia, they were wary of Jews, who, it was felt, were susceptible to having mixed loyalties. Although before the revolution the Bolsheviks had agreed to the Bund's platform of cultural autonomy, a highlight of which was education in Yiddish, when they came to power they changed their minds. One of their first campaigns was to disband the Bund. The point man for this effort was Trotsky, who, for one of the few times in his life, publicly defined himself as a Jew.

This must have been an excruciatingly difficult period for the Bundist leaders. Frumkin was one of those who counseled folding their beloved organization into the Bolsheviks, and it was her view that prevailed. The Russian Bund dissolved itself in 1921. Jewish Communists then agreed that, to set an example, they would strike the blows against Jewish institutions.

The former Bundists gained one important concession, however. The Bolsheviks made good on their old promise to respect Yiddish. At first it might just have been common sense. With 108 nationalities and twenty-two lesser ethnic groups in the new Soviet Union, it was obvious that creating the new Soviet citizen was going to take resources and time. Changing a people's language was too much of a luxury for early Soviet days. In 1919 Lenin called for "support not only for real equality in rights, but also for the development of the language, the literature of the toiling masses of the formerly oppressed nations." And who had been more oppressed under the tsars than the Jews?

The Communist Party created special Jewish sections whose task it was to disseminate propaganda and carry out party policy among Jewish workers in the Yiddish language, and "to see to it that the Jewish masses have a chance to satisfy all their intellectual needs in that language." Yiddish was formally recognized as being integral to the legal identity of the Jewish nationality. It was a remarkable moment for the language. The old oppressors were gone, and it looked like the new Communist government might understand their needs. As all the varied people of the new Soviet Union gathered, Yiddish speakers would have a place at the collective table.

For Frumkin, the years that followed the revolution must have been bright with hope. She was the only woman in the eleven-person Central Bureau of the Jewish Sections of the Communist Party, becoming commissar for political education. She was in charge of closing synagogues and religious schools, as well as of stripping Jewish religious leaders of their rights. "Taking the revolution to the Jewish street" was the slogan for this sort of activity.

Because all enterprises were now under state control, it was possible to eliminate the jobs of rabbis, *cheder* teachers, and yeshiva teachers, as well as *shochets,* ritual slaughterers, and *moehls,* ritual circumcisers. With private enterprise abolished, there would be no way for religious functionaries to earn a living. It was an efficient way to both dismantle the *kehiles* and suppress religion.

Frumkin was in the forefront of the anticlerical campaign, her slogan "Down with the rabbis!" Although similar drives were being waged against the Russian Orthodox Church, the attacks against Jewish institutions were carried out with a special vengeance. Frumkin told an American Jewish visitor: "You do not understand the danger Jews face. If the Russian people begin to feel that we are partial to the Jews it will be harmful to the Jews. Jewish Communists must be even more ruthless with rabbis than non-Jewish Communists are with priests."

Frumkin supported what might now be called guerrilla theater actions, in which activists demonstrated noisily in front of synagogues on solemn holidays or broke into services on Yom Kippur, the Day of Repentance. While congregants were fasting and praying, the interlopers made a great show of eating, waving unkosher sausages in front of the noses of the worshipers.

But even as Frumkin was dismantling the Jewish religion, she was building an infrastructure for the Yiddish language. With her background in education, she set to work establishing a state-supported Yiddish educational system. This was a remarkable achievement. For the first time, Yiddish-speaking children could receive a complete, free secular education in their native tongue.

Frumkin translated Lenin into Yiddish. She was instrumental in having Yiddish designated as one of the four national languages of the new Soviet Union. And she supported the state-run Yiddish schools, which at first enjoyed great popularity. For example, in Belarus and Ukraine, two of the new Soviet republics in what had been the Pale, by the end of the 1920s half the Jewish children attended these new institutions. This was an extraordinary moment in history. Yiddish, the underdog of languages, had been granted official status by one of the world's largest, most powerful nations. Idealistic Jews from around the world came to see and to send home their reports.

In 1928 Avrahm Yarmolinsky, a Russian-born American Jew, traveled to the new Soviet Union on such a mission. He found the Soviet recognition of Yiddish a cornerstone of Jewish unity. It impressed him much more than the assimilationist outlook he had come to expect in the United States:

> The 106 soviets |governing councils| set up in small areas often were Jewish. One post office was named for Sholom Aleichem. In the Jewish soviets, all transactions are in Yiddish. There are a number of lower courts |thirty-six in Ukraine and five in White Russia| where the business is conducted entirely in Yiddish. In some of the larger cities, as, for example, in Kiev and Odessa, there are station houses where a man can file a complaint in Yiddish and have it written down by a Jewish policeman. Likewise, marriages, births and deaths may be registered at the Government Bureau of Records in Yiddish.

The effect of this cannot be overemphasized. This was the first time in almost two millennia, since the destruction of the Temple in Jerusalem, that a Jewish language was functioning in officially sanctioned and state-funded institutions.

But the Communists did not give the Jews carte blanche. They favored a policy they described as being "national in form, socialist in content." This meant that ethnic groups like the Jews were perfectly welcome to use their own language as long as the thoughts they expressed in it were socialist. The old Yiddish literature from pre-Soviet days was almost never read in the schools; religion existed only as an object of derision. The book that taught children their *alef beys*, their alphabet, began with a big picture of Lenin.

If older Jews were dismayed by the wholesale destruction of their religious and secular heritage, younger ones were more likely to go along. And with great rapidity, a new Soviet Yiddish culture took shape. State-supported Jewish theaters opened in Moscow, Kiev, and sixteen other cities. Marc Chagall produced stage sets and murals for the Moscow State Yiddish Theater. Some 850 Yiddish books were published between 1917 and 1921, many of them the product of the new, state-run Yiddish publishing house. The number of Yiddish newspapers doubled between 1923 and 1927.

Many Russian Jewish writers and intellectuals who had fled their homeland before and during the years of upheaval returned to help create this new populist Yiddish world. Poets Dovid Bergelson, Peretz Markish, and Der Nister came home from Western Europe. Another poet, Dovid Hofstein, returned from Palestine. The Yiddish poet Shmuel Halkin wrote a poem called "Russia — 1923," which read, in part,

> Each blow of your hand is precious to us,
> And painfully hard to bear —
> But however great the misfortune or shame,
> We turn to you and implore:
>
> What is the promise that lies overseas?
> What lands and what countries?
> Here on Russia's happy streets,
> We'll gladly live out our lives.

Unfortunately, Jewish lives with their Yiddish dreams did not always dovetail with Communist plans. The new state-supported Yiddish schools were, first and foremost, agents of propaganda. Their goal was to educate Jewish children to take their place in the new Soviet society. Studying Jewish history or religion was, of course, out of the question, although it was permissible to study the role of the Jewish proletariat in the revolution. Yiddish literature was useful only when it held the old shtetl culture up to ridicule. As soon became obvious, the slogan "National in form, socialist in content" meant just what it said. If Jews wanted to fold themselves into the new Soviet Union, that was fine. If they did not, too bad. Their traditional communities and religious institutions had already been dismantled. Now there was nowhere for them to go.

Yet even this new deracinated Yiddish education was not carried any farther than the elementary level. Higher education in Yiddish was not allowed. Colleges and universities operated strictly in Russian. The lesson was clear: Yiddish would not lead its speakers to the bright industrial Soviet future. Frumkin's vision of Yiddish as the unifying force of a powerful Jewish proletariat was fading fast.

Even as the Soviets underwrote Yiddish education, they undermined its base. Their policies gave Jews no incentive to study in Yiddish and every reason to abandon the language. In 1926, a quarter century after the first Russian census, over 70 percent of all Soviet Jews still listed Yiddish as their primary language. By 1939, however, that number had fallen by almost one-half. As the Soviet sociologist Yankl Kantor described it in 1934, "The mother speaks Yiddish, but when |her child| is of nursery age she breaks her teeth and speaks Russian to him to make him equal to the others."

The Soviets — and we must keep in mind that for decades Jews were well represented and active in Communist circles — dealt Yiddish a serious blow by even changing the language itself. They developed something called Soviet Yiddish. Words that retained a Hebrew-derived spelling, with its typical lack of vowels, were changed to a more European orthography. For example, the Yiddish word for "truth" is *emes*. Traditionally, it is spelled with three letters — an *e* sound, an *m* sound, and a *t* sound, because it comes from the Hebrew word *emet*, spelled with the Hebrew equivalent of *e-m-t*. The Yiddish pronounciation softened the final *t* to an *s* sound. So the Soviet spelling rationalized the word, writing it as it sounded: in essence, *e-m-e-s*, thus weakening the link to Hebrew. So now, when Yiddish speakers saw *emes*, they no longer saw the link to the Hebrew of their prayers — if, in fact, any of them still said the old prayers.

There were other changes as well. Many words that had a religious source were expunged, even if they were used only symbolically. Words that had a Germanic base were replaced with those of Slavic background. Some language planners and politicians (often one and the same) suggested replacing the Hebrew-derived alphabet with a Cyrillic one, although this was never carried out.

Although some of the reforms, such as abandoning the separate forms of letters found at the ends of words, were attempts to simplify and rationalize the language, they began to run on their own steam. Language planners became so enamored of creating new words that they made some fifteen hundred of them, almost all Russian derivatives. Yiddish moved farther from being a folk language toward becoming a political-speak. A joke made the rounds that the only people who read Yiddish books were the author, the typesetter, and the censor.

In 1933 a Communist educator, Judah Darak, proudly reported on the success of the Yiddish schools:

> Assisted by all means at the government's disposal, the school won one victory after another. First, the Sabbath day of rest was abolished. Secondly, all books with a nationalistic coloring were removed. . . . Work in school follows the general program of the People's Commissariat for Education. The very concept of "Jewish history" is alien to the school. Any general course in the history of the class struggles may include sections describing the struggles of Jewish artisans against their employers and of Jewish workers against the Jewish or any other bourgeoisie.

Although Frumkin had at first envisioned a reworking of Jewish holidays and history into a new Communist framework, she was forced to give that up. Headquartered in the heart of the Communist bureaucracy in Moscow, she probably spent most of her time maneuvering her way between ideology and realpolitik. Already in the 1920s Joseph Stalin, a man with deep anti-Semitic feelings, was beginning to consolidate power.

In all fairness, though, it must be said that throughout this turbulent period, Hebrew fared much worse than Yiddish. As the language of religion, it was totally suppressed. The American Yarmolinsky described its fate thus: "In their fight against the influence of the synagogue and all it stands for, the Communists found more effective means than the jeers and arguments of so-called 'anti-religious propoganda.' They secularized the schools. . . . The language of the new Jewish culture is the spoken idiom of the masses, while Hebrew and all things Hebraic are frowned upon and in every way discouraged."

Still, the new era did produce one enormous gain for the Jews: the final dissolution of the Pale of Settlement. Under Communism, Jews were free to live in cities. In 1920, three years after the revolution, twenty-eight thousand Jews were already living in Moscow. Just six years later, some 131,000 Jews called Moscow home. By 1939 almost 40 percent of Jews had left the former Pale.

City Jews gained new freedoms but lost their old communities. With synagogues forbidden, rabbis unable to function, and religious schools closed, it was not possible to establish new Jewish institutions. The old Yiddish culture functioned only informally. Much more readily available and appealing was the new Soviet world. In 1924 the Yiddish newspaper Der emes (The Truth) reported on a meeting of transport workers: "One comrade, a porter, takes the floor and comes out categorically against any work in Yiddish." When challenged, he answered, "The matter is quite simple — For many years I have carried hundreds of pounds on my back day in and day out. Now I want to learn some Russian and become an office worker." Yiddish, which had long been a link among all Jews, was instead becoming the language of only the backward, unsuccessful ones. Ambitious Jews learned Russian and moved on.

Frumkin recognized the consequences of the changes she had set in motion. At a 1926 Conference of the Jewish Sections of the Communist Party she said, "Very likely the process of assimilation will engulf all the national minorities scattered in the cities. . . . Considering the probability of such assimilation, we must, by our approach, indoctrinate the Jewish workers and leaders not to judge each particular activity from the standpoint of national self-preservation, but rather from that of its usefulness to socialist reconstruction."

From this distance we cannot know if Frumkin was abandoning the Jewish identification that had been such a core part of her personality, or if she was making the compromises necessary to maintaining a public presence in a dangerous time. It is also possible that she believed contradictory things either sequentially or concurrently. She was a woman who defined her life in terms of public ideology. She left no personal notes.

Although Yiddish made tremendous strides in the decade after the revolution, this period of state support did not last long enough to create long-term Yiddish institutions. The heritage of anti-Semitism was too strong; it ran too deep in the Russian psyche. Other linguistic groups in the Soviet Union might have been able to keep their native tongues. But other linguistic groups were not Jews.

After a decade of widespread state sponsorship of Yiddish institutions, the government began to scratch its Jewish itch. In 1930, in what some have called the rising to the surface of the seemingly endemic Russian strain of anti-Semitism, the Jewish Sections of the Communist Party were accused of having nationalist tendencies and were disbanded. The Jews no longer had a locus of power. Some historians have concluded that the Jewish sections had never been meant to be anything other than agents of cultural destruction.

First little by little, and then abruptly, Yiddish schools were shut down, Yiddish theaters closed. The news reported most often in Yiddish newspapers was of the "exposure" or "unmasking" of Yiddish writers, editors, dramatists, and politicians who were discovered to have been "enemies of the people." Public figures began to disappear. If the 1930s were a time of insecurity for the Russians, they were that much more unsettling for Russian Jews.

Still, Frumkin managed to land on her feet. She became head of the Jewish Department of the University of the National Minorities of the West. But that job lasted only until 1936, when the department was closed. The early experiments of the Soviet period were ended, and the Stalinist purges began. Frumkin found herself yet another job, but she was arrested in 1938 and sent to a forced-labor camp in Siberia. Although she was diabetic, she received no treatment. Her daughter, now married, was imprisoned along with her husband. In 1943 friends managed to obtain Frumkin's release, but by then, at sixty-three, her health had been ruined. She died a few months later, a victim of the government she had helped to establish.

Virtually all the members of the Jewish Sections of the Communist Party were liquidated, to use a particularly expressive Soviet euphemism. They were jailed, exiled, executed, or simply subjected to inhuman conditions until they killed themselves or went mad. For Frumkin and her colleagues, their death was also the death of a dream.

CHAPTER 8

The Soviet Union: Marching and Singing to Birobidzhan

אַ דערטרינקענדיגער מענטש כאַפּט זיך אָן אפֿילו אויף אַ שפּיץ פֿון אַ שווערד.

A dertrinkendiger mentsh khapt zikh on afilu oyf a shpitz fun a shverd.

A drowning man will grab even for the point of a sword.

One piece of Soviet policy toward the Jews and their language was so remarkable that it merits a separate telling, for it is the whole convoluted tale writ large — as large, in fact as the nation of Belgium, some fourteen thousand miles square. This vast project made little sense in the context of the Communist/Yiddish enterprise. But in this part of the story, sense is in short supply.

In the 1920s, as part of the Soviet plan to erase the distinctions of the old regime, the Communists decided to "normalize" or "productivize" the Jews. This meant encouraging them to do precisely what they had been barred from doing under the tsars: working the land as farmers. This opportunity would wean Jews away from their previously "parasitic" jobs as merchants and artisans, the only lines of work that they had been allowed to pursue.

The Soviets set to work abolishing the old system of landownership and organizing agricultural collectives. In 1924 they established a Commission for the Rural Settlement of Jewish Toilers, to organize the separate Jewish cooperatives. Having closely linked Jewish agricultural settlements would serve several purposes: It would separate Jews from the general Soviet population as well as from their old "parasitic" occupations. And if the Jews were tied to the land, it would be that much easier for the government to keep an eye on them.

The Jewish Sections of the Communist Party favored the plan as well. From their point of view, the settlements would help to establish secular Jewish institutions while draining off any lingering Zionist sentiments. The physical reclamation of the land had become an important part of the Zionist dream, and this new Communist version fed off the old ideal of Jews living healthy outdoor lives. Moreover, concentrating the Jewish population could help the Jews.

As Frumkin enthused, apropos of this Jewish agricultural plan, "Under the dictatorship of the proletariat, there is an opportunity for the Jewish people to consolidate itself as a nation." If it all seemed highly unlikely, it must also have appeared to be an opportunity worth pursuing. Certainly, at this time no other government was offering the Jews any opportunities at all.

The plan was first tried in the Crimea, the region bordering the Black Sea in what is now Ukraine, an area that was close to traditional centers of Jewish population. In these new Jewish cooperatives, families controlled their own small plots of land, a logical transition between the old shtetls and the new Communism. But this sort of gradual change seems to have been out of step with the drama of the time, and by 1928 all the farms had been both "collectivized" and "internationalized." This meant that the farms became communal, and that members of the Jewish "nation" were integrated with members of other "nations," such as Russians or Ukrainians. Families were forced to give up the land they had recently received, the first land they had ever controlled, and the Jewish colonies were forcibly merged with neighboring non-Jewish groups. The Communists paid particular attention to breaking down the Jews' distinct identity.

The party published photos of happy Jewish children raising

pigs, which might have gone over well with the Moscow bureaucrats but not with the parents of the young pig farmers, who were incensed by this frontal assault. Jewish farmers left the project in droves, and the effort was soon abandoned. But the seed of an idea had been born.

It is said that Stalin himself came up with a more ambitious and far-reaching plan. At the same time that the farms in the Crimea were saying good-bye to their Jews, the central government made a remarkable announcement. Jews would be given incentives to settle on agricultural land of their own, on territory specifically set aside for them. On this land they could also keep their own language. There was more: a promise that hung in the air. Stalin's government let it be known that, if all worked out as planned, this new project would become a Jewish autonomous region, which would mean special prerogatives for Jews. In time, it might even evolve into a Jewish republic, with its own offical status in the Union of Soviet Socialist Republics — a Yiddish-speaking republic at that. It was a breathtaking dream. And it was 180 degrees away from the now-moribund pig-farming scheme. Unfortunately for the Jews, there was the slight problem of location. This happy homeland was in eastern Siberia, five thousand miles away from where any Jews lived at all.

It can be difficult for Westerners to imagine the vastness of the Soviet Union. It stretched across two continents and eleven time zones. Although almost the entire Soviet Jewish population lived in the western Soviet Union, the new region was about as far from the Jewish centers as was possible to go. Even today, the train ride from Moscow takes seven days.

The location of the Jewish Autonomous Region was not an accident. It served several government aims. Unfortunately, none of them corresponded with the interests of the Jews. Located near the Chinese border, the new settlement would provide a bulwark against the encroaching Chinese and Japanese. By transporting Jews so far from their traditional homes, it would make it that much easier to wean them from their cultural ties. Over time, Jews were much more likely to lose their particular identity and assimilate into the general Soviet citizenry, one possible solution to the endless Jewish Problem. And for all this, the Soviet Union could score points on the international scene at a time when it desperately needed them.

But even if we suspect the Soviet planners and politicians of having only the basest intentions, we must give them credit. The Communists were doing more for the Jews than any capitalist or Western country at the time. Jews had no nation of their own, and even Palestine was a wasteland mired in international politics. Even if this particular godforsaken land was hardly a solution, it was at least a new development. Jews would be able to speak their own language and exercise some control over their local government and institutions.

This tiny spark of hope was not lost on American Jews, many of whom responded with moral and financial support. Several hundred idealists even joined the new settlers, who were, for the most part, transplants from the western Soviet Union. One American couple, Morris and Rosa Becker, who had earlier emigrated to the United States from their birthplace in tsarist Russia, gave up a farm in California and, with their two young children, headed off to follow a dream.

In 1928 the region, which soon became known by the name of its principal city, Birobidzhan, was little more than a stop on the Trans-Siberian Railroad. With a population of only about twenty-seven thousand Russians and Ukrainians, it was covered by virgin forests and plagued by extremes of temperature. Winter produced endless snow. In summer the disease-ridden swamps reminded one American visitor of the Florida Everglades. Still, Jews were offered free passage and food. They were promised housing, land, and everything else they would need in order to farm. They would also be supported in their expectation of speaking Yiddish, the language that, despite the inroads made by Russian, was still the primary language of two-thirds of Soviet Jews.

Six years after the project was first proposed, in 1934, even though the area's Jewish population still had not reached more than 20 percent, the Presidium of the Central Executive Committee of the USSR issued a decree that created the Jewish Autonomous Region. Jews took this as an extremely positive sign. Documents uncovered since the fall of the Soviet Union indicate that this venture was never really meant to succeed. But contemporary Jews did not know that. For them, a bit of land and the hope of living among their own people was the best offer they had yet received. In fact, apart from the state of Israel, the Jewish Autonomous Region represents the only Jewish civic entity in modern times.

Unfortunately, things did not work out well. When Jews arrived, mostly from the former Pale, they found conditions ranging from primitive to dismal. There were no houses, no tools, no tractors, no horses, no medical care. The land was boggy and insect-ridden, the forests absolutely untouched. Almost none of the Yiddish-speaking arrivals knew anything about farming. Families lived in mud huts. The area was as difficult to farm, to make a living in, as Palestine — without having the benefits of reviving the ancestral Holy Land. Even though many of the settlers who came were escaping dire poverty, with conditions near famine level in the Ukraine, half of the settlers who arrived in the first years turned around and left.

Ilya Bliecherman was one early settler who stayed despite the arduous work. "We were tremendously enthusiastic because we had been dreaming about the revolution, and now we were being offered a chance to participate in building it," he recalled. "The conditions were brutal, but despite the hardships, I was doing exactly what I wanted to do."

Another early settler said, "I thank you, comrades, for sending me here. Here I am getting settled and will stop living life like a 'Jew,' that is, as a luftmentsh." This Yiddish term, meaning "one who lives on air," was a deprecatory term for a Jew without profession or trade.

Many of the leading Yiddish poets wrote odes to the project. Here is a section of Isaac Feffer's "Birobidzhan March":

> We are building our home on the edge of the land,
> On the banks of the Amur our country will stand,
> The taiga draws back when it hears a man
> Go marching, singing to Birobidzhan.
>
> We waken the roads, the forests we clear,
> No one is old who joins us here.
> Villages rise, and wherever you go
> Are streets being built and new towns grow.
>
> Lift up your voices and swing your ax,
> Tame this land, lumberjacks,
> With all other peoples, hand in hand,
> We have our home here, a Stalinite land.

Unfortunately, conditions in that "Stalinite land" remained poor. Most of the Jews who stayed gave up the attempt to farm and moved into the capital city. Not that it was much of a metropolis: In 1937 Birobidzhan, a city of ten thousand, still had no public sewage or public lighting system. But the trend continued. By 1939 only one-quarter of the region's eighteen thousand Jews remained on the farms.

Still, the experiment had great propaganda value, and whatever other mistakes they made, the Soviets managed that part of the enterprise with great efficiency. The central government in Moscow circulated some thirty different periodicals, along with brochures, books, and films showing strong, happy, healthy Jewish farmworkers. And Jews around the world continued to respond, writing Yiddish poems and novels lit with an idealistic glow. Jews who had abandoned Russia for Western Europe, the Americas, and even Palestine returned to settle this new Jewish land. Even some non-Russians, Jews and Christians alike, were drawn by the project's vision.

In 1937 a group of left-wing American Jews presented a portfolio of lithographs, *A Gift to Birobidjan,* that spoke of "the flowering of a new social concept wherein the artist becomes moulded into the clay of the whole people and becomes the clarion of their hopes and desires."

There is no question that Jewish international desires were becoming more pressing as the 1930s rushed on. Even as idealistic Americans were moved by the possibility of a Soviet Jewish homeland, Jews in Germany were being stripped of their rights. There was some talk of settling German Jews in Birobidzhan, but the project never materialized.

Still, the Yiddish language did benefit from the Soviet colony in the east. From the beginning, both the settlers and the central government saw Yiddish as an integral part of the Jewish Autonomous Region. From its inception, the region was completely bilingual, which meant that Yiddish and Russian coexisted on an equal basis. All government documents were required to be published in both Russian and Yiddish. Railway station signs, street signs, even postmarks were written in both languages. Jewish children attended 128 Yiddish-language elementary schools. Even in the Russian-language schools, Yiddish was a required subject. Jewish children also learned Russian out of necessity; it was of course the language of the Soviet Union. Any books, pamphlets, edicts, or films that came from beyond Birobidzhan were written in Russian. Yiddish might have been available locally, but in the greater Soviet world, Russian remained the primary tongue.

Still, Birobidzhaners could count on state funding to create many of their own Yiddish institutions. A state-supported Yiddish newspaper debuted in 1930. The region became the center for a Jewish theater group that toured the Soviet Far East. There were Yiddish libraries, a Yiddish teachers' training college, even a Yiddish medical school.

But the elementary schools illustrated the region's real drawback. As in the Yiddish-language schools back in the more settled western areas of the Soviet Union, the content was purely Soviet. Schoolchildren might have been reading in Yiddish, but they were reading about Lenin and the glories of the revolution, the same as their Russian counterparts. A visiting American, Hayim Greenberg, wrote in 1938, "If national culture is simply a linguistic variation of something which is called 'general Soviet culture,' then why does one have to have it? The young Jew is well able to learn Russian." The schools, like the culture at large, expressed the disjunction of form and substance. Just as in the schools that Frumkin had established back home in the former Pale, simply speaking Yiddish turned out not to be enough. If the content of the schools, theaters, books, and newspapers was determinedly non-Jewish, then what was the sense of saving the Jewish language?

Because, as we have seen, language is inextricably linked with identity. Separate it forcibly from religion, custom, and self-expression, and its value plummets. Pre-Soviet Yiddish had grown organically from an all-encompassing culture. Cut off from that culture, the language of the Soviet period was diminished and dimmed. How could you understand a Yiddish saying like *if you don't like the cantor, you can still say amen,* without knowing anything about prayer?

The dreamers and idealistic pioneers who had left their old lives and families had bought into a hard bargain. They had been offered this region as Jews, but once they got there, any expression of that Jewishness was severely limited. Religion was out, of course, and Jewish history likewise prohibited. The classics of Yiddish literature, like the works of Sholom Aleichem, were tolerated only as illustrations of the unfortunate pre-Soviet past. Articles in the newspaper *Birobidzhaner shtern* (Birobidzhan Star) attacked Jewish holidays and customs. The Jewish theater group made fun of traditional Jews. Yiddish was used as an anti-Jewish tool.

The year 1937 saw the scheduling of a state-sponsored Yiddish conference "to result in the establishment in Birobidzhan of academic and educational institutions empowered to supervise the

Yiddish language and Yiddish culture in the Soviet Union." But by the time the conference was set to open, Soviet policy had once again shifted. The Stalinist purges had begun, and the conference never took place.

The entire leadership of the Jewish Autonomous Region was liquidated, beginning with Joseph Liberberg, the first chairman. In a move that would have been funny if it hadn't been tragic, he was accused of trying to place Birobidzhan at the center of Jewish culture in the Soviet Union.

By this time, Yiddish schools were being closed throughout the Soviet Union. In the Jewish Autonomous Region, Yiddish schools and newspapers — even the *Birobidzhaner shtern* — were peremptorily shuttered. Settlers who had survived the hard work, hardships, and disease wondered why they had journeyed so far.

They had come lured by the promise of some breathing space, some help in creating their own version of the new Soviet world. Now all that was gone. The old Soviet vision of a harmonious linking of people of varied ethnic, national, and religious backgrounds had been superseded. From now on, the Soviet Union would be one proletarian people united by ideology and language. The language would be Russian. There would be no place for Yiddish in the new Soviet world.

Birobidzhan, along with the rest of the Soviet Union, suffered through World War II. At war's end, the exhausted Soviet population looked to the area once again. Soviet Jews had been hit particularly hard, with massacres and anti-Semitic violence adding to the chaos of war. Hundreds of thousands of Jews had been murdered by the Germans, their Soviet neighbors, or a combination of both. They were eager to start anew. Because emigration outside the Soviet Union was impossible, any new beginning would have to take place within Soviet borders.

Once again, Communist policy reversed course and gave the green light to the Jewish Autonomous Region. Party officials began touring Jewish areas in the west, encouraging people to migrate to

Birobidzhan. Once again, Jews were offered free passage, as well as guarantees of housing and work. The promise of a Soviet Socialist Jewish Republic with its own language and culture was once again heard. By 1948 some ten thousand additional Jews had moved to Birobidzhan, bringing the total number to about thirty thousand. (The population of the region had grown to 185,000, making Jews a minority in the Jewish Autonomous Region.)

But Yiddish enjoyed new support as well. The Yiddish-language newspaper in Birobidzhan not only was started up again but also received orders from Moscow to increase circulation. Government directives were once again published in Yiddish. Yiddish was again a required subject in the schools. A Yiddish-language publishing house was opened, and the Jewish Theater once again performed. In 1946 a major celebration, with concerts and lectures, marked the thirtieth anniversary of the death of Sholom Aleichem. His name was given to the main street of Birobidzhan.

Still, Soviet goals came first. The next year saw a competition for a "Soviet-Jewish song to mark the thirtieth anniversary" of the revolution. According to its guidelines, the song "must reflect 1) the basic socioeconomic changes that have taken place in the life of the Jewish people during the years of Soviet power; 2) the active participation of Jewish toilers in socialist construction and defense of the homeland; 3) the construction of Soviet Jewish statehood; and 4) the boundless loyalty of Jewish toilers to the Bolshevik Party and the Great Stalin." One can only imagine the boot-thumping refrains. A typical Yiddish story of the era was Shifra Kochina's "How We Achieve Large Vegetable Crops."

Overseas supporters once again responded with enthusiasm and generosity. The American Committee for Birobidzhan held a fundraising concert at Carnegie Hall in 1948 to celebrate the region's twentieth anniversary. A precarious Jewish state might have just been established in Palestine, but here was a Jewish region that had existed already for two decades, one that enjoyed the backing of a superpower.

By this time, though, the years of indifference had taken their toll. Even though two small Yiddish-language schools had remained open in Birobidzhan throughout World War II, in the postwar era the numbers of their students dropped. In the intervening years, almost all Soviet Jews had learned Russian. Despite the on-again, off-again support for Yiddish in the Jewish Autonomous Region, it was only too clear that Russian was the language of the Soviet Union.

And then, as suddenly as it began, it was all over. In 1948 the brief, tantalizing window of opportunity shut once more, as Stalin's paranoia focused in on the Jews. We now know that the Soviet leader envisaged Birobidzhan as a good location for a concentration camp for Jews. He saw it as a way, once and for all, to free the Soviet people from the Jewish presence.

Stalin ordered the arrest of the leading Birobidzhan Jews in government and the arts on charges of "bourgeois nationalism" and "rootless cosmopolitanism," Russian code words masking anti-Semitism. Contacts with their American supporters had made them easy targets, and they were branded "lackeys of Western bourgeois culture." Most of those arrested were sent to the Siberian gulag. Few ever returned. Ilya Bliecherman, an early settler who had so enthusiastically cleared the land, remembered the bad times as well: "One by one, the people began to disappear from our commune. At first, I assumed that those arrested really were enemies of the people. But then they began arresting people who were close to me, who I knew had done nothing wrong. But no one could open his mouth. We were all deathly afraid we would be next."

Once again, Yiddish schools, libraries, and theaters were closed. The staff of the *Birobidzhaner shtern* was arrested en masse. The paper continued to be published, but there was no more Jewish content in it at all. It shrank to a mere two pages of translation of the Russian-language state organ, most likely a bone thrown to those Birobidzhaners whose only language was Yiddish.

When the original *Shtern* editor, Boris Miller, was released in

1956 after eight years in the gulag, he wrote bluntly, "The Jewish Autonomous Region did not fulfill our hopes; it became instead a factory for Jewish assimilation." Assimilation, of course, had all along been one of the possible uses for the region, a place where Jews could be concentrated for whatever fit into the Soviet plan.

It now appears that, at the time of his death in 1953 (on Purim no less, the Jewish celebration of topsy-turvy), Stalin had been planning to exile *all* Soviet Jews to Birobidzhan and Siberia. Luckily, that never happened. But over the decades this region, like the Jewish Problem itself, could not be integrated or placed in any kind of context. Too dry and too wet, too hot and too cold, its extremes only mirrored the violent swings of the Soviet attitude toward the Jews and their language.

CHAPTER 9

Israel: Language Wars in the Holy Land

גאָט, שוץ אונדז פֿון גוישע הענט און פֿון ייִדישע צינגען.

Got, shutz undz fun goyishe hent un fun yidishe tsingen.

God protect us from gentile hands and Jewish tongues.

Half a world away from the Yiddish shtetls and Russian steppes, the obsession of one Jew who emerged from that background would have an extraordinary influence on the fate of *mame loshn*. Eliezer Perlman was born in 1858 in Luzhky, which was then in tsarist Russia and is now in Lithuania. Because of a lucky accident of timing and a frighteningly intense dedication to a lucid, resonant vision, he set in motion a shift that, in the years to come, would largely determine the future not only of the Yiddish language but indeed of the Jewish people. If his mythic stature has waxed and waned over the years, if his godlike aura has dimmed, there is no question that he was at least present at the Creation.

He certainly would not have looked that important when, as a desperately ill twenty-three-year-old consumptive, he arrived in Palestine with his bride, Deborah, in 1881. Most Jews who arrived at that time were either religious fanatics or sick and elderly pious folk who dragged their bones to the sacred soil to die. The liberal, modern Perlmans, however, arrived in thrall to a different dream. They would live in Eretz Israel and resurrect the sacred language, Hebrew, on its hallowed ground.

It had been almost two thousand years since Jews in any numbers had lived there or used Hebrew for their daily speech. But Perlman, a man who was looking death in the face and who tended toward messianism under less intense circumstances, was convinced that repopulating the ancient land and renewing its ancient language was the only way for Jews to survive as a people.

He was a brilliant, discontented character who had left the civilized world to pursue his one chance at living out his dream. Deborah was a devoted, comparatively learned woman who had given up a comfortable home to accompany her husband to this decaying corner of the failing Ottoman Empire. One mark of her dedication was extreme: She had agreed that, if they had a child, they would speak to him only in Hebrew.

This grandiose sense of purpose was all very well, but there were a few hurdles to overcome. First, Jews had so far evidenced no desire to leave the known problems of Europe for the unimaginable difficulties of settling an undeveloped land. Second, Mrs. Perlman knew almost no Hebrew. And third, Hebrew as a spoken, contemporary language did not really exist.

Like the other Jews in tsarist Russia, Perlman had grown up speaking Yiddish and studying Hebrew. He was a devoted student, but he had come up sharply against the limits of traditional Orthodoxy. First, when one of his teachers had tried to teach him Hebrew grammar, the man almost lost his job. (The rabbis saw language as a path to meaning, not something to be studied for its own sake.) Then, when the boy had dared to read *Robinson Crusoe* in a stilted Hebrew translation, his family had thrown him out. Taken in by a well-to-do cosmopolitan family, he fell in love with the oldest daughter, Deborah, who had taught him Russian and French. This Deborah was now his wife.

In between, Perlman had gone off to Paris, where instead of studying medicine as planned, he had imbibed the political ferment of that turbulent, invigorating time. Russian-born Chaim Weizmann, who would later become the first president of the modern state of Israel, described the intellectual ferment of Western European student life in that era. He recalled his own time as a physics student in Berlin: "I think with something like a shudder of the amount of talking we did. We never dispersed before the small hours of the morning. We talked of everything, of history, wars, revolutions, the rebuilding of society. But chiefly we talked of the Jewish problem and Palestine. We sang, we celebrated such Jewish festivals as we did not go home for, we debated with the assimilationists, and we made vast plans for the redemption of our people."

For Jews, redemption has always been associated with a place — Eretz Israel, where the Messiah will come when he ushers in the End of Days. And the place Israel has always been linked with the people Israel, *Am Israel*. God's covenant with Abraham, the core of Jewish identity, includes God's promise, "Unto thy seed have I given this land." Jews face Jerusalem when they pray. Every Passover seder ends with the pledge, "Next year in Jerusalem!"

Even though, by this time, Jews had been exiled from the land for almost two thousand years, they always believed they would one day return. By the time that Perlman was a student in Paris, some modern Jews began to think of actually going there. As we have seen, other ethnic, national, and linguistic groups in Europe were demanding control of their own states. Why not the Jews?

But the question of language was complicated. Of course they had always carefully guarded Hebrew, their sacred language. Since the *Haskalah,* a century before, it had even gained a new cachet. For one thing, it was respected by gentile intellectuals; for another, some Jews thought it could be harnessed in the service of modernism. Its lofty phraseology, so removed from what they saw as the degrading aspects of day-to-day Jewish life, might be a way to wean Jews from old superstitions.

At this point, though, Hebrew was an archaic, little-used tongue. Writing in it meant stringing set biblical phrases into standard combinations. It was used for legal documents, business contracts, and, if all else failed, basic communication between Jews from different backgrounds. It was a second or third language; it was nobody's mother tongue. Even though the occasional obsessive Jew made an effort to speak only Hebrew on the holy Sabbath, the result must have been many long Sabbath naps and quiet days.

In the intellectual ferment of the nineteenth century, however, a few European journals began to appear in a sort of pidgin Hebrew. We can get a feeling for the pained and ponderous quality of the language by looking at this one-sentence paragraph found in a preface to an 1859 Hebrew work of fiction. Although the author is undoubtedly trying to say something here, it is almost impossible to wade through the Bible-speak to find out what that is:

> Who among our people, knowing that the splendor of the language is the splendor of her people and in her honor they too will be honored, will not rejoice to see today that our Holy Tongue — which, since honor was exiled from Israel, suffered the decline of her honor also, and she was exiled from the face of the earth and imprisoned between two covers |of a book|, in her few holy books and her few holy places — now God's spirit began to revive her in these generations, by the hand of her writers, few and scattered, that she might return to her past state and, little by little, begin walking on the face of the earth too, and she returned to speak again of all the works of the Lord and all His creations in heaven and on earth.

So modern Hebrew existed in only the most rudimentary sense. But it was enough to spark Perlman. He conceived a plan of linking the language to the dream of rebuilding Eretz Israel. As he put it, "Late one night, after several hours of reading newspapers and thinking about the Bulgarians and their approaching freedom, I suddenly felt as though a flash of lightning had passed before my eyes. My thoughts flew from the Shipka Pass in the Balkans to the banks of the Jordan in the Land of Israel, and I heard a strange voice within me calling: The Revival of Israel and its Language on the Ancestral Soil!"

The messianist had met his ideal. In 1880 Perlman published the first of several articles, "A Worthy Question," in the Warsaw-based Hebrew journal *Hashahar* (The Dawn). The question, of course, was Jewish survival. At first he was vague about whether his plan involved reviving just Hebrew literature or spoken Hebrew as well, but it did not matter for the moment; his writings produced little response.

Perlman, however, had no time to refine his ideas. With a diagnosis of advanced tuberculosis, he decided to head east. Deborah agreed to marry him, and together they started out.

Nineteenth-century Palestine was a backward and barren region ruled with utter indifference by the Ottoman Turks. Their empire was on the brink of collapse, and this desert outpost had little to recommend it to them. Interestingly, it had been the weakness of the Ottomans that had encouraged the nationalistic movements in Eastern Europe that inspired Perlman. He understood that with the end of Ottoman rule, Western powers would be looking to divide up the spoils, which included this land of little physical value but of infinite symbolic worth to the Jews. Their claim would be strengthened if they could demonstrate the "normal" attributes of a nationality — common territory and language.

In the meantime, for all its grand history, Eretz Israel looked like no-man's-land. Great chunks of its property went unclaimed; the legal term was "dead land." The area was plagued by yellow fever, typhus, typhoid, malaria, and trachoma, not to mention awful heat and a lack of fresh water.

Of the two hundred thousand people who lived there, most were Arab. Only about 10 percent were Jewish. Some Jews had remained in the area ever since the destruction of the Second Temple. Others had drifted back there from Europe over the centuries. Most Jews lived in Jerusalem and Safed, where some scholars, mystics, and holy men continued to speak an extremely diminished version of Hebrew.

Most Jews in nineteenth-century Palestine had come from Europe or were descendants of people who had. They spoke Ladino, Yiddish, Russian, or Arabic. They were, for the most part, horrified at the thought of using *loshn koydesh,* the holy language, for everyday speech. Some of these pious Europeans who had made the journey to Eretz Israel to pray and to die received some support from their congregations back home. But these contributions hardly sustained their remaining widows and orphans or their descendants. When Perlman arrived, Jerusalem was full of Jewish beggars.

The new arrival got right to work. He began to use the Hebrew surname he had created for his article, Ben Yehuda. Meaning "son of Judah," it comes from his father's Yiddish name, Leib, or lion, the symbol of the tribe of Judah. He went to the Turkish authorities, handed in his Russian passport, and insisted that they issue him a new birth certificate. He later wrote, "I felt I had been reborn. My link with the diaspora had been severed." His goal became "resurrection for the people of Israel and the Hebrew tongue in the land of the forefathers!"

Perlman/Ben Yehuda's health began to stabilize in the warm climate, and for a time he found work at one of the few Hebrew publications. But money problems were unending for the young family. When Deborah became pregnant, she found lodgings directly across from the Western Wall, where the sounds of wailing and mourning filled their ears day and night.

But as the proverb says, *every baby is born with a loaf of bread in his mouth.* (In the case of the Ben Yehuda family, this would have been a literal necessity.) Deborah found better lodgings; no more lamentation, only an entrance marked by seven courtyards filled with garbage. Soon a group of twenty-six young Europeans appeared at their doorstep. They had read Ben Yehuda's article and, in response, had traveled to the Middle East. They called themselves Biluyim, an acronym from the Hebrew words for "Sons of Jacob, Come, Let Us Go." Their plan was to buy land and reclaim the earth, ending centuries of alienation from the soil. They also planned to link the rebuilding of the country with the revival of Hebrew. Ben Yehuda had found his first disciples.

But they went north to look for land, leaving Ben Yehuda to pursue his mission in Jerusalem. He wrote: "I speak Hebrew, only Hebrew, not only with the members of my household, but even with every man or woman whom I know to more or less understand Hebrew, and I do not take care in this matter to abide by the [Talmudic] laws of common respect or courtesy to women. I act in this with great rudeness, rudeness that has caused many people to hate me and has engendered much opposition to me in Eretz Israel."

His home life was difficult as well. A new modern language did not spring to his lips fully formed. A visitor, Yosef Klauzner, reported that Ben Yehuda communicated with his wife mainly in gestures and signs. When he wanted her to pour him a cup of coffee with sugar, "he lacked the words for cup, saucer, pour and spoon, so he said, 'Take that and do that and bring me that and I'll drink.'"

When it was time for Deborah, by now lonely and sick, to give birth, Ben Yehuda would allow only Hebrew speakers to help her. There were almost none in Jerusalem. As Ben Yehuda later wrote: "We were afraid of the walls of the house, afraid of the air in the room, lest it absorb the sounds of a foreign tongue emanating from the servant girl, which would enter the child's ears and damage his Hebrew hearing and the Hebrew words would not be absorbed as they should be and the child would not speak Hebrew." There would be no servant girl, no doctor or midwife, and precious few friends. Not for them the Yiddish joke about the woman in labor:

How can you tell when a woman is ready to deliver? When she calls out in French, *mon dieu*, you send for the doctor. When she cries in Russian for her mama, *mamushka,* you know her time is approaching. But when she screams in Yiddish, dear God, *gottenyu,* you know she is ready to deliver.

While Deborah labored, Ben Yehuda stood guard at the door giving prospective helpers impromptu Hebrew exams. Luckily, one woman was able to pass, and Deborah gave birth to a healthy boy. When the infant was placed in her arms, she managed to call up a Hebrew word, *yaldi,* my child. But the eventful day was not yet finished. A telegram arrived from Ben Yehuda's young disciples. They had bought land outside of Jaffa for a settlement they would call Rishon le-Zion, the first settlement of Zion. The Ben Yehudas gave their child two names: Itamar and Ben Zion, son of Zion. The first village and the first child were born on the same day.

Little Itamar grew up with no playmates, no lullabies, no games. When Ben Yehuda wasn't working, he stood by the child's crib, reading to him from the Bible. Deborah, whose health continued to decline even as her husband's stabilized, was not allowed to have a servant. Because her friends could not speak Hebrew, they could not talk to her when the child was around. And she never learned more than a rudimentary Hebrew. It should come as no surprise that for more than three years little Itamar did not utter a single word.

He later described the central event in his young life. His rendering, which comes perilously close to a primal scene, gives some sense of the psychic cost of his father's devotion to his idea. It helps us to understand the emotional burden of renouncing the mother language, *mame loshn,* in favor of the new father tongue.

It seems that after years of obedience to her husband's demand that the child hear nothing but Hebrew, Deborah gave in to her worries that her son would remain permanently mute. Maybe she herself felt the need to connect with her past. And so, in secret, she began to sing to the boy the Russian and Yiddish lullabies of her youth.

One day, her husband came home without warning. As the younger Ben Yehuda recalled it, his father said,

> "What have you done? All that we've built in the first Hebrew household — you've destroyed in a single day!" . . .
>
> Seeing my father raging and storming, and seeing my mother whimpering like a child who has been caught red-handed — I suddenly understood everything that was hap-

pening in the house, stood up straight before my father with the will of a boy defending his mother, even against his father, and screamed, "Father! *[Abba]!*"

Mother covered me with kisses. They both realized that good had emerged from evil, and that from my great shock at seeing my father enraged and my mother sobbing, the dumbness had been removed from my lips and speech had come to my mouth.

The Ben Yehudas had produced a mythic being, the First Hebrew Child.

The couple went on to have four more children, but the family's continuing poverty and the terrible conditions took their toll. Deborah, who had contracted tuberculosis from her husband, died ten years after their arrival in Eretz Israel. Three of their children died very young.

Still, Ben Yehuda held on to his dream. He sent for his widowed mother, Faygele Perlman, to care for his remaining two grief-stricken youngsters. Two versions of his next dictum exist: In the first, he forbids the seventy-year-old woman from speaking anything but Hebrew to the children, even though she did not know the language. In the second version he relents slightly, allowing her to speak to them in Russian, but absolutely forbidding a word of Yiddish. *Mame loshn,* even from the mouth of his aged *mame,* had become the enemy.

Ben Yehuda then took a second wife, Deborah's youngest sister, Pola, who chose a Hebrew name, Chemda, beloved. Like her sister she was a loyal supporter, and like her she paid a price. Of the six children she bore, two died in childhood.

Ben Yehuda produced more than the First Hebrew Family. In 1884 he began to publish a newspaper called *Hatzvi* (The Deer). (The name had been borrowed from another publication that had been approved by the Turkish officials.) He ran the enterprise single-handedly for over a decade, providing news as well as an example of the new conversational Hebrew. He created the first Hebrew dictionary — seventeen volumes with over eight thousand double-columned pages, published over the course of fifty years. The only example of a humorous statement from him concerns this enterprise: "He whom God wishes to severely punish, He decrees upon him to be a dictionary compiler. The life of the compiler is like living in Hell."

Wherever possible, Ben Yehuda harvested words from the existing literature, recycling old terms. Song, *zemer*, and sing, *zamer*, share the *z-m-r* Hebrew root. To invent a new word for "orchestra," Ben Yehuda expanded the root to create *tizmoret*. The word for "traffic light" comes from the words for "beckon" and "light." He adapted international technical words, like *telephone* and *telegraph*. Sometimes he found cognates in Arabic, which, like Hebrew, had grown from Semitic roots. When necessary he made up words, at least a thousand, including terms for "banana," "beer," "blanket," and "bus." He even took a few of the First Hebrew Child's babyish inventions, including the words for "spinning top" and "napkin." It is said that the very first word that Ben Yehuda invented was the term for "dictionary," *milon*.

By design, there are few borrowings from Yiddish. Those that entered the language tended to come in under the radar of the Hebrew language police. Because Hebrew had come down through the centuries as what linguists call a "high-function language," meaning that it exists in the formal or public realm, it had few words for intimate, emotional speech. So affectionate diminutives and baby talk percolated up from "low-function" or informal Yiddish. There is also the occasional more neutral word like *kumzitz*, which in Yiddish is two separate words meaning "come" and "sit." In Hebrew this command has become a noun, its meaning expanding from "the rest a group might take after a hike" to its current meaning of "a get-together, a bit of a party."

Creating a modern language under difficult conditions was, however, no picnic. Even the matter of pronunciation was intensely political. Early on, Ben Yehuda decided to follow Sephardic speech patterns. (Jews who had lived in Spain during the Middle Ages spoke Hebrew with a markedly different pronunciation.) Yiddish speakers pronounce their Hebrew much as they pronounced their Yiddish, full of *oys*, while the Sephardic pronunciation tends to more openmouthed *ohs*. Yiddish speakers change the typical Hebrew *-ot* endings to a softer *-os* sound. And Sephardic speakers accent the last syllable, while Yiddish speakers move the accent one syllable forward. But in Israel, these differences were never expressed neutrally. The Ashkenazic pronunciation was always described as being whining or weak; the Sephardic, forceful and strong. It was obvious which one was approved for a new generation of strong, proud Jews.

Arguably as important as creating the new language was getting people to use it. And because of the region's politics, people had to begin using it fast. Hebrew became a tool for uniting the new settlers and giving them some hope of consolidating their claim against the Turks in the court of public opinion.

If changing the linguistic associations of a lifetime was difficult, then moving an entire society into a language that barely existed was a monumental undertaking. Ben Yehuda soon realized that the most efficient change would come through the schools. At the time, most of the Jewish schools in Palestine were funded by European philanthropic groups. This was a fairly recent development. As some Western Europeans had achieved a measure of stability and success, they wanted to help impoverished Jews in the Holy Land. Being citizens of Britain, France, and Germany, however, they each insisted on providing education in the language of their "home" country, further flaming the linguistic fires.

When Ben Yehuda convinced the French school in Jerusalem to let him teach his new Hebrew to their pupils, he taught it using only Hebrew. Although he did not invent this total-immersion system (the Berlitz method already existed in France), it made particular sense for this language, which had to quickly unite such a varied population. Besides, there was no time to try any other method.

Linguists were too busy inventing the language to painstakingly translate it for others to learn.

Linked with building the new country, Hebrew words expressed the new mentality. *Sabra,* the name of the cactus fruit that is prickly on the outside but soft on the inside, became the designation for those born in the new land.

And there were soon many more of these proud Hebrew-speaking youngsters. Ben Yehuda arrived at the head of the first wave of Zionist settlers. As Russian pogroms worsened, Jews left in droves. In the last two decades of the nineteenth century, twenty thousand European Jews emigrated to Palestine. In the twentieth century the numbers continued to rise. Healthy, idealistic, and young, these newcomers were the opposite of the old-style religious pilgrims. They were determined to shake off their background of (as they saw it) city-dwelling, intellectualizing, cowering fear. Into this mix they added passivity, femininity, and Yiddish.

They formed agricultural colonies and set to work remaking both the land and themselves. These succesive waves of emigrations were named *aliyahs,* a term that gives some hint of the depth of meaning of this population transfer. *Aliyah* in Hebrew means literally "going up." It is used to describe the coming up to the *bima,* the raised platform in the synagogue, to read from the Torah. It has come to mean emigrating to Israel.

Although the new Hebrew language took root in the new agricultural settlements, the lack of standardization, even lack of vocabulary, continued to be a problem. Settlers joked that Hebrew was the first language that parents learned from their children.

In 1912 the Zionist theoretician Ahad Ha'am visited from Europe and reported, "In every school I now find a word-coining factory. Every teacher is coining with gay abandon, this one calls a certain something a so-and-so and that one a such-and-such. . . . Even within the same school different classes are using different words."

The first language instruction books had appeared only in 1900. At first, many more men than women mastered Hebrew, because they had learned biblical Hebrew as children. A misogynistic joke expressed satisfaction that, finally, instead of speaking without understanding, women would understand but not speak. But with a new generation, little girls grew up speaking Hebrew as naturally as did little boys.

The bond between language and land can be seen in this 1904 declaration establishing the Hebrew Teachers' Federation in Palestine: "Whether the children in the village school learn more or less of the rudiments of elementary grammar, more or less of history, more or less of science, does not matter. What they have to learn, though, is this: to be strong and healthy villagers, to be villagers who love their surroundings and physical work, and most of all to be villagers who love the Hebrew tongue and the Jewish nation with all their hearts and souls."

A succession of language organizations set standards for spelling, grammar, and usage and settled linguistic disputes. The first group, formed in 1889, was called Safa Berura, the Plain Language Society. It quickly morphed into a joke name, Safa Arura, the Cursed Language Society, because of the inability of its members to agree, but its successors gradually became effective. The Sephardic pronunciation was officially adopted in 1907. By 1918 the Assembly of the Yishuv, the official representatives of the Jewish community in Palestine, voted that no one could be elected to that group who did not understand Hebrew.

Adopting a new language meant changing one's associations at the most basic level. The scholar Maurice Samuel went to Palestine in the 1920s: "For me, too, in spite of my sympathy with the revival of the language, Hebrew had been mostly the vehicle of great religious, ethical and spiritual communications. How queer it was, for a time, to buy a round-trip bus ticket from Tel Aviv to Jerusalem in Hebrew, or to discuss with the tailor, in Hebrew, the alterations I wanted made in a pair of trousers." He remembered visiting a restaurant in the Holy Land: "I looked at the posters on the wall. I had been reading Isaiah that morning, and I was still aglow with the tremendous denunciation of the hypocritical bringers of sacrifices, a denunciation which reaches its climax in the thundering phrase: Dirshu mishpat! Seek justice! And on a poster in front of me, in letters a foot tall, was an advertisement, Dirshu glidah! Seek ice cream! I could not but feel an inward grimace of discomfort."

But he understood the lure of the language, its place in a people's rebirth. When he saw a group of schoolchildren listening to a story in Hebrew about a biblical event that had happened right where they were sitting, he understood that "the triple cord of people, land and language was woven into their minds, and a triple cord shall not easily be broken. To these children the Bible is not only sacred; it is the source of their first awareness of their childhood surroundings."

It was the education of this new generation of Jewish children that precipitated one of the most dramatic battles of the language wars. When in 1913 the German-language Hilfsverein schools were planning the curriculum for their new Technion, a university-level scientific school, they assumed that it would function in German, the undisputed international language of science. By this time, the supporters of Hebrew had grown numerous, vocal, and organized. All over Palestine, students and teachers walked out in protest. Jewish newspapers around the world carried word of the strike and vociferously took sides. Only the outbreak of World War I upstaged this heated conflict. By the time the new institution opened after the war, the word *technion* had been imported into Hebrew, and Hebrew was the language of the new scientific school.

In a census taken at that time, a quarter of the Jewish adults and more than half the Jewish children who lived in Palestine listed themselves as speakers of Hebrew. When the Balfour Declaration was issued in 1917 announcing Britain's support of "a Jewish homeland in Palestine," it recognized three official languages: English, Arabic, and Hebrew, with Hebrew the language of the Jewish settlement. Now that language would become even more closely identified with *hatikvah,* the hope, with Hebraists feeling entitled to do whatever was necessary to make sure that the new language took root in the newly irrigated desert soil.

In the meantime, Yiddish was the hardy native species that had to be yanked out and replaced. Hebraists routinely disrupted Yiddish gatherings, telling people they had to speak Hebrew. Yiddish conversations overheard on the street would be interrupted by jeering passersby. Occasionally real violence flared. Kiosks whose owners dared to sell Yiddish newspapers were repeatedly trashed or burned.

At Yiddish literary evenings, lectures, and plays, performers were routinely pelted with tomatoes or rocks. When Chaim Zhitlovsky, the leading Yiddish-language theorist of his day, visited Palestine in 1914, crowds of militant Hebraists prevented him from delivering his lecture. In 1927, when the Hebrew Writers Union held a conciliatory dinner to welcome visiting Yiddish writers, a firestorm erupted in the press.

It is not hard to understand the desire to rescue the Hebrew past and weave it into the new Jewish future. The tragedy is that the new settlers could find no way to include the strands of Yiddish in the new sheltering cloth. The violence with which Yiddish was excised shows how deep the identification must have been. Samuel characterizes new Israeli settlers as "a pathetically schizophrenic group aspiring to complete Hebraization but tied by habit and inclination to Yiddish. I have seen Yiddish-speaking pioneers enduring agonies of frustration in order to 'pass' completely into Hebrew. At the communal table they would point dumbly to what they wanted — knife, apple, kettle — waiting to be reminded of the Hebrew *sakin, tapuakh, kumkum,* rather than utter the Yiddish *messer, epl, tchanik.*"

No other language was rejected with such utter contempt. English, French, German, Russian, Arabic, and Ladino were also commonly spoken in Palestine. But they did not have to be rooted out of the Jewish soul.

A typical Yiddish joke of the pioneering era describes two old men walking along the beach in Tel Aviv when one gets caught by an undertow. As he struggles in the water he calls out in Hebrew, "Help! Help!" His companion shouts back to him, in Yiddish, "So! Hebrew you learned! Now you will also have to learn how to swim!"

A memoir of Isaac Bashevis Singer by Dvorah Telushkin has Singer publicly complaining to Menachem Begin that, although Israeli Jews have resurrected Hebrew,

> "Vith Yiddish, you took a living language vhich vas alive for some eight or nine hundred years and managed to kill it."
>
> Menachem Begin, who had himself grown up in a Yiddish-speaking home, began pounding his fist on the glass coffee table while spittle flew from his lips. . . .
>
> "With Yiddish," he shouted, "we could have not created any navy; with Yiddish, we could have no army; with Yiddish, we could not defend ourselves with powerful jet planes; with Yiddish we would be nothing. We would be like animals!"
>
> Isaac sat with his hands folded in his lap and shrugged his shoulders. "Nu," he said sweetly to the hushed crowd, "since I am a vegetarian, for me to be like an animal is not such a terrible thing."

A whole school of stories circulated about famous Hebraists who were found out — caught in the act of speaking Yiddish. There were always excuses. If the person was boarding a bus, for example, the reason was that Yiddish was faster; if at home, Yiddish felt comfortable, like a pair of old slippers. In 1930 one of these incidents gained international prominence when the Brigade for the Defense of the Language tried to ban the Yiddish film *A yidishe mame,* a tearjerker made in New York. The Jewish press in Europe and the United States shouldered arms in the language war, and the British army had to step in to guarantee the safety of audiences who wanted to see the film. Yiddish, for all its warm associations, perhaps even *because* of its warm associations, had to go.

The poet Jacob Glatstein was acutely aware of the precarious state of his language. In his poem "Red tsu mir yidish" (Speak Yiddish to Me), he wrote with bitter irony about the language being silenced in, of all places, Palestine. Here he places the first Jewish family, Abraham and Sarah, in the modern Jewish settlement.

> God help us, Grandpa-Grandma.
> Abraham is crossing the street in silence.
> Don't take it to heart, Yankele,
> Says Sarah, he understands every word.
>
> That's the way it goes here.
> A man has to stifle his Yiddish.
> But a Jewess from the yidish-taytsh
> Still has something to say.

She would be hard pressed, however, if she wanted to continue speaking Yiddish in the Holy Land. By the time Eliezer Ben Yehuda died, in 1922 at the age of sixty-four, Hebrew was firmly established as the center of the new Zionist identity. In Europe, Jews hoping to move to Palestine studied the new tongue before they left. Stories, poems, songs, nonfiction of every type, an entire literature was being produced. The speed of the transformation was miraculous.

Unfortunately, there was a price to pay for creating this longed-for new home: There would not be room for two Jewish languages. To nourish modern Hebrew, Yiddish would have to starve. The nurturing *mame loshn* would have to die so the new virile Hebrew might live.

CHAPTER 10

America:
The Golden Land

אמעריקע גנב

Amerike ganef

America the thief

At the same time that Ben Yehuda left Europe and headed east, millions of other Yiddish-speaking Jews fanned out in other directions. Beginning in the 1880s, they chose new beginnings in England, Canada, South Africa, Australia, and South America. But for the bulk of the transplants, the ultimate destination was the United States.

On their arrival, the Statue of Liberty was not always what overwhelmed. Sometimes new immigrants were more impressed by the images of Ivory soap or Crisco shortening. H-O oatmeal, Coca-Cola, Bayer aspirin, and Dutch Master cigars all displayed their products on giant billboards directly in the line of the arrivals' sight. They printed bold Yiddish newspaper ads and bilingual recipe booklets, targeting campaigns at Yiddish-speaking Jews.

These newcomers were dazed, dazzled — and quick to adapt. They might not have disembarked in some bucolic *Gan Eydn,* Garden of Eden, but many were convinced they had arrived in its urban equivalent. Unlike the countries they had come from, which could seem to revel in devising more ways to shut Jews out, America worked at luring them in. Immigrant life brought dislocation, crowded housing, and endless work, but even the lowliest slum dwellers could look forward to a better time.

If the price of entry to this new land was a downplaying of where and what they had come from, if new arrivals were busy throwing the baby out with the bathwater, it was a tariff most Yiddish speakers were ready to pay. The bathwater had been brown and turgid, drawn from a dirty stream. And the baby? It hadn't been so cute either. Here there would be a new baby — a real American.

We see the immigrant's first wide-eyed view in Abraham Cahan's 1917 novel *The Rise of David Levinsky:*

> I led the way across Battery Park and under the Elevated railway to State Street. A train hurtling and panting along overhead produced a bewildering, a daunting effect on me. . . . Where were we to go? What were we to do? . . . I mustered courage to approach a policeman, something I should never have been bold enough to do at home. . . . I addressed him in Yiddish, making it as near an approach to German as I knew how, but my efforts were lost on him. . . .
>
> At this moment a voice hailed us in Yiddish. . . . Prosperity was written all over his smooth-shaven face and broad-shouldered, stocky figure. He was literally aglow with diamonds and self-satisfaction. But he was unmistakably one of our people. It was like coming across a human being in the jungle.

The man, learning that the new arrival is a religious scholar by occupation, tells him, "that's no business in America." But he also tells him not to worry.

> "You will be all right. If a fellow isn't lazy nor a fool he has no reason to be sorry he came to America. It'll be all right."
>
> "All right" he said in English, and I conjectured what it meant from the context. In the course of the minute or two which he bestowed upon me he uttered it so many times that

the phrase engraved itself upon my memory. It was the first bit of English I ever acquired.

The Jew David encountered had abandoned his beard and perhaps his learning, and was certainly jettisoning his language. But he had diamonds and a big smile. Cahan was a novelist, journalist, memoirist, and historian whose true territory, whether he was writing in Yiddish or English, was the immigrant experience. For half a century, as the micromanaging editor of the *Forverts,* known in English as the *Daily Forward,* the most influential of the American Yiddish newspapers, he shaped that experience to a remarkable degree. While writing in Yiddish, he moved his readers toward English. He held open the doors to the New World, and the people rushed eagerly through.

He was born in 1860 in a small town near Vilna, in what is now Lithuania but was then tsarist Russia. His father was a *melamed,* a teacher; his mother, unusual for her time, was also a teacher who could read and write German and Russian as well as Yiddish. Cahan was trained at the state-run Vilna Teacher Training Institute for Jewish Students, which, incredibly, forbade its students to speak Yiddish, much as, slightly later, U.S.-run schools for Native Americans forbade the use of their native tongues. Cahan's main interest in teachers' training was avoiding the hated tsarist army; left-wing politics engaged his mind and heart.

But on the verge of being arrested for his activism, he fled Russia in 1881. In that same year, the liberal Tsar Alexander II was assassinated, ending the hopes of a generation of Jews. The new regime outlawed Yiddish newspapers and theaters, and Jews began voting with their feet. Cahan arrived at the head of a huge cohort of Yiddish speakers.

Adept at languages, Cahan studied a Yiddish-English dictionary on his transatlantic trip and was soon translating between passengers and crew. Two weeks after his arrival in New York, he attended a meeting of the Propaganda Association for the Dissemination of

Socialist Ideas among the Immigrant Jews. He described hearing a stirring speech in Russian, responding with one of his own, and then asking the speakers why, if their organization was aimed at Jewish immigrants, the talks were in Russian and German.

> "What language do you suggest?" [the speaker] asked derisively. "What Jew doesn't know Russian?"
> "My father," I replied.

The next week, Cahan delivered a two-hour lecture on Marxism in Yiddish, an act that would have landed him in jail back home.

But Yiddish did not make the journey unchanged. Cahan described the first family he lived with in New York:

> All, except Mrs. Zass, spoke poor Yiddish overlaid with American pronunciations and idioms. For example, one evening when I was exchanging jokes with the eight-year-old, she said to me: *"Du kenst nit machen mir lachen"* [you can't make me laugh].
> The use of the familiar, informal *"du"* [you] shocked and amused me. I was uncomfortable with the non-Yiddish Yiddish they all spoke, even though my landlady explained to me that in America everyone is addressed with the *"du"* because the language has no counterpart of the Yiddish polite form, *"ir."*

Later he described how "the Yiddish of American-born children grated on my ears." The Americanized Yiddish of the immigrants, studded with English expressions, was no better: "My anger rose when I heard such expressions as *'er macht a leben'* [he makes a living] or *'er is vert tsehn toisend dolar'* [he is worth ten thousand dollars]. Or such horrors as *'vindes'* [windows] or *'silings'* [ceilings] and *'pehtaytess'* [potatoes]." The first two phrases are English idioms translated literally into Yiddish. Then the three words he holds up for rebuke — *vindes, silings, pehtaytes* — are all Yiddish-sounding pronunciations of English words that replace perfectly adequate Yiddish ones *(fenstern, sufitin, bulbes)*. The Yiddish terms had apparently been thrown overboard on arrival in New York Harbor.

Cahan supported himself by giving language lessons (Yiddish and Hebrew and soon enough English, one step ahead of his pupils). He also wrote for English-language New York newspapers, giving gentile readers an insider's view of the teeming immigrant neighborhoods that were mushrooming in their city. In the years between 1870 and 1914, more than two million Jews came to the United States, 60 percent from Russia. Their living and working conditions horrified native-born Americans. But for the Jews who lived on New York's Lower East Side and the equivalent neighborhoods of other large American cities, the new life at least offered hope. Back home, the Russian government was shutting Jews out of even more occupations while supporting a series of pogroms that savaged their communities. While the rest of Europe entered a period of prosperity, more and more Russian Jews were sinking into desperate poverty.

In America they had sufficient food, and if an entire family was crammed into one room, at least it was one family per room, not several families crammed into a basement hovel. In the United States, Jews were not excluded by law from entering professions or living in major cities. They were allowed to own land. Children were not conscripted into an alien army. Tacit exclusion from clubs, neighborhoods, and professions was hardly worth complaining about compared to the targeted conscription and state-sanctioned murder under the tsars.

So the Jews enthusiastically set about making a place for themselves. If their neighborhoods were dense and poor, the sense of freedom made them feel rich. When Yiddish theater was banned in Russia, one of the most prominent troupes picked up and moved to New York, where it thrived. Without censors, theaters could present a Yiddish translation of Hamlet as easily as a melodrama like *Dos yidishe harts* (The Yiddish Heart). There were even competing Yiddish plays on the subject of birth control.

Yiddish culture exploded with years of pent-up artistic and political yearnings. Yiddish theaters played to packed houses. Vaudeville triumphed. There were lectures, "literary evenings," concerts, and debates. Politicians of every stripe held forth every night. After working long hours in factory or shop, a Jew could go out to hear Yiddish speeches and debates across the political and social spectrum.

Many of these parties and interest groups started their own newspapers. *Der tog* (The Day), *Di varheit* (The Truth), and *Morgen journal* (Morning Journal) were centrist. *Arbeiter tsaytung* (Workers' Newspaper) and *Ovent blat* (Evening Bulletin) were Socialist Labor. *Tageblat* (Daily Bulletin) represented the Orthodox, *Freiheit* (Freedom) the Communists, and *Di zeit* (The Times) Labor Zionists.

But beyond the Yiddish neighborhoods, Americans regarded the language with contempt. German Jews who had arrived a generation earlier had already established a place for themselves. Still smarting from the German/Yiddish conflicts of a century earlier, they were mortified by their *Ostjuden* cousins. They made every effort (sometimes with impressive philanthropic generosity, sometimes with disdain) to help them learn English so they could move up in the world.

This was also the prevailing wisdom among gentiles. The public schools attended by almost all Jewish children had no bilingual programs and few teachers who understood Yiddish. The liberal American reformer Jacob Riis, writing in *Scribner's Magazine* in 1892, expressed the enlightened view when describing a group of new arrivals: Most, he said, "could only make themselves understood to each other, never the world around them, in the strange jargon that passes for Hebrew on the East Side but is really a mixture of a dozen known dialects and tongues and some that were never known or heard anywhere else. In the census it is down for what it is — jargon, and nothing else."

President Theodore Roosevelt, describing the need for the acculturation of the great streams of immigrants, said in 1919, "We have room for but one language here and that is the English language, for we intend to see that the crucible turns our people out as Americans and not as dwellers in a polyglot boarding house."

The bargain could not have been stated in balder terms. The Jews would be welcome, but only if they learned to fit in.

Many of the cultural institutions established by the Yiddishspeaking immigrants thus proved to be the agents of their own demise. The immigrants' newspapers, theaters, movies, clubs, and settlement houses might have assuaged the pangs of sorrow for *der alter heym,* the old home, but they helped *di griener,* the greenhorns, to move more confidently in the new one.

Of all these institutions, one of the most successful was a newspaper. *Der Forverts,* the *Daily Forward,* was founded in 1897 as a party organ of the Socialist Unionists. It was edited by that old leftist, Cahan. By all reports he was a dictatorial, petty, arrogant man. The paper soon split into factions, and Cahan lost out.

He went to work for the English-language press, getting to know some of the most respected American writers and editors of the day. He published muckraking journalism as well as colorful fiction. Writing in Yiddish and in English, he explained the immigrants to the native-born and to themselves.

In his Yiddish short story "The Imported Bridegroom," a wealthy New York businessman returns to his hometown in Europe to find a pious young student for his daughter, Flora, who, not surprisingly, cannot bear her intended's old-fashioned ways. The tide turns, however, when the yeshiva student discovers the New York Public Library and begs Flora to teach him the English he needs to read its treasure-house full of books.

> He could not wait. He was in a fever of impatience to inhale the whole of the Gentile language — definitions, spelling, pronunciation, and all. . . .

"Oh, do hear me read — may you live long, Flora! It somehow draws me as with a kind of impure force."

An impure force, and an unstoppable one. By the end of the story, the American landscape has totally consumed the formerly holy young man, who joins forces with his intended in a way that Flora's father never had in mind. It was the archetypal Cahan tale.

By 1902 the *Forward* was in such bad straits that Cahan was offered his old job back, this time with absolute authority. A man with a difficult marriage and no children, his life became the paper. He ran it until 1946.

Cahan the novelist saw the rich human comedies and dramas acted out on the streets of the Lower East Side. Cahan the journalist knew he had a ringside seat for an extraordinary period of social change. Cahan the socialist hoped that by informing his readers about relevant news, they would better themselves and their world. Cahan the emerging American knew that he could do all these things and turn a profit. Cahan the egotist was confident that he could mastermind it all.

Although he never forgot his socialist background, even translating Marx's *Das Kapital* into Yiddish and running it in installments in the *Forward,* he made sure the paper could compete in New York's marketplace of ideas. He insisted on clear, simple Yiddish. Taking his cue from contemporary American realist fiction and from the yellow journalism around him, he excised the paper's political harangues.

Cahan's readers responded with voracious enthusiasm. The *Forward* became their guide. No subject, no style was out of bounds. Serious literary criticism, first-rate fiction, and strong reportage shared space with running soap operas, photo essays, advice columns, and lessons on science and history. There were reviews of the latest Yiddish plays and films. There was literature — Yiddish originals as well as translations of both new and classic works by Americans and Europeans. In the period before World War II almost all Yiddish writing, of whatever genre, appeared first in newspaper form.

When Trotsky arrived in New York in 1916, he was interviewed by the *Forward*. Cahan himself visited the new Jewish colonies in Palestine in 1923 and reported back. The most popular living Yiddish writers of the 1920s and 1930s, Sholem Asch and I. J. Singer, were on staff. Singer's novels, including *The Brothers Ashkenazi* and *Yoshe Kalb,* were serialized in the *Forward*. When Cahan refused to print Sholem Asch's 1938 novel *The Nazarene* because of its pro-Christian theme, it ignited a controversy that lasted for a decade.

The *Forward* was not the only Yiddish paper to prosper. At the market's height, the United States supported at least ten Yiddish dailies. (Many of the large ones, headquartered in New York, ran regional editions.) In 1914 the New York Yiddish papers had an estimated circulation of 646,000, which meant a readership of two million. *Der tog,* perhaps the *Forward*'s toughest competitor, ran the bulk of Sholom Aleichem's work in serial, as well as the complete translation of the Bible into Yiddish by Yehoash (Yehoash Solomon Bloomgarden).

But whatever their ideology, the Yiddish papers ran on dollars. The period of the great migration, roughly the last quarter of the nineteenth century and the first quarter of the twentieth, was for the most part a boom time for American industry, which often targeted the emerging Jewish market. A handy pocket book of Yiddish phrases for English speakers included these formulas: "Where is the buying office? . . . I have some new samples to show you," and "We can promise delivery in ___ days."

A 1912 advertisement for Crisco vegetable shortening in the Yiddish papers capitalized on Jews' need, according to dietary law, to separate dairy products from meat. Because Crisco could be used for both, the ad trumpeted, "for Jews it is especially a great invention." Borden's condensed milk, Aunt Jemima pancakes, and Rice Krispies ran special Yiddish ads. For newcomers, the sharp graphics and catchy text made these ads one of the most appealing parts of the paper. More accessible than news, they were an entrée into the new culture, an easy step on the road to assimilation.

The *Forward* staff was well aware of the power of both editorial and ads. They argued over whether or not to accept advertising from the Ford Motor Company, since Henry Ford was a well-known anti-Semite. But ad dollars coming in meant editorial dollars that could go out, and the *Forward* ran the ads.

Above all, the paper prospered. At its height, in the 1920s, the *Forward* had a kingly editorial budget of $250,000 a year. *The Day* was not far behind at almost two hundred thousand dollars. At one point, the Forward Foundation had amassed a nest egg of three million dollars, all from profits from the paper, which it doled out, over the years, to a variety of left-wing causes.

Cahan set the tone for this enormously profitable enterprise. His approach was like the language itself — *heymish* and homespun. Despite his own early distaste for "Americanized Yiddish," he became its most influential proponent, much to the dismay of many of his writers, who preferred a more literary Yiddish. But Cahan had an unerring sense of his audience. They needed practical information as well as intellectual and literary stimulation. Above all, they wanted a safe haven as they threaded their way through this confusing new world. The *Forward* took the place of the trusted relatives and revered institutions his readers had left behind.

Here is Cahan's editorial on the occasion of the opening of the new *Forward* building in 1912, at ten stories high the tallest edifice on the Lower East Side: "Our old religious Jews here have their synagogues. Where is the synagogue of our Jewish workers? Where is the temple of freedom, of equality, of brotherhood? The Forward building will be the home of the Jewish socialist movement. The Forward building is the temple of the worker's religion."

That religion was expressed in a style derisively called "potato Yiddish," because it used terms like *pehtayteh,* as we've seen, in place of the perfectly adequate Yiddish *bulbe*. In time, it went even farther.

When it published "art sections" with photos of the European world its readers had left, it included English notes and captions. Eventually, this expanded to an English section as the *Forward* readers' families became bilingual. Where immigrants freely mixed English into their Yiddish, some of their children spoke little or no Yiddish at all. Whether Cahan, with his enormous influence, was setting a trend or following his audience can be argued ad infinitum, and was.

Any children who spoke Yiddish at home learned English when they began public school. Even in the religious-run day schools that a minority of Jewish boys attended, which continued the tradition of discussing sacred Hebrew texts in Yiddish, students learned English to pass government-mandated exams. With time, even this traditional learning largely gave way. Most boys, as well as some girls, attended afternoon Hebrew schools. In Conservative and Reform schools, the holy tongue was taught in English, and one more link to Yiddish was gone.

The watershed year was 1924. The Johnson Act essentially shut down immigration from Southern and Eastern Europe, and the supply of new Yiddish speakers dried up. Still, for the foreseeable future, the United States contained a sizable pool. In the American climate of freedom and enterprise, these people supported a range of choices. By 1920 the Jewish population of New York had ballooned to a million and a half, making it the world's largest Jewish city. The metropolis supported sixteen different Yiddish-language radio stations. There was also a wide variety of Yiddish schools. Although they never established a network of day schools, weekend and afternoon Yiddish schools were parsed by political and cultural affiliation.

The Sholom Aleichem Yiddish schools gave a broad education in politics, literature, and the arts. Here is Alan Lelchuk's description of his school days from a slightly later era:

> My Sholom Aleichem school in Brownsville |Brooklyn| was my true learning center, for Yiddish, Jewish culture, and for living. My teacher was "Chaver" |friend| Goichberg, who, it

turned out was . . . a Yiddish poet of some renown. He was a serious educator and, I felt, a father-figure and friend. . . . I learned Jewish history, geography, literature; and was reading short stories by Sholom Aleichem, the Singer brothers, Peretz, Mendele at age 9 and 10; I acted in Yiddish plays; I read regularly the Kinder Journal, all through the school and my wonderful Goichberg. I did this for 5 years, in late afternoons, after my regular public school days. And while I complained aloud of my long school day, I always showed up, and was secretly delighted to be there.

As well, the Idish-nationaler Arbeiter Farband (Jewish National Workers' Alliance) and the Poale Zionists (Labor Zionists), both left-wing groups, ran some four hundred Yiddish language and culture schools. Arbeiter Ring (Workmen's Circle), another left-wing group, had over one hundred schools with twenty thousand pupils at its height in the mid-1930s. True to their secular left-wing outlook, the Arbeiter Ring's approved schedule of holidays included no Jewish holy days. Even the few holdovers from the traditional Jewish calendar picked up a new, nonreligious spin. Passover became "the holiday of the liberation of the Jews," and Chanukah was celebrated not because of the miracle of the eight days of light but because of the "breaking of the Hellenistic yoke." They shared calendar space with May Day and the anniversary of the Russian Revolution.

Drama societies, children's newspapers and books, summer camps for families and for children, all maintained a Yiddish identity. The Workmen's Circle boasted that, in the decade between 1925 and 1935, some 140,000 adults and fourteen thousand children attended their seven camps. *Landsmanshaftn,* organizations of people who came from the same shtetl or area, helped their members get jobs, spouses, or proper burial in the society's corner of the graveyard.

Also, because Yiddish was the language of the proletarian masses, it was linked with a variety of left-wing utopian visions. This enduring coalition held even when immigrants loosened or abandoned their ties to traditional religion. New York produced a short-lived but fiery school of Yiddish *svetshop poetn,* sweatshop poets. These immigrants fused the personal with the political, strengthening the identification of Yiddish with the left. In 1893 Morris Rosenfeld wrote:

> So loudly the roar of the noisy machines
> Overcomes me and drowns me without any sense
> And I who am shrunken, and I who am sunken,
> Am lost in the end — I become a machine.

> Es royshn in vork-shop zo shtark die mashinen
> Az oftmol in tummel ferlir ikh dem zinn,
> Ikh ver in zikh zelber ferzunken, ferloren,
> Mein "Ikh" vert dan bettel — ikh ver a mashine.

Mani Leyb's poem "I Am" draws on that old Yiddish duality — the discrepancy between a Jew's worldly stature and his very different sense of himself:

> I am Mani Leyb, whose name is sung —
> In Brownsville, Yehupets, and farther, they know it:
> Among cobblers, a splendid cobbler; among
> Poetical circles, a splendid poet. . . .

> O Poets, inspired and pale, and free
> As all the winged singers of the air,
> We sang of beauties wild to see
> Like happy beggars at a fair. . . .

> In Brownsville, Yehupets, beyond them, even,
> My name shall ever be known, O Muse.
> And I'm not a cobbler who writes, thank heaven,
> But a poet who makes shoes.

Sadly, the sweatshop poets were never able to make the leap beyond the immigrant neighborhoods, and these desperate idealists were well aware of their marginal position in American life. Here is Moshe Nadir's description of an "evening" in honor of the poet Abraham Reisen, whom we last saw publishing a literary journal in Warsaw: "I collect some money and buy him a gold watch. . . . I only wanted to make sure that, just in case . . . he would be able to pawn it. Reisen, dressed in a black tuxedo with the gold watch chain gleaming from his pocket, has no patience with the 'honor' and no money for his rent." After the event, Nadir says, "I fling the bouquet over my shoulders. . . . We wander around for half an hour. . . . We pass Columbus's monument on Fifty-ninth Street and Reisen says, 'You know what, Nadir? Put the wreath on him. It's his America.'"

His America, and the immigrants' children's. No other group of foreigners would come so far so fast. No other people would feel such ambivalence about what they had left. Isaac Bashevis Singer described his first day in New York in the spring of 1935:

> Here, the climate was different and so the life-style — eating, dressing, the attitude toward people. Only the Yiddish writers remained the same as in the old country, but their children all spoke English and were full-fledged Americans. . . .
>
> We ate with our landlord and his family. Although he was the brother of a well-known critic and fervent Yiddishist, his children knew no Yiddish. They sat at the table in silence.

Silence could at least be read as neutrality. Within a generation of immigration, the Yiddish language and accent became a ready source of humor. Although European Jews, and sometimes their children, maintained their link with Yiddish, the mark of the American was fluid, unaccented English speech. Consider this excerpt from the tremendously popular 1920s dialect book *Nize Baby* by Milt Gross, which parodied the Yiddish accent for a Jewish audience: "So I went by de jenitor I should feex de car so I esk him a ceewilized quastion so I sad, 'Do you got here plizze a ranch?' So he geeves me a henswer, 'Wot kind from a ranch you want?' So I sad, 'A monkeh ranch.' So dot dope geeves me a henswer so he sad, 'Hm — I hoid from maybe a cettle ranch odder a sheep ranch bot I deedn't hoid never from a monkeh ranch!'"

In one generation Yiddish slid from being the golden key to Jewish tradition to being an easy laugh at the immigrants' expense. The children of newcomers often served as their parents' translators. But only a small percentage of this first American generation made sure that *their* children could read and write or even speak Yiddish. The language that had been a people's link with its history, the language through which they had discovered the modern world, the language that was creating a vibrant popular culture and the beginnings of a literary tradition was reduced to nostalgia if not summarily dropped. America taught Jews to be ashamed of their language. In the relative security of their new home, Jews no longer had such a desperate need for the protection of Yiddish. And so quite often, they let it go.

The poet Jacob Glatstein wrote,

> In reality, it is one of the greatest puzzles. From the very outset tens of thousands of readers read a language with the thought that they must be weaned from it. Frequently, the sure sign of a "better" neighborhood was a gradual but constant estrangement from Yiddish. . . . In the "old" neighborhoods, that seemed to be so full of Jewish life, parents still deigned to accept Yiddish for their own few remaining years. However, they protected their children against contamination from themselves [the parents] and from the words on their own lips.
>
> No other people has ever squandered its national treasures in the way that Jews have done by resigning from Yiddish.

With steady consistency over the years, scholars found that Jews were among the fastest of all immigrant groups to drop their native tongues. The 1940 U.S. census measured how much of the second and third generation still spoke the "Old World" language. Out of a field of eighteen different immigrant groups, Yiddish, a culture with a great tradition, came in almost at the bottom — an amazing fifteenth.

One explanation is that, by and large, Yiddish-speaking immigrants had a very different relationship with the countries they had left behind than did immigrants from, for example, Italy or Sweden. Yiddish speakers fled not only grinding poverty but governments that ranged from indifferent to hostile to, by the time of that study, genocidal. Often, the very villages they had come from had disappeared. Within decades of their arrival, "Yiddishland" was gone.

The Soviet era presented its own set of problems. As the regime became more oppressive and xenophobic, Jews in the Soviet Union were often reluctant to keep up contact with their relations in the West. And so American Jews lost another thread back. With the exception of a small number of Zionists, Jews who had settled in the United States felt they had made the best choice. And once here, the mandate was clear: Learn how to fit in.

Cahan described an important rabbi who had just arrived from Vilna: "It was only his second or third sermon since his arrival and already he was making a clumsy attempt to accommodate himself to his audience by using American Yiddish. Once he used the word 'clean' for 'rein,' and it was easy to see this was purposely done to show he was not a greenhorn."

And so it was Yiddish that lost out. It is the tragedy of the language that its blossoming was so short, its cultural life so relentlessly under siege. The *Forward* kept printing, but beginning in the hard days of the Great Depression, its circulation numbers slipped steadily down. Meanwhile, the percentage of Americanized words continued to climb. Year after weary year, its readership grew more old and frail.

1) The *Tsenerene* (Tsena Urena in Hebrew), a Yiddish book of Biblical commentary intended for women, who were often unable to read Hebrew. This edition was published in 1848. (YIVO Institute for Jewish Research, Strashun Collection)

2) The Ba'al Shem Tov, eighteenth-century mystic and founder of Hasidism. (YIVO Institute for Jewish Research)

3) A traditional Eastern European shtetl. (YIVO Institute for Jewish Research)

4) Sholom Aleichem with his wife and children. (YIVO Institute for Jewish Research)

5) A postcard of some of the leading lights of the Czernowitz conference. Right to left: D. Nomberg, Chaim Zhitlovsky, Sholem Asch, Y. L. Peretz, and Abraham Reisen. (YIVO Institute for Jewish Research)

6) Official portrait of the Czernowitz conference, August 1908. Nathan Birnbaum and his wife are seated in the first row to the left; Y. L. Peretz and his wife are seated in the front row to the right. Chaim Zhitlovski stands at the right, wearing a light-colored suit. The banner reads "Yiddish Culture," the name of the student organization that sponsored the event. (YIVO Institute for Jewish Research)

7) In this illustration from a 1911 Yiddish humor magazine Hebrew, depicted as a wealthy dowager, complains that Y. L. Peretz is romancing Yiddish, the servant girl.

8) As part of a 1936 photo spread about Birobidzhan, the *Forward* ran this photo of Mordechi Azimov selling the Yiddish newspaper *Birobidzhaner shtern*. (YIVO Institute for Jewish Research)

9) The First All-Union Conference of the Commision for the Rural Settlement of Jewish Toilers, November 1926. This group promoted Jewish collective farms in Ukraine. Esther Frumkin is in the front row. (YIVO Institute for Jewish Research)

10) Children in Birobidzhan in front of a bilingual sign in the 1930s. (YIVO Institute for Jewish Research)

11) A biplane in Birobidzhan, 1935. The Russian says, "Birobidzhan Maksim Gorki Special Propaganda Squadron." The Yiddish says, "The Birobidzhaner." (YIVO Institute for Jewish Research)

12) A 1920s Paris bookstore. The French advertises foreign books and newspapers; the Yiddish offers language manuals. (YIVO Institute for Jewish Research)

13) Shimon An-ski on the Russian Front during World War I. His Russian hat bears a Red Cross insignia. (YIVO Institute for Jewish Research)

14) Postcard showing the dedication of the new YIVO building in Vilna, 1929. (YIVO Institute for Jewish Research)

15) Abraham Rechtman sitting on the porch of his grandfather's house while the old man dictates his memoirs. Rechtman was part of the expedition organized by the Jewish Historic-Ethnographic Society of St. Petersburg in the early 1910s. (YIVO Institute for Jewish Research)

16) Max Weinreich with his sons Uriel and Gabriel in the 1930s. (YIVO Institute for Jewish Research)

17) *Di khalyastre,* "the Gang." Warsaw, 1922. Peretz Markish is in the center; I. J. Singer is at the right. (YIVO Institute for Jewish Research)

18) Historians at a YIVO conference, 1935. Simon Dubnow, with a white beard and cane, is at the center. Emanuel Ringelblum sits at the right end. (YIVO Institute for Jewish Research)

וואָס זאָל זיין גרעסער ווי
די וועלכע ליגט אין דעם
אלטן פעדאגאגישן
געבאָט.
איז דען דא א ליטערא-
רישערע שאפונג, וועל-
כע דערביט צו עקל צו
דער קנעכטשאפט, צו
פרייהייט ליבע, מער
ווי די געשיכטע פון
פארשקלאפונג און
יציאת מצרים?
איז דען דא אן אלטע
דערינערונג, וואָס זאל זיין
דער סימבאל פאר דער
געגנוווארט און צוקונפט

19) A page from *A Survivors' Haggadah*, originally produced by the U.S. Army occupational forces in Germany in 1946. Note the drawing of Hitler standing on a corpse in the lower right. (Jewish Publication Society)

20) Yiddish books and materials confiscated by the Nazis and recovered by the u.s. Army. Here they arrive at yivo in New York in 1947. (yivo Institute for Jewish Research)

21) Aaron Lansky at the National Yiddish Book Center. (National Yiddish Book Center)

22) Isaac Bashevis Singer, at left, being awarded the Nobel Prize for Literature by King Carl Gustaf of Sweden in 1978. (© Bettman/COR-BIS)

23) A still from *American Matchmaker* (Amerikaner shadkhin), 1940, in which a modern matchmaker is picketed by protesters carrying both English and Yiddish signs. (National Center for Jewish Film)

24) A still from *East and West* (Mizrekh un mayrev), 1923. Molly Picon, playing an Americanized Jew, returns to the traditional shtetl. (National Center for Jewish Film)

דו זעהסט די גאָלד'נע שטראַהלען ?
די לערכע זינגט און טרילט, —
עס וועלען לוסט און פרייודען
בעהערשען אונזער וועלט !

לשנה טובה

25) A New Year's card from early-twentieth-century Poland. The Yiddish reads, "You see the golden rays? The lark sings and trills. Cheer and joys will rule our world." (YIVO Institute for Jewish Research)

Still, Cahan kept writing and editing: more stories for the *Forward,* a Yiddish-language book of U.S. history, an impressive body of fiction. His best-known novel, written in English, *The Rise of David Levinsky,* tells the classic tale of a man who gains riches but loses his soul. The last chapter of this five-hundred-page opus begins, "Am I happy? There are moments when I am overwhelmed by a sense of my success and ease." But soon enough he admits, "I am lonely. . . . Sometimes when I am alone in my beautiful apartments brooding over these things and nursing my loneliness, I say to myself: There are cases when success is a tragedy."

Cahan stepped down from his editorial post only when his health failed at age eighty-six. (To give a sense of how quickly Yiddish was declining, in that same year, 1946, the proportion of children enrolled in Yiddish schools as compared with all children enrolled in Jewish schools was 5 percent.) Cahan lived on for another five years, until 1951. Ten thousand came to his funeral to pay tribute to an era that had passed by.

Poland: Drinking in the World

אָט בין איך דאָך, אַן אויפגעבליטער אין מײַן גאַנצער גרײַס.

Ot bin ikh dokh, an oyfgebliter in mayn gantser greys.

Here I am, sprouted to my full height.

Abraham Sutzkever

In 1938 a Warsaw film company produced a series of travelogue shorts that showcased the five major Jewish cities of Poland. In them, a narrator points out the local sights — historic synagogues, modern hospitals, busy commercial districts. We see crowds dressed in stylish European fashions and families promenading through city parks. In a summer camp program, children perform calisthenics while, in the old ethnic neighborhoods, bearded men in quaint dark garb scurry quickly past the camera's intrusive eye. What strikes a present-day observer is how unremarkable it all is, how familiar the texture of modern urban life. The only unusual aspect is that the local accents described, the narrator's speech, the modern life, all took place in Yiddish.

This is where the story of *mame loshn* is most likely to intersect with the twenty-first-century reader's frame of reference; where it is easy to recognize the faces in the photos as ourselves. Unfortunately, that sets off a common response. Watching these scenes unfold from across the chasm of the Holocaust, we tend to see in these glimpses of piercing ordinariness the prelude to destruction. But if that is all we perceive, we are shortchanging ourselves. In focusing on the historical forest, we are missing a glimpse of an extraordinary stand of colorful and varied trees.

The political map of Central and Eastern Europe was substantially redrawn at the close of World War I. The Austro-Hungarian Empire was dismantled, and Poland, which had been dismembered as a kingdom a century and a quarter before, was reborn as a republic. Stretching from the Baltic in the north to Czechoslavakia and Romania in the south, and picking up some of the eastern territories that had previously been under control of the tsars, the new Polish nation included some three million Yiddish-speaking Jews. The end-of-war settlement obligated the new Polish nation to support primary education for minority children in their own language. But the Poles regarded this treaty as an insult and, with little or no international oversight, largely ignored it.

So, in the two decades before war once again engulfed Europe, Polish Jews created an unofficial shadow government of their own. They established, maintained, and funded up-to-the-minute health, educational, political, cultural, religious, and recreational systems. Unlike the old *kehiles,* they functioned at a national level. But like the local community system, their medium was Yiddish — a language that now formed a conscious part of their group identity.

In Yiddish, banks, hospitals, businesses, and schools provided the necessities of life in the bustling cities. Some words, like *bank-konte* for "bank account," or *bank-kasir,* "teller," reflect terms that are similar to those in other European languages. But a bank holiday was called a *legaler yontev,* a "legal holiday," which distinguished it from *yontev,* the holiday defined by Jewish law or custom. (*Yontev,* by the way, comes from the words *yom tov,* which mean "good day" in Hebrew.) As well, hundreds of new words like *telefon, telegraf, fotografye, gazolin,* and *motosikel* described the Yiddish speakers' new world.

Thus Yiddish continued its age-old mission. It expanded as needed, keeping an ear tuned to the languages around it. At the same time, it reinforced the separateness of the people who spoke it.

Jews continued to appreciate having *a yidishe vort,* a Jewish word, in their mouths. Now they could have many more. Yiddish was no longer just the language of the traditional. It kept pace with change, staying relentlessly up to date. In the arts, it was the language of the avant-garde. It was the voice of technological, medical, political, and philosophical advance. Yiddish life in interwar Poland is most often described as being *zaftik.* A word now confined to one meaning, "buxom," in the 1920s and 1930s it had a wider connontation. Although the word for "juice" in a variety of Eastern European languages is *zaft,* the Yiddish ending gave it a meaning of "juicy," "brimming with life."

The scene for this life was set by World War 1, which had devastated much of Europe. It had been particularly hard on Eastern European Jews. The civil wars that followed unleashed pogroms both official and ad hoc. In their wake, in the small towns and the large cities, Jewish poverty, even starvation, became endemic. Often the only sustenance was charity (food, clothing, Yiddish books) from the *goldene medine,* the golden land of the United States, where more than two million Jews had emigrated from the Polish provinces before hostilities had broken out. One Yiddish supplication went, *God, if you don't help me, I'll ask my uncle in America.*

The new Polish Republic in which the Jews now found themselves was a diverse place — almost a third of its citizens were non-Poles, primarily Jews and Ukrainians. But in this period of intense nation building, Poles saw diversity as a defect. The Jews fared worst of all. Because they had always been part of the Polish landscape but not really part of its society, being neither peasants nor landlords, the Jews were singled out for special disdain. Things only got worse with time. By the 1930s anti-Semitism became official government policy.

This course of events created a bizarre situation for Polish Jews, many of whom had built both the Polish economy and Polish nationalism. Polish Jews therefore identified themselves at many points along the spectrum of being more or less Jewish or Polish.

POLAND: DRINKING IN THE WORLD 149

One of the contradictions of this overheated era was that they became both more Polish and more Jewish at the same time. Historically, Judaism had been a complete life system. But modernists could also describe it as being a religion, a nationality, or an ethnic designation. A very few of the most assimilated Jews began to call themselves Poles of the Mosaic faith, but most Yiddish speakers continued to greet one another with the standard, *"Vus makhst a yid?"* How's a Jew doing? — a question that was to assume a cosmic dimension.

One way to understand how deeply the well of Yiddish continued to water all these various Jewish selves is to check in on an event that Franz Kafka, the great and tormented writer who lived in nearby Prague, had organized in 1912, just before World War I. Kafka saw himself as a European and was deeply conflicted about his Jewish identity. Yet he developed a forceful connection with the Yiddish theater, and with the language itself, that helped him strengthen his own work. This depressed and antisocial man organized an evening in Prague's town hall during which an actor friend of his recited Yiddish poetry and dramatic speeches. In his introduction (recorded in his diary), Kafka spoke to an audience of modern city dwellers like himself, people who had put what they considered a provincial, old-fashioned language and its culture behind them:

> I should like, ladies and gentlemen, just to say something about how much more Yiddish you understand than you think.... So many of you are so frightened of Yiddish that one can almost see it in your faces.... You begin to come quite close to Yiddish if you bear in mind that, apart from what you know, there are active in yourselves forces and associations with forces that enable you to understand Yiddish intuitively.... If you relax, you suddenly find yourselves in the midst of Yiddish. But once Yiddish has taken a hold of you and moved you — and Yiddish is everything, the words, the Hasidic melody, and the essential character of this Eastern Jewish actor himself — you will have

> forgotten your former reserve. Then you will come to feel the
> true unity of Yiddish, and so strongly that it will frighten you
> — yet it will no longer be fear of Yiddish but of yourselves.

Most often, these cosmopolitan sophisticates feared regressing into what they saw as the closed, superstitious, shtetl-defined past. Now, with the world in flux, they could move much more freely, reinventing themselves both as people and as a People. It was the Mr. Israel/people Israel equation again.

In Poland more and more of the Mr. and Mrs. Israels were living in cities. Although the urban centers had been off limits to Jews until 1862, by this time some three-quarters of them had moved to the metropolitan areas. By the late 1930s, although Jews made up about 10 percent of the Polish population, they accounted for an extraordinary 40 percent of Warsaw, the capital.

Here worlds collided. A Jew could send his child to public school, marry a non-Jew, abandon Jewishness altogether. Some moved back and forth, for example, writing for both Yiddish and Polish newspapers or singing both opera and religious music.

But if most remained steadfastly Jewish, their Jewishness could now be more individually delineated. The new urban Jewish centers could support a variety of what we might now call lifestyles or special-interest groups. One could attend the Yiddish theater (some twenty different Yiddish troupes regularly toured) for a Yiddish translation of Ibsen or Molière. One could catch the latest avant-garde production by the Vilne Trupe (Vilna Troupe) or see what Yung Teater (Young Theater) was up to. The latter's play about the American trial of Sacco and Vanzetti played over two hundred performances in Warsaw. One could even see Yiddish plays translated into Polish. (Jews made up the majority of Polish theatergoers.)

Politics presented an even more bountiful smorgasbord. Along with the usual *a*-to-*z* suspects, the Autonomists created the Yidishe Folks-partey in Poylin (Jewish People's Party in Poland), whose goal was a separate Polish-Jewish parliament, while Territorialists worked for a Jewish state not linked to any existing country. And all these varied parties sponsored a full complement of cultural institutions. The Zionists even founded model *kibbutzim* to prepare their members for life after they made *aliyah*.

But even with this tempting buffet of modernism, the Hasidim — that living link with tradition — remained strong. About a third of Polish Jews remained Orthodox, although not all Orthodox were Hasidim. But it was said that in 1937 in Warsaw, eighty thousand people turned out to hear the Hasidic Gerer *rebe blozn shofer,* blow the ram's horn that marks the Jewish New Year.

The other end of the spectrum was also expanding. The Bund, which had disbanded in the Soviet Union, grew stronger in Poland. In Vilna members of its youth group celebrated the Jewish New Year with a decidedly antireligious twist. Lucy Dawidowicz, an American visitor, described their gathering on Kol Nidre, the most solemn evening in the Jewish year, a time traditionally for fasting and penitential prayer: "A goodly crowd — perhaps 200 or so boys and girls in their teens, all wearing their red neckerchiefs — cheerfully milled about. The guest speaker . . . delivered an old-fashioned firebrand exhortation against religion. The young people applauded him heartily. The meeting closed with the singing of the Bund anthem."

To the Bundists, the Hasidim, and everyone in between, Yiddish remained an intimate part of what it meant to be a Jew. Even the most assimilated Jews, who took great pains not to speak it, demonstrated by their avoidance that Yiddish remained the Jewish tongue. In the 1931 census 80 percent of Polish Jews identified Yiddish as their primary language. In 1937 Polish Jews supported twenty-seven daily newspapers and one hundred weeklies in Yiddish. Even the non-Jews felt it. Poles had a typically disparaging saying that one spoke Polish, but one jabbered in Yiddish.

Among the many families who left the shtetls at this time, the Singers moved to Warsaw when Isaac Bashevis was five. Once in the Polish capital, the Singers continued to live in a Hasidic environment. Isaac did not learn Polish until he was fifteen. He later wrote, "Rarely did a Jew think it necessary to learn Polish; rarely was a Jew interested in Polish history or Polish politics. Even in the last few years [before World War II] it was still a rare occurrence that a Jew would speak Polish well. Out of three million Jews living in Poland, two-and-a-half million were not able to write a simple letter in Polish and they spoke [Polish] very poorly. There were hundreds of thousands of Jews in Poland to whom Polish was as unfamiliar as Turkish." Even when Jews did learn the language, their accents and usage gave them away, leaving them open to anti-Semitic jokes and worse.

But unlike the United States, which made it only too easy for Jews to abandon Yiddish, the climate in Poland led Jews to dig deeper into their Yiddish souls. They looked at the way the religion was changing and decided to take the change even farther, redefining Jewishness (the term in Yiddish is *yidishkayt*) itself. They removed God from the equation and called the system of morals, culture, history, and language that remained "secular Judaism." Where the heart of the old religion had been Hebrew, the heart of the new nonreligion would be Yiddish.

Chaim Zhitlovski, whom we have met before, was the chief theoretician of *yidishkayt,* also known as Yiddishism or the Yiddish Language Movement. A socialist activist and theoretician, Zhitlovski had been born in tsarist Russia in 1865. He described how he had come to his role by referring to his father: "My father, greatly learned in rabbinic literature, a sharp mind and a thorough one, was just as ignorant as the shoemaker or tailor of Western culture." The younger Zhitlovski wanted to find ways for people like his father to at least understand, if not embrace, the rest of the world. Where Cahan had invoked his father in a linguistic context, Zhitlovski had bigger fish to fry: "The question facing me was to decide in which language to appeal to Jews, not just the ignorant masses, but the whole people, to train an avant-garde to fight for the ideals of universal progress and for their realization in Jewish life. . . . We, the carriers of ideas of universal human progress, had to appeal to the people with our message about quite a new world, the world of modern, progressive Western European culture."

Zhitlovski eventually settled in New York, but his message found an eager audience throughout the Yiddish-speaking world. In Poland it resonated deeply. By 1930 he described with glowing enthusiasm the advances in Yiddish that he had seen:

> Before our eyes, simultaneously battling both Hebraism and assimilation, a wonderful culture has sprouted in the Yiddish language, works of which are already included in the spiritual wealth of all mankind. One hundred and fifty daily newspapers in Yiddish, theatres in every Jewish settlement, art-theatres around the world which the English press writes about and points to as an example. In every Jewish community islands of Yiddish culture have emerged as links which join Jewish life and the Jewish people of Buenos Aires, New York, Paris, Warsaw, Kovno, and of every community where life pulsates and where the song of the Yiddish word is heard.

He saw things as only getting better:

> The growth of our culture in Yiddish is proceeding with such zest that perhaps in a generation or two we will be able to match the most cultured of peoples. . . . Modern Yiddish secular culture is already a colossal oak tree deserving of equal rights with other cultures; it is our national home which binds the entire people together, the intellectuals with the masses in one international unity. And as our ability to withstand assimilation grows, we gather strength with which to fight for the principles of progress, for personal freedom and fulfillment, for cultural enrichment, for social justice and equality, for international brotherhood, equal rights for all nations.

He called Yiddish the "national spritual home." He went even farther: "A Jew who lives in the language sphere of Yiddish can be a Jew by religion, a Christian by religion, of no religion or even against religion."

This was heady stuff. As the Marxist journalist and historian Isaac Deutscher described the climate of interwar Poland, "Here something like a new Jewish cultural consciousness was forming itself, and it was doing so through a sharp break with the religious consciousness."

In Poland much of this consciousness was formed through the Bund. Here the Jewish Socialist Party developed its strongest base. Its anthem, "The Oath," written by Shimon An-ski, whom we will get to know later on, shows the intensity of its followers' devotion:

> Brothers and sisters who work and who need,
> All who are scattered and spread,
> Together, together — the flag awaits,
> It waves in anger, with blood it is red,
> An oath, an oath, in life and in death!

> Heaven and earth will hear,
> Our witness the brightest stars,
> An oath of blood, an oath of tears —
> We swear, we swear, we swear!

> Brider un shvester fun arbet un noyt
> Ale vos zaynen tsezeyt un tseshpreyt.
> Tsuzamen, tsuzamen, di fon zi iz greyt
> Zi flatert fun tsorn, fun blut iz zi royt
> A shvue, a shvue, oyf lebn un toyt!

> Himl un erd vet undz oyshern,
> Eydes veln zayn di likhtike shtern,
> A shvue fun blut un a shvue fun trern —
> Mir shvern, mir shvern, mir shvern!

For a generation of Polish Jews, the Bund was a trade union, a political party, an ideology, an alternate reality. It provided Yiddish schools, camps, health care, occupational training, cultural and sports activities, and self-defense for children and adults.

A film was made in Poland in 1935 called *Mir kumen on* (Here We Come), known in English by the title *Children Must Laugh*. With the goal of raising American funding for the Medem Sanatorium, a Bundist residential facility for poor Jewish children at risk for tuberculosis, it showcased children working and playing outdoors, eating healthy food they had grown. In between the chess games and the talent shows, we see the children's council helping to run the institution, then voting to reach out to the children of striking Polish miners. Comradeship and a Jewish-based universalism were served up with the plates of fresh rolls.

The new Yiddish culture flourished all across the political and religious spectrum. In Warsaw there was a Yiddish Writers' Club, also a Yiddish section of PEN. It was said that the Yiddish pickpockets had their own *shul,* synagogue, where, even though Jews were supposed to shut their eyes while reciting the *Shema,* it was done at one's own risk. In the Polish countryside, American film producers like Joseph Green and Adolph Mann shot Yiddish dramas and musicals, taking advantage of the "Old Country" settings and lower production costs.

Throughout, the old continued to rub shoulders with the new. At the Singer home in Warsaw the father, as pious and impoverished as always, advised the followers who consulted him in his rabbinical court. But the older son, Israel Joshua, began hanging around with an artistic crowd, supporting himself as a writer. (One assignment had him reporting on Jews in the new Soviet Union for the *Forward* in New York.) Then, depending on your viewpoint, Israel either corrupted or enlightened his younger brother Isaac Bashevis by giving him secular books like the Yiddish translation of *Robinson Crusoe*. When Israel Joshua moved out of the family apartment and into an artists' studio, he invited the youngster to visit him.

There Isaac Bashevis found a world unlike anything he had known. "The girls posed nude with no more shame than they would have about undressing in their own bedrooms. In fact, it was like the Garden of Eden there, before Adam and Eve had partaken of the Tree of Knowledge. Although they spoke Yiddish, these young people acted as freely as Gentiles."

The artists, taken with the young man in his long Hasidic coat and *peyes,* earlocks, even asked him to pose for them. "No one, in my Hasidic background, had ever mentioned my red hair, white skin, and blue eyes, but here the body was respected; there was more to a boy than the ability to study." One more traditional Yiddish-speaking Jew had discovered the world.

One marker of this new sense of choice was the variety of educational systems. No longer did all boys attend the same religious-based *cheders* and, for the more advanced, yeshivas, with girls picking up their knowledge piecemeal. Interwar Poland had four kinds of schools for Jews. First, there were public schools. Although the Polish government never met its treaty obligations, it did establish Polish-language schools that, in a nod to the Jews, were closed on Saturdays. Anti-Semitic incidents were endemic, however, and these "Saturday schools" were eventually shut. But Jews established three different nationwide, nongovernmental school systems — one that offered a traditional Orthodox education (Yiddish discussion of Hebrew texts), a modern Zionist Hebrew-based system, and an innovative secular Yiddish system.

But one major stumbling block to the expansion of both the Yiddish and Hebrew school systems was the fact that, with the exception of a few Jewish-run institutions, higher education took place in Polish. The universities and professional schools with merit-based entrance requirements attracted those Jews who could speak Polish. Even there, however, during the 1920s and 1930s Jewish quotas shrunk. Eventually, officially tolerated anti-Semitic violence made higher education impossible for Jews in Poland. Even as Jews developed a spectrum of new institutions, they became more aware of their lack of power outside their own sphere.

In Polish society at large, they were a minority that was increasingly derided and despised. Sometimes there was little they could do except to argue among themselves, to put finer and finer points on differences of theory or style.

Here is how Isaac Bashevis Singer described the Yiddish Writers' Club, where nearly everyone

> bore some passion and was blinded by it. The young writers all aspired to become literary geniuses and many of them were convinced they already were, except that the others refused to acknowledge the fact. The Communists waited impatiently for the social revolution to start so that they could exact revenge upon all the bourgeois, Zionists, Socialists, petit-bourgeois, the Lumpen-proletariat, the clergy, and most of all the editors who refused to publish them. The few women members were convinced that they were victims of male contempt for the female sex.

But somehow, through all this segmentation, Polish Jews maintained their cohesion. Their old village *kehiles* had been transformed, in the cities, to elected community councils. They oversaw hiring rabbis, running hospitals, providing charitable help for indigent Jews. Sometimes they were the site of internecine disputes, like the time, at a meeting of the Warsaw *kehile,* that the Zionist representative hit the representative of the Orthodox Agudath Israel Party in the face with a water pitcher. More often, though, they were expressions of the way that, as communities of newcomers and outsiders, the Jews of the great modern metropolises had to stick together.

Because no matter how many books and plays and pamphlets they wrote, the world beyond the *yidishe gas,* the Jewish street, ranged from indifferent to threatening. A Yiddish joke made the rounds that a bear escaped from the circus, and the police had orders to shoot him. Upon hearing the news, a Jew immediately went inside his house. Not because he was afraid of the bear, he told his friends, but because the Poles would shoot a Jew and then, surprise!

discover that the creature they had shot hadn't been a bear at all.

As Poland's economy plunged from bad to worse, Jews were reminded, in case they had forgotten, of their favored scapegoat status. A 1927 Polish law required that all artisans pass examinations in Polish, even though a third of the artisans were Jews, many of whom could not speak or read Polish at all. City authorities in Vilna taxed shop signs by size, so that Jewish owners were compelled to pay more for their signs, which were of necessity bilingual. Eventually, Yiddish signs were forbidden altogether.

The Polish Parliament passed a mandatory Sunday closing law, which meant that Jews would have to close their businesses two days a week if they wanted to honor the Jewish Sabbath. Another law specified that all business signs had to display the name of the owner as it appeared on his birth certificate, in effect proclaiming that the owner was a Jew, even if he took the tack of posting only Polish signs. The growing anti-Jewish boycott became easier to enforce.

And if Jews did not like conditions in Poland, it was not at all clear where else they could go. As noted earlier, the United States had closed its doors in 1924. In 1931 the British, who controlled Palestine, pretty much shut Jews out. And the Jews' precarious economic situation gave them little latitude. In a world that continued to be indifferent or hostile to their interests, there was no escape valve. So the bubbling new secular Yiddish culture was always on the point of overheating. Sometimes it seemed that the only stability was the old *mame loshn*. Scores of verses were penned to the beloved, threatened Mother Yiddish. In a sort of linguistic chivalry, dozens of poets vowed to fight for it to the death. Many of these poems express more heartfelt longing than poetic art: "My lungs thrive on Yiddish no less than on air." Or, "The Yiddish language — our accumulated treasure — is a gleam forever blazing, brightening."

But even the most committed Yiddishists, when they were not out organizing or speechifying, were intently peering at the wall, trying to make out the writing scrawled there. Even as they worked for a better Yiddish world, they and their children still had to get ahead in this one. In his typically acerbic way, Isaac Bashevis Singer later described one facet of the time, which was similar to what he saw in the United States: "There was an unwritten law among the wives of Yiddish writers and of the great number of so-called Yiddishists that their children should be raised to speak the Polish language. My brother's wife was no exception. The husbands had to accede. Only Chasidim and the poor, especially in the small towns, spoke Yiddish to their children."

But in Poland, unlike the United States, assimilation was no guarantee. Julian Tuwim, one of the most important Polish-language poets of the time, was accused of debasing the language with Yiddishisms because he was Jewish.

As Polish society became even more closed off to Jews through the 1930s, the Bund picked up support. Despite its rigid opposition to Zionism and its stiff-necked refusal to make any compromises with traditional religious practices, it was becoming the Polish Jews' last best hope. Jewish workers signed up in droves for its self-defense programs; strikes and protests mobilized hundreds of thousands. But the Polish government consistently protected the anti-Semitic thugs who attacked Jews.

Even as the range of ideological choices was multiplying, the real-world choices were quickly shrinking. This people poised for action could move in only the most limited spheres — their own self-defined institutions, their own groups of comrades, their own fevered minds.

A Yiddish poem called "The Newborn," written in the interwar years by Shmuel Halkin, shows how much Jews were prepared to work for, and how little they expected they would actually get:

> Let our newborn child be blessed.
> May it take in with mother's milk
> A thirst for bringing light to all mankind,
> Light that will also shine for us.
> But when it will discover a new star in the world,
> At least let not things grow darker for its own people.

CHAPTER 12

Eastern Europe: Language as History

אַ שפּראַך איז אַ לעבעדיגע זאַך, זי וואַקסט צוזאַמען מיט דער נשמה פון פאָלק. זי ווערט רייכער ווען די נשמה פון מענטשן, וואָס רעדט אויף איר, צערייכערט זיך.

A shprakh iz a lebedige zakh, zi vakst tsuzamen mit der neshome fun folk. Zi vert raykher ven di neshome fun mentshn, vos ret oyf ir, tseraykhert zikh.

A language is a living thing which grows together with the soul of a people. It is enriched when the souls of the people who speak it are enriched.

Ba'al Makhshoves (Isadore Elyashev)

One extraordinary institution that transcended boundaries and simple definitions sprang to life in this difficult time. Through this visionary organization known as the Yidisher Visnshaftlekher Institut (Yiddish Scientific Institute), or YIVO, Yiddish-centered Jews worked at breakneck speed to recover and reinterpret their past, restructure their present, and create a future. While the civilized world failed to protect them against a new, virulent strain of anti-Semitism, Yiddish speakers feverishly built their own cultural house. It was an extraordinary edifice, constructed on the strong foundation of a great heritage, its rooms open to invigorating modern breezes. But the land it stood on did not belong to the builder. And its owners would soon take it back.

The idea behind the edifice can be traced back to 1891, when the historian Simon Dubnow of Odessa wrote a pamphlet in Russian, *On the Study of Russian-Jewish History,* and in Hebrew called *Let Us Search and Inquire.* He said Jews should educate themselves about their historical, chronological past, instead of seeing themselves as existing only outside the historical continuum. Dubnow called for the Jewish people to mount an archaeological expedition to collect what he called "the natural resources of our history." He argued that because Jews had not been aware of themselves as a historical group, they had not bothered to save important documents such as *kehile* records, or the minutes of trade or craft organizations. Although they had kept careful note of philosophical and theological arguments down through the centuries, they had not chronicled their comings and goings in the temporal world. They had not collected folktales or songs. They had no sense of how their people had lived in different times. This folk with an obsessive sense of remembering, an unbroken tradition of theocratic call-and-response, had let the records of their earthly time disappear.

"I appeal to all educated readers, regardless of their party: to the pious and to the enlightened, to the old and to the young. . . . Not every learned or literate person can be a great writer or historian. But every one of you can be a collector of material and aid in the building of our history." Although Dubnow, aiming for a scholarly tone, had issued his appeal in Russian and Hebrew, the history that he so much valued had been spoken, written, recited, and sung largely in Yiddish.

Dubnow's writing was a wake-up call. Jews throughout Eastern Europe became volunteer *zamlers,* collectors. The most ambitious and far-sighted of the first generation was a Russian named S. Anski, whose name is often written in English as Ansky. Born Shloyme-zanvel Rappoport in 1863, as a young man he abandoned his Jewish background for left-wing politics, living and working among Russian peasants (hence his Russified pseudonym). In time, he followed the intellectual's siren call to Paris. Once there he began reading Peretz, the Yiddish modernist who had mined Jewish folk themes and Hasidic lore.

An-ski was transfixed. This was the vision that would knit together the disparate strands of his life. He took the energy and focus that had fueled his earlier devotion to the Russian "people" and applied them much closer to home. He became obsessed with the Jewish people — their visions, ideas, and mythic themes. As he described it, "When I first began writing, my striving was to work on behalf of the oppressed, the laboring masses, and it seemed to me then — and that was my error — that I would not find them among Jews. . . . Bearing within me an eternal yearning toward Jewry, I nevertheless turned in all directions and went to labor on behalf of another people. My life was broken, severed, ruptured. Many years of my life passed on this frontier, on the border between both worlds."

An-ski celebrated his return to his people by organizing a mammoth roots trip. In 1911 he commenced a five-person, three-year-long search for what his colleague Abraham Rechtman called "the priceless gems of a beautiful folklore." Under the auspices of the Jewish Historic-Ethnographic Society of St. Petersburg, he compiled a questionnaire of over two thousand parts covering the whole Jewish life cycle from conception to death. Rechtman recalled:

> [We] roamed into the remotest corners of the Ukraine, everywhere collecting the remaining treasures of our past; notated stories, legends, historical events, spells, charms, remedies; tales about dibbukim, demons, and evil spirits; songs, proverbs, maxims, sayings; recorded on phonograph discs: old melodies, prayers, and folksongs; photographed old synagogues, historic places, gravestones, prayer houses of zaddikim, various ritual scenes; picked up and purchased: Jewish

antiques, documents, communal record books, ceremonial objects, jewelry, clothing, and all sorts of Jewish antiquities.

Perhaps as impressive, upon their return, An-ski was able to take some of the premodern myths they had gathered and use them to create a Yiddish play of stunning power. *The Dybbuk* tells the tale of a Hasidic woman about to be married who is "inhabited" by a *dybbuk,* the spirit of a dead lover. (*Dybbuk* means "attachment." It was thought that the spirits of the dead could attach themselves to the living.) The subtitle of this work is perhaps as important: *Between Two Worlds.* As the haunted woman lived between the worlds of the living and the dead, so An-ski dwelt between the modern political present and the mythic Yiddish past. By allowing the old themes to attach themselves to him, he harnessed their allegorical power. In mining the Hasidic legends, An-ski created a modern work that has been continuously reimagined and performed.

It was a decade after An-ski's great expedition and subsequent play, after the massive destruction of World War I, that the Jewish attempt to both save and reuse its cultural past found its most ambitious form. In interwar Poland the extraordinary institution known as Yidisher Visnshaftlekher Institut blossomed in a compressed period of time. The product of many strands, YIVO bore the stamp of its founder, a dynamic polymath named Max Weinreich.

Weinreich was born in 1894 in a small Baltic town where his ambitious German-speaking parents transferred the precocious boy from his *cheder* to a secular school. But when anti-Semitism made it impossible for him to continue, he returned to a Jewish *gymnasium.* It was there that he discovered Yiddish politics, becoming a leader in the Junior Bund.

After studying language in St. Petersburg and in Marburg, Germany, where he wrote his dissertation on the history of Yiddish linguistic studies, he settled in post–World War I Vilna, which was then part of Poland. Vilna had a long history of Jewish learning; it had been a center of the *Haskalah,* Enlightenment, and was home to the Strashun Library, the most important in the Jewish world. But the city had fared badly during the Great War, coming under the control of a succession of occupying armies — Russian, Lithuanian, German, and at war's end, Polish. None of these nations had the interests of the Jewish population at heart. But with Yiddish-speaking Jews making up 30 percent of the city, the Yiddish environment remained strong.

As Lucy Dawidowicz, an American who spent a year in inter-war Vilna, described it:

> At the Jewish banks, you could write a check in Yiddish. Trade unions and craft guilds managed their affairs in Yiddish. Doctors talked to their patients in Yiddish. Political parties competed with one another in Yiddish and posted Yiddish placards on the streets. Young poets wrote their verses in Yiddish and composers set Yiddish songs to music. Nature-study hikes had Yiddish-speaking guides and Maccabi boxing matches had Yiddish-speaking referees. Even the Jewish underworld, the pickpockets and the horse thieves, plied their trades in Yiddish.

By the time Weinreich moved there, in the 1920s, the economy had gone from bleak to disastrous, but Vilna, which was called the Jerusalem of the North, had retained its cultural edge. Its multiethnic makeup even made it easier for Jews to exist as one more national or racial minority. Weinreich taught at the Yiddish Teachers Seminary, edited a Bundist newspaper, and began a Jewish scouting movement whose activities included coining Yiddish names for flowers and fauna. In time he had a wife and two sons.

In 1924 a group including Dubnow, the historian, floated a proposal for a dual-purpose Yiddish academy. This institution would standardize and regularize the language, establishing a scholarly base that would increase its status, giving the lie once and for all to the canard that Yiddish was inferior to other tongues. But linguistic advance was not to be an end in itself. Scholarly work would also serve the Yiddish-speaking masses, the people who would be the scholars' source and their strength. Raising the status of the Yiddish language and culture could only benefit the Jews, who knew they had no choice but to take their future into their own hands. *Mir hobn gornisht gehat, ober es hot unz gornisht gefelt.* We had nothing, but we also lacked for nothing.

The Jews of interwar Poland were growing desperately poor; the political situation was becoming increasingly bleak. Yet they had a great tradition of learning and a population of deeply committed, newly secularized scholars. If "Yiddishland" had no political boundaries, no concrete reality, these people who were just beginning to appreciate the role of Yiddish in Jewish history would have to create a Yiddishland of the mind.

Although YIVO was technically born in Berlin and later had branches in Warsaw, Paris, New York, and Buenos Aires, thanks to Weinreich its real home was Vilna. Full of enthusiasm, erudition, and connections, he set about creating an institution of daringly ambitious scope.

He wrote, "We want to fathom Jewish life with the methods of modern scholarship and, further, whatever modern scholarship brings to light, we want to bring back to the Jewish masses." As a linguist who had studied psychoanalysis in Vienna and sociology at Yale, who had translated Freud and Homer into Yiddish, Weinreich understood the deep meaning of the language as cultural lodestone, icon, and glue. It had given him focus as a teenager; it was a matter of pride in his adopted city; it was an organizing principle in a forward-looking period of Jewish life.

The Yiddish Scientific Institute grew swiftly into a unique institution. *Visnshaftlekher* means "scientific"; it also means "educational." Weinreich drew the parallel with *visn vos shaft,* knowledge that creates. YIVO was born with no money but with a rich agenda. Its honorary board included Dubnow, Zhitlovski, Einstein, and Freud.

Weinreich's plan was to continue An-ski's prewar work of rescuing and collecting Jewish artifacts and documenting folkways. To this would be added studies of Jews using the latest methods of the new social sciences. Sections for history, economics, and linguistics would be interwoven with the organization's other foci — education and Jewish youth. In 1933 the institute moved into its new headquarters, a renovated villa outside the old, traditional Jewish neighborhood, set on the hightest point of the city. Dawidowicz recalled: "This YIVO building was utterly unlike the institutions for the Yiddish world I knew in New York, most of which were housed in cramped, dingy, and dilapidated quarters. Everything about the YIVO — its location, its landscaped setting, its modern design, the gleaming immaculateness of the place — delivered a message. . . . YIVO was no relic of the past; it belonged to the future."

Building on Dubnow's idea, YIVO enlisted an army of volunteer *zamlers* to find books, documents, and objects of historic, religious, linguistic, or ethnographic interest. There was also an archive, a publishing house, and a department of psychology and pedagogy. Professional historians, especially a young man in Warsaw, Emanuel Ringelblum — a name to remember — created new fields of study and new ways of working. They published studies of Jewish-Polish relations; they sponsored field trips to document important buildings and collections. YIVO's synergistic quality made it easy for the excitement of one area to ignite the imagination of another. The organization quickly attained the status of myth.

"No one who would examine it as a mere institution at which a few dozen people did their prescribed job and were paid for it a certain (and more often, an uncertain) salary, would ever understand its role," Weinreich wrote. "I do not mean this pejoratively, for I have nothing against institutions where people earn a decent living. But I want to convey a difference. The young man from the town of Grodno, who roamed the streets for weeks with a group of beggars, so that he could write down their sayings and stories, did not get a penny for his pains, but he earned a *mitsve,* a substantial share in the world to come."

In the early 1930s Weinreich conceived a devilishly clever scheme to involve the next generation of Yiddish speakers in YIVO, as well as to produce sociological work from the inside out. YIVO sponsored a series of autobiographical contests in which young people were awarded cash prizes for essays describing what they saw as the important issues in their own lives.

Then, in another tactic to elevate the status of Yiddish while ensuring its centrality to Jews, in 1935 YIVO produced a set of standards for Yiddish. It was the first time any organization had regularized its grammar, spelling, and usage — a remarkable achievement for a fledgling institution whose only authority was self-defined. It also had real-world consequences. The spelling standards were adopted by the central organization of Yiddish schools in Poland, which served tens of thousands of pupils. Yiddish had indeed become scientific.

But not all Yiddish speakers were ready to accept YIVO's program. In the first place, the YIVO standard language was arbitrary. It had to be. Spelling reflected a middle-ground pronunciation, something on the order of broadcast English. Yiddish, like other major languages, included a variety of regional pronunciations, so this new standard was no one group's particular speech. It leaned heavily toward the Litvak, the Lithuanian or northern style that was spoken in Vilna. But like all people, Yiddish speakers stereotyped each other by regional accent. Litvaks were said to be coolly intellectual — so clever that they repented before even committing a sin. Galitzianers, on the other hand, those who came from what had been the Austro-Hungarian province of Galicia, were held to be impulsive. Western Europeans who spoke a Yiddish that was closer to German were said to share the stereotypically Germanic traits. But impassioned disagreement among Jews was nothing new. *If Jews all agreed, the Messiah would have come long ago.*

There is an apocryphal story that surfaces repeatedly about a group of Yiddish writers taking the train from Warsaw to Vilna to protest the new standards. In some versions, they throw rocks and break YIVO's new windows. Apocryphal tales are, in some sense, true. Meanwhile, it is objectively certain that Yiddish newspapers and publishers ignored the whole issue, continuing to use whatever spelling and usage they pleased.

It is easy, in hindsight, to fault what looks like these holdouts' narrow vision. We must remember the compressed time frame involved. Institutions, artistic schools, ways of thinking that in other cultures took generations or centuries to build, had to be jury-rigged in the two decades between one European war and the next: less than one generation. If the interwar Yiddishists had had the luxury of time, their reforms would probably have been accepted in the natural course of events, as children graduated from the new Yiddish schools and began to staff the institutions their parents had founded. But that never happened.

No matter how vibrant and alive Yiddish culture was in the Poland of the 1920s and 1930s, the world beyond the Jews was closing in. The Jews both knew it and did not. For centuries, they had lived with anti-Semitism and managed to survive, even thrive, on its margins. Their response, which had always worked before, was to ignore it as much as possible and, in a brilliant act of bravery and denial, to live in their own parallel world.

Inside YIVO, this concept was known as *dokeyt,* roughly translated as "hereness." Given their options, it made absolute sense for Jews to create a satisfying world for themselves where they were. With our contemporary knowledge of the impending Holocaust, it is easy to wonder why the Jews didn't leave. From their vantage point, though, there was nowhere safe to go. And if they spent their lives always escaping, they would never truly be living. Weinreich put *doikeyt* in the context of modern psychological theory, describing it as a matter of emotional maturity, of facing one's situation squarely and doing something constructive about it.

Unfortunately for YIVO and the European Jews, the destructive forces of European anti-Semitism were moving faster and with infinitely greater force. In 1933 anti-Semitic elements gained control of Germany, Poland's neighbor. And Poland, which centuries before had invited the Jews in, now wanted them gone. Although it ignored treaty obligations to provide education to Jews, right up until 1936 it repeatedly asked the League of Nations for help in getting rid of them.

As Isaac Bashevis Singer wrote about this period, "I had always believed in God, but I knew enough of Jewish history to doubt in His miracles." Bashevis managed to get himself to New York, where his brother, who had landed a staff job at the *Forward,* had moved his family a few years before. But most Jews were stuck. The whole wide world, which the Yiddish speakers had been hungrily imbibing, now seemed to have no place for them.

When war erupted in 1939, just fourteen years after the founding of YIVO, something like eleven million people, three out of every four Jews in the world, spoke Yiddish. Weinreich, who was attending a linguistic conference in Finland, could not get back home to Vilna. He and one of his sons made their way to New York; his wife and second son followed, but the sizable YIVO archives remained behind. Weinreich established a temporary headquarters for the organization in New York, began to organize research about American Jewish youth, and worked on another lifelong project, a history of the Yiddish language. He assumed that he would return to Vilna as soon as the war was over.

At the same time, Weinreich's young colleague, the Warsaw historian Emanuel Ringelblum, found himself in Geneva attending the Zionist Congress. Speaking at that meeting when Germany invaded Poland, Chaim Weizmann expressed what was surely everyone's fear when he said, "I have no prayer but this: that we will all meet again alive."

PART 3

Annihilation

CHAPTER 13

Singing in the Face of Death

אונדזערע צרות, זיכער, זײנען געווען אין ײדיש.

Undzere tsores, zikher, zaynen geven in yidish.

Our troubles, surely, were in Yiddish.

Remark of a survivor

If the speakers of a language are killed, then surely that language
will die. Although the elimination of Yiddish was not the primary
aim of the Nazis who gained control of Germany in 1933 and went
on to decimate much of Europe, the destruction of the language was
a certain consequence of the annihilation of its speakers. During the
decade or so that the Nazis were in power, they came terrifyingly
close to their avowed goal of ridding Europe of Jews. Their murder
of six million of them meant the destruction of two-thirds of the
nine million Yiddish speakers in Europe. (Virtually all Eastern
European Jews spoke or at least understood the language. It was
comprehensible to a majority of Western European Jews.) The
Nazis killed more than half of the eleven million Yiddish speakers
in the world.

Even for those who survived, their language was so intimately
bound up with the time of their weakness and terror that whatever
life they were able to construct when it was over would forever be
defined as before and after, with the "after" most often taking place
in a new tongue. Yiddish speakers called the Holocaust *der driter
khurbn,* the third destruction, recalling the destruction of the First

and Second Temples in Jerusalem. This was the first time in two thousand years that an event was cataclysmic enough to even merit comparison. Some said this one was worse.

The Nazis rose to power out of the wreck of World War 1 and the turmoil that erupted in its wake. The defeat of Germany and the collapse of its economy left its citizens prey to simplistic hate mongers. The Nazis preached a backward-looking ideology of racial purity — a bizarre concept given the multinational, multi-ethnic, multilingual conditions in Central Europe. As Germans sought out "impure" elements, they did not have to look very far. The Jews had been living among them for more than a thousand years. For well over a century they had been tightly enmeshed in German society. They were the outsiders who had managed to make a place for themselves, the Germans who were, somehow, not real Germans at all.

This us-but-not-us aspect of the Jews was painfully evident in their language. Even eight or nine hundred years after diverging from German, Yiddish was still obviously related to it. So the Nazis had to stamp out Yiddish just as they had to stamp out the Jews. As they conquered neighboring countries, the German of the Third Reich was the only language allowed. Nazis screamed orders in it and expected to be obeyed. They never worried that a conquered people might not understand them. Non–German speakers were subhuman by definition.

Yiddish speakers fared especially poorly because their language was, to the Nazi ear, a debased, corrupted version of the language of the Fatherland. If they tried to speak German, their Yiddish accents were derided, and they were often punished for their efforts. Even though Nazis ordered them to speak it, they found nothing more insulting than a Jew speaking German.

Speaking Yiddish was worse. Because almost no one but Jews spoke the language, Yiddish became an easy marker for enemies look-ing to root them out. Story after story is told of how a life was saved because the Jew in question was able to either keep his mouth shut or else had sufficient command of another European language to pass undetected. Just as Yiddish speakers had used the language for centuries to seek each other out for comfort and protection, their words, tones, and accents now gave them away. A language learned in childhood and spoken for an entire life can be teased out and laid bare in the torturer's cage. Anyone possessing Yiddish books, writing Yiddish letters, singing Yiddish songs was an obvious candidate for death.

The war began with Hitler's army invading Poland, the throbbing center of Yiddish life. Once the Nazis had taken control, they began their campaign of eradicating both the Jewish people and their culture. In Vilna by 1941, the Germans had squeezed the area's Jews into a ghetto. They collected the Jewish books as well. They brought all forty thousand volumes of the Strashun Library, as well as assorted books and sacred items from the area's three hundred synagogues, into the YIVO building, where the riches of generations were stacked and stuffed. The Nazis' plan was to destroy most of the books, Torah scrolls, and priceless manuscripts. The bulk of the materials, the treasures of centuries, would be shredded. A small selection would be sent to Frankfurt's new Institute for the Study of the Jewish Question. The plan was that, at the successful conclusion of the war, the institute would specialize in Jewish studies without Jews.

The Nazis forced some forty Yiddish scholars, including the poet Abraham Sutzkever, to sift through the riches and make heartbreaking decisions about what must be destroyed and what might be saved. The Jewish workers, well aware of what their captors had in store for their treasures and for them, worked with desperate efficiency. They formed themselves into a *papir brigade,* paper brigade, bent on sabotage and rescue. They managed to hide more than five thousand items in the YIVO building itself. Thousands of others, including manuscripts by Peretz, Sholom Aleichem, and Herzl, as well as drawings by Chagall, were smuggled out of the YIVO building and hidden in the ghetto.

As they feared, almost all of the *papir brigaders* were murdered. The Nazis also killed the great historian Simon Dubnow that same year in nearby Riga. There are several more or less apocryphal accounts of his death. We are told that the eighty-year-old scholar marched with his fellow Jews to a mass grave. In one report his final words were, *"Yidn, shreibt un farshreibt."* Jews, write and record.

Throughout the Nazi-occupied countries, Jews who weren't killed outright were herded into ghettos. In the Warsaw ghetto (or, as it is said in Yiddish, *in ghetto Varshe*) another historian took Dubnow's message to heart. Emanuel Ringelblum was thirty-nine when the Nazis invaded in 1939. He was a gregarious man with a good sense of humor, boundless energy, and a wife and young son. A respected historian with the broad perspective of a social scientist and the community consciousness of a left-wing activist, he had helped establish YIVO's historical section. He also worked on the Warsaw staff of the American Joint Distribution Committee, a philanthropic organization that channeled funds from American Jews to their needy Polish brethren. As mentioned earlier, the outbreak of war found him in Switzerland, but he came back to his family and his people. Because of his connections, he would have been able to get a visa to leave. But he chose to stay and bear witness.

Although anything written in Yiddish was inherently suspect, Ringelblum began systematically collecting, in Yiddish, documentation of the campaign being waged against the Jews. He organized a secret society known as the O.S., for *oyneg shabes,* delight in the Sabbath. The Yiddish version of a Hebrew phrase, the term is used to describe Friday evening, the beginning of the Sabbath, when Jews gather together with family and community to take special pleasure in that time and those activities that define them as Jews. It was an extraordinary choice of name. At one level it was a bit of subterfuge. The entries were written in the form of letters, or as pieces to be read at *oyneg shabes* gatherings. At another level it was pure heartbreak, given the proverb about *shabes* keeping the Jews, and the very real question of who, or what, would survive. The O.S. became a clearinghouse and archive. Its members collected information from towns, ghettos, and camps, and produced regular reports that were smuggled out to both Jews and non-Jews — anyone who would listen. They also produced a thoroughly professional record of information about the day-to-day happenings in the Warsaw ghetto, conducting interviews and surveys, as well as compiling information from diaries and reports into news releases. In addition, Ringelblum maintained his own volume of personal notes. Here he described how the O.S. laid out its procedures: "At hour-long editorial sessions we mulled over the main points in each of the themes. What we wished to do was to draw the author's attention to specific trends, and to indicate the lines along which he could develop his theme — not that we wished to force any of the authors to follow a particular line of our own. . . . We drew up special questionnaires designed to elicit information on such subjects as the relations between Jews and non-Jewish Poles, smuggling, the situation in various trades, the special problems affecting young people and women."

The group recorded ghetto life — the attempts at normalcy, even the long string of jokes: "A Jew alternately laughs and yells in his sleep. His wife wakes him up. He is mad at her. 'I was dreaming someone had scribbled on a wall: "Beat the Jews! Down with ritual slaughter!"' 'So what were you so happy about?' 'Don't you understand? That means the good old days have come back! The Poles are running things again!'"

An apocryphal story that seems to have made the rounds concerns a German officer who was boasting to Jews about all the foreign cities the Germans had already taken. The Jew asks if he has taken *a mise meshune*, and the German answers that he doesn't think so, but he is sure that it will be taken soon. The joke is on him, because the expression, *nemen arayn a mise meshune*, is a curse meaning "to suffer from (literally, take) an unnatural death."

As conditions worsened, Ringelblum and his group, which by now included dozens of members, maintained their high standard of reportage. On March 18, 1941, he wrote: "The number of the dead in Warsaw is growing from day to day. Two weeks ago some two hundred Jews died. Last week (the beginning of March) there were more than four hundred deaths. The corpses are laid in mass graves, separated by boards. Most of the bodies, brought to the graveyard from the hospital, are buried naked. In the house I lived in, a father, mother, and son all died from hunger in the course of one day."

Ringelblum took pains to distinguish what he had seen or heard himself from information that had been passed on to him:

> Heard that when They [the Germans] were seizing Poles for forced labor, a number of Jews with an Aryan appearance were ordered to speak Yiddish as proof that they were Jewish.
>
> Heard that there are signs in both Yiddish and German in Lublin. Requests from Jews to the German authorities must be written in German.

He was fastidiously observant, as in this excerpt from May 1942:

> Jonas Turkow acted this season in a Polish repertoire. The reason: There are no good plays in Yiddish. Besides, this is evidence of the marked assimilation so discernible in the Ghetto. The Jews love to speak Polish. There is very little Yiddish heard in the streets. We have had some heated discussions on this question. One explanation advanced is that speaking Polish is a psychological protest against the Ghetto — *you* have thrown us into a Jewish Ghetto, but *we'll* show you that it really is a Polish street. To spite you, we'll hold on to the very thing you are trying to separate us from — the Polish language and the culture it represents. But my personal opinion is that what we see in the Ghetto today is only a con-

tinuation of the powerful linguistic assimilation that was
marked even before the war and has become more noticeable
in the Ghetto. So long as Warsaw was mixed, with Jews and
Poles living side by side, one did not notice it so acutely; but
now that the streets are completely Jewish, the extent of this
calamity forces itself upon one's attention.

Still, the Yiddish penchant for language-based jokes continued.
The German group Werkschutz (Work Guard) was routinely
referred to as *werkshmutz*, work filth. One popular set of definitions
played on the similarity of the word Nazi to the Polish word for
Germans, *niemcy,* which sounded like the Yiddish phrase *nehm-zu,*
take away, while *Allemagne*, Germany, meant *alles mein,* all mine.
Yiddish speakers were nothing if not experts at gallows humor.

As we know from survivors, in the early days of the various
ghettos, Yiddish theater, poetry readings, and artistic "evenings"
continued. Prewar songs were brought up to date to reflect the current situation. The frankly sentimental song "Afn pripetshik,"
which describes a charming scene of a rabbi teaching young children to read their *alef beys*, their *abc*'s, was updated:

> At the ghetto gate
> a fire burns. Inspection is fierce.
> Jews are coming
> from the work brigades
> sweating buckets. Should I go ahead
> or stand still?
> I don't know what to do.
> The little commandant
> in his green uniform
> takes everything away.

In the Lodz ghetto, singers made fun of Western European Jews
who clung to the remnants of their previous life. "*Es geyt a yeke, oy, mit*

a teke" describes a German Jew wandering the ghetto clutching his briefcase searching in vain for butter or margarine. Polish Jews were not above making fun of their German coreligionists, who, being less accustomed to privation and poverty, died at a much higher rate.

But singing the old Yiddish songs had deeper meaning as well. A young woman named Leah Hochberg remembered the way her prewar youth group continued to meet in the Lodz ghetto: "During weekdays we sat together, and in the evenings we sang songs by the light of a small burner. . . . We tried to forget the bad times, so we sang. It worked wonderfully! I think it was one of the things which helped us to survive. The problem of physical hunger is not so difficult as psychological hunger. It is common knowledge that a hungry person is not hungry in his stomach but in his head. There is no doubt that the singing helped."

But the Jews would need more than tuneful aid. As Ringelblum and his comrades reported with painful precision, the noose continued to tighten. In the fall of 1942, when the Jews were reduced to starvation diets when they weren't being rounded up and shot, he made a list of "The Signs of Modern Slaves." Number one was "Numbered and stamped," number two, "Live in barracks without their wives." The list continued to number seventeen: "Worse than slaves, because the latter knew they would remain alive, had some hope to be set free. The Jews are *morituri* — sentenced to death— whose death sentence [has been] postponed indefinitely, or has been passed." And eighteen: "The sick and the weak are not needed, so ambulatory clinics, hospitals, and the like have been liquidated."

As conditions worsened, his reports became more telegraphic and brief. The community sent spies to confirm the rumors they had heard of a death camp. Ringelblum wrote: "The news about Treblinka brought back by the investigators sent out by the families of those deported there. — The story about the tractors: According to one version, tractors plow under the ashes of the burned Jews. According to another version, the tractors plow the earth and bury the corpses there."

As it became ever clearer that the Germans intended nothing short of total extermination, the tattered remnants of the Warsaw ghetto planned their revolt. To ensure the safety of the O.S. archive, the entire project, now numbering something like seven thousand entries, along with Ringelblum's notes, was packed in three milk cans and buried within the confines of the ghetto. Ringelblum himself was spirited out; his comrades insisted he was too important to be sacrificed.

The uprising lasted for almost a month, beginning on the eve of Passover 1943. After killing almost all the remaining Jews, the Nazis methodically destroyed the ghetto, blowing it up street by street, house by house, until not a soul or a building was left. Ringelblum, in hiding beyond the ghetto walls, began working on a new book. This one described Polish-Jewish relations during the course of the war. He wrote this new book in Polish, so it could be read by non-Jews.

There are two versions of how Ringelblum met his death, both of which probably contain elements of myth. In one, despite his strenuous objections, his fellow Jewish prisoners bribed the police to let him go free, explaining that he was a good shoemaker. But even with the bribe he was executed. Later on, the officer slyly offered that he knew that the man had been no shoemaker.

In the second version Ringelblum, his wife, and their thirteen-year-old son were tortured by the Gestapo in an effort to find the ghetto archives, but none of them talked. They were then taken to the ruins of the ghetto. After being forced to witness the murder of his wife and child, Ringelblum was killed. In both versions Ringelblum, his family, and his comrades all shared a common grave.

In other parts of war-torn Europe, Yiddish continued to bind together those Jews still alive. The simple Yiddish statement *"Ich bin a yid,"* I am a Jew, was the most direct, foolproof way to identify oneself as a comrade, no matter what protective disguise one might be wearing. Partisans spoke Yiddish in their forest haunts and, for one extraordinary military unit, Yiddish became the official language.

The Lithuanian Divison of the Soviet Army contained a plurality of Jews throughout the war, the number sometimes rising as high as 80 percent. In this division, officers gave orders in Yiddish and used the language to rally the troops. Their battle cry was *"Far unsere tates un mames,"* for our fathers and mothers. Dov Levin writes:

> To the Jewish soldiers, the use of Yiddish was so natural that at first they were not even self-conscious about it, and certainly they did not view it as special, since there were so many of them in the division. . . . However, as a result of their contact with Jewish soldiers from other Red Army units who did not conceal their astonishment at this mass use of Yiddish, and from a few, albeit minor, incidents within the division over this phenomenon, the division's Jewish soldiers began to realize that they enjoyed an advantage over the Jewish soldiers in other units of the Red Army.

The record of the division was outstanding. Its members chose dangerous assignments often enough that they were repeatedly commended for bravery by the Supreme Soviet Command. Ninety percent of the casualties in the Lithuanian Division were Yiddish-speaking Jews.

Still, the Nazi war machine ground on. As Jews were rounded up, they were sometimes able to call upon their reserves of *yidishkayt* to inspire each other. Here is a report of the last words, in Yiddish, of the beloved Rabbi Nokhem Yanishker of Slobodke in Lithuania. According to a survivor, when his townsfolk were being rounded up and he knew his end was near, he put on his shroud under his *shabes* clothes and addressed his followers:

> And if peace will return to the world, you should continuously tell of the greatness and wisdom in Torah and morals of Lithuania, what a fine and honorable life the Jews led here. But don't dissolve into tears and mourning! You should also

recreate your speech in letters. That will be the greatest revenge you can take on the evil ones. In spite of them, the souls of your brothers and sisters will live on, the martyrs whom they sought to destroy. For no one can annihilate letters. They have wings, and they fly around in the heights — into eternity.

Another survivor, Eliezer Berkovits, reported this event that took place in Poland:

> The Germans came to Lublin to set up a "Jewish area" and ordered the chairman of the *Judenrat,* Jewish committee, to assemble the Jewish population in an open field outside the city for a "general parade." As the Jews presented themselves at the appointed time, the German commander ordered them to sing a gay and happy Hasidic tune. The crowd was fearful and confused, but one hesitant voice started singing the moving song: *Lomir zikh iberbetn, ovinu shebashomayim* — Let us be friends again, Our Father in Heaven. The crowd remained unresponsive. The German soldiers threw themselves with murderous blows upon the Jews who would not obey their command. Suddenly, a voice broke from among the crowd singing the same tune with might and joy, but with the words now changed to: *Mir veln zey iberlebn, ovinu shebashomayim* — We shall outlive them, Our Father in Heaven. The song gripped the crowd. They sang it with enthusiasm and danced to it ecstatically. It became for them the hymn of Jewish eternity.

This letter, found on a Polish street leading to a death camp, detailed atrocities suffered by the writer and her group. Addressed, "Deliver into Jewish hands," it concluded, "I am writing in Polish, because if someone finds a Yiddish letter they would burn it. . . . We say good-bye to you, we say good-bye to the world, calling for revenge!"

After the forced marches and the horrific train rides, Jews from all over Europe found themselves thrown together in *lagers,* concentration camps. They whispered to each other: Are you Jewish? Where are you from? What should I do? They had, in their shared misery and terror, a common tongue. Although their accents varied, and the language was not by any means universal, Yiddish was common enough to be a ready source of communication.

The language also had the value of being close enough to German that Yiddish speakers could usually, by listening closely, get a general sense of the Nazis' words. Jews from Italy or Greece, for example, tended not to know Yiddish, and so were handicapped. One young Italian Jew showed just how this worked. Primo Levi was a graduate student in physics when he was arrested by the Germans in 1944:

> We immediately realized, from our very first contacts with the contemptuous men with the black patches, that knowing or not knowing German was a watershed. Those who understood them and answered in an articulate manner could establish the semblance of a human relationship. To those who did not understand them the black men reacted in a manner that astonished and frightened us: an order that had been pronounced in the calm voice of a man who knows he will be obeyed was repeated word for word in a loud, angry voice, then screamed at the top of his lungs as if he were addressing a deaf person or indeed a domestic animal, more responsive to the tone than the content of the message.
>
> If anyone hesitated (everyone hesitated because they did not understand and were terrorized) the blows fell. . . . for those people we were no longer men. With us, as with cows or mules, there was no substantial difference between a scream and a punch. . . .
>
> Whoever did not understand or speak German was a bar-

barian by definition; if he insisted on expressing himself in his own language — indeed, his nonlanguage — he must be beaten into silence and put back in his place.

Levi was soon transferred to Auschwitz. The vast majority of its inhabitants were Eastern European and German Jews, people who could speak either Yiddish or German. Levi, who had not learned either, was at a real disadvantage. "This 'not being talked to' had rapid and devastating effects," he wrote.

> To those who do not talk to you, or address you in screams that seem inarticulate to you, you do not dare speak. If you are fortunate enough to have next to you someone with whom you have a language in common, good for you, you'll be able to exchange your impressions, seek counsel, let off steam, confide in him; if you don't find anyone, your tongue dries up in a few days, and your thought with it.
>
> Besides, on the immediate plane, you do not understand orders and prohibitions, do not decipher instructions, some futile and absurd, others fundamental. . . . The greater part of the prisoners who did not understand German — that is, almost all the Italians — died during the first ten to fifteen days after their arrival: at first glance, from hunger, cold, fatigue, and disease; but after a more attentive examination, due to insufficient information. If they had been able to communicate with their more experienced companions, they would have been able to orient themselves better: to learn first of all how to procure clothing, shoes, illegal food, how to avoid the harsher labor and the often lethal encounters with the ss, how to handle the inevitable illnesses without making fatal mistakes. I don't mean to say that they would not have died, but they would have lived longer and had a greater chance of regaining lost ground.

Levi found what he called "our natural interpreters," Jews who could translate the German orders into French, a Romance language that the Italians could more easily understand. These people "translated for us the fundamental commands and warnings of the day, 'Get up,' 'Assembly,' 'Line up for bread,' 'Who's got broken shoes?'" Levi continues: "I implored one of them, an Alsatian, to give me a private and accelerated course, spread over brief lessons administered in a whisper, between the moment of curfew and the moment when we gave way to sleep, lessons to be recompensed with bread, since there was no other currency. He accepted, and I believe that never was bread better spent." Levi credits these language lessons with raising the odds of his survival.

Sometimes the Nazis used the warm associations of Yiddish as just another form of torture. Frieda Aaron reported that, in the camp where she found herself, "Every Sabbath night, as we were marched to the camp, the guards enacted a ritual of beating and killing to the accompaniment of a recording of the Yiddish song *Gut vokh* [Have a Good Week] that in better times greeted the new week."

In a place whose goal was the destruction of an entire people, the mood most often was one of desperation and despair. A survivor, Yoysef Vaynberg, described an Auschwitz scene one Kol Nidre, the most solemn night of the year. Here Hebrew slips into Yiddish for one final time, for these men who know that soon they, too, will slip from life to death.

> For a long time already we have been promising each other to observe the Kol Nidre service this year. A Jewish Block elder has allowed us to pray in his block. Someone has brought a *talis* [prayer shawl] from the clothing warehouse. The seriousness of the moment is felt in camp. It seems that the entire world is preparing for Kol Nidre.
> The rabbi prays.
> He was only recently brought into camp. Those who knew him helped and supported him in any way they could. So

many rabbis have died already; not another one is left. This one at least must remain alive.

Wrapped in the talis, he says the Prayer of Purification. Everyone hears his voice clearly. Everything is frozen — as if our bodies are placed on top of the altar to be willingly accepted by the almighty, as a sacrifice dedicated completely to God. Through the boards of the barrack I look at the crematorium, from which smoke reaches into the gray heavens.

And I hear the voice of the rabbi, as though it no longer came from his heart, but as if his heart itself had opened and wept:

"And a portion of our fat and our blood."

He wraps himself more tightly, and repeats the words; but now his heart bleeds, and he omits "and a portion"; "our fat and our blood." The congregation repeats "our fat and our blood." As if under a spell, everyone stops at these two words. The rabbi cannot go on. Louder and louder the congregation repeats: "our fat and our blood."

Now the words of the makeshift congregation switch from the formal Hebrew into heartfelt Yiddish.

Someone shouts: "The blood and fat of our parents, children, and relatives."

Tears pour from everyone's eyes. The weeping flows together, like a river. Hearts of stone have given way.

Survival in the death camps was often a matter of luck, but for most European Jews, luck had long since run out. Yet even in the face of certain death, Yiddish continued to be a bond, helping Jews to express whatever remained of dignity, devotion, faith, and fellow feeling. Stories are told repeatedly of groups of Hasidim breaking into fervent Yiddish song and dance in front of the crematoria where they knew they would meet their doom. These martyrs were transported beyond themselves by love for their fellows and their God. They breathed their last, as Mendele would have said, with both nostrils, the Yiddish mingling with the Hebrew ecstatically, one last time.

PART 4

Aftermath

Europe: Life from the Ashes

איך האָב געזען טויזנטער ייִדן, וואָס יעדער אײנער פון זײ איז א צאַפּלדיקע
טראַגעדיע אָדער אַן אומגלויבלעכער נס.

Ikh hob gezen toyznter yidn, vos yeder eyner fun zey
iz a tzapeldike tragedie oder an ungloyblekher nes.

I have seen Jews in thousands, and every one of them is a
fresh tragedy or a miracle of survival.

Jacob Pat

The war ended with silence — the silence of millions of people
dead, schools destroyed, presses smashed, books burned. Yiddish
theaters, movies, and radio programs had been stilled. Half of the
world's Yiddish speakers were no more. Many traumatized survivors had been rendered mute. But as they emerged from death
camps and from hiding places in cellars and barns, others were
eager to bear witness. For those who looked for a meaning in the
chaos, many latched onto this: They would speak. They would
write. They would tell their stories. Those who survived would
take on the voices of the generations of dead.

Out of nine million Jews who lived in Europe in the mid-1930s,
spread from the British Isles to the far reaches of the Soviet Union,
only three million remained. Most of those killed had come from
Central and Eastern Europe, Yiddish culture's home. Many of the

buildings and most of the political, economic, educational, and cultural institutions were gone. No matter how bad the centuries of entrenched anti-Semitism had been, no one could have imagined anything like this.

Soviet and American soldiers who liberated the death camps searched for words to describe what they saw. For the soldiers who were themselves Jews, the situation was even more fraught. One American soldier, Michael Elkins, was a journalist. Growing up in New York in the interwar period, he had distanced himself from his Yiddish-speaking parents. He described his childish tirades against them thus: "'Be American!' I yelled, 'Americans speak English! English not Yiddish!'" But in 1945, in an American military uniform, he found himself at Dachau.

> One of the skeletons came up to me and babbled something. I couldn't understand him and I held him up and held him close, and said:
>
> "It's all right, you're safe now, you'll be all right. Only, I just don't understand you. I speak only English. I'm an American." And then he said to me:
>
> "Du kenst nicht redden mamaloshen? Bist du nicht ein Yid?"
>
> And memory came surging out of my childhood.
>
> "Can't you speak the mother-tongue? Aren't you a Jew?"
>
> This I understood and was ashamed.
>
> And began, at that moment, the long voyage home.

The liberators of the death camps found fifty thousand souls alive. More continued to die from the sudden influx of food, or the lingering effects of starvation and disease. Even among the healthy, many were too dazed or frightened to leave the camps. And they had no idea where to go. Jews who tried to reclaim their old homes in Poland were murdered by their former neighbors. Palestine was off limits, the United States effectively closed.

Thousands of orphaned Jewish children wandered aimlessly

across Europe. Many of those who found no one to claim them made their way to Italy and southern France, back the way their ancestors had come almost two millennia before. Other Jews helped smuggle them into Palestine.

But the first stop for many suvivors was their prewar home. They hoped against hope that they would find family, community, friends. What they discovered was almost as horrifying as what they had already lived through.

Nokhem Krumerkop recalled his journey to his hometown:

> Finding myself in Lublin when the war ended, I began to think about ways in which I, as a Jew, could travel to Tarnogrod, which entailed great dangers. At that time the Kelts pogrom also took place, costing the lives of 40 Jews, and the anti-Semitic bands terrified every surviving Jew. Jews were warned not to ride trains until the hooliganism stopped.

Krumerkop decided to disguise his Jewish appearance. In the spring of 1945 he cut off his beard, put on peasant boots and a peasant cap, and set off for Tarnogrod by train via Bilgoray.

> When I arrived at Bilgoray, Polish coachmen stood in front of the station. They fell upon me, asking me where I was headed; each one wanted to take me. I stood mute for a while, searching with my eyes: perhaps Mendle Roshe's |Roshe's son, Mendle| would appear, or Mendl Avel, or another of the Jewish coachmen of Tarnogrod, who used to drive to Bilgoray and back each day.
>
> But my search was fruitless. None of them was left. Gentile wagons had taken their place. Having no other choice, I approached one of the Polish Coachmen, and we settled on a fare to Tarnogrod. For a short while we both sat silently. He was the first to speak: I tried to answer as little as

possible, so that he wouldn't realize I was a Jew. Then he pointed in front of himself with his whip and said:

"See, on both sides of the road are buried Jews whom the Germans shot. Jews from Tarnogrod, Bilgoray, and the surrounding villages lie there. The Germans knew what they were doing when they shot all the Jews. It was a good thing they did, and we should be grateful to them for it."

The gentile sat talking with his back to me, and I sat as if petrified. As I looked around I saw that the entire road from Bilgoray to Tarnogrod was the same as before. Nothing had changed: the same houses, the same gentiles, the same women drawing water from their wells, just as before. Only the coachman wasn't the same. I no longer heard the rich Yiddish tongue and the Yiddish *"Vyo, ferdelekh! Giddyap!"* I no longer heard the melody of the prayer, "Let us give strength to the holiness of this day," which Yoysef Magid used to sing as he rode with his passengers to Bilgoray. Depressed, I thought to myself: Where am I going, and to whom? Is there really no one left? Is it possible that an entire city of Jews was slaughtered?

The answer, often, was yes.

Hundreds of thousands of the survivors converged on the American-run displaced-persons camps in Germany, searching for loved ones, looking for comfort, hoping for passage out of Europe. In those camps, Yiddish flourished. No longer the language of fear, it became an agent of unity. Driven by a need to see who was left, to arrange some kind of lives for themselves, and to tell the world what horrors they had seen, one of the survivors' first requests, after food and medicine, was for Yiddish typewriters.

Luckily, the American forces in charge of the camps understood the overwhelming need for the *sharit ha platah,* the surviving remnant, to communicate with each other and with the world. According to their records, the Information Control Division of the

American Military Government "would confiscate printing plants that had belonged to the Nazi party and Nazi individuals and lease them to the new publishers, search out supplies of newsprint and ink, arrange for the salvage of bombed out presses |and| supervise a swap of Bavarian cheese for British-Zone zinc needed for making photographic plates."

The newly formed Central Committee of Liberated Jews of Bavaria immediately began publishing lists of survivors and by October 1945, five months after liberation, were publishing a Yiddish weekly, *Unzer weg* (Our Way). Within half a year, it had grown to sixteen pages.

Leo Schwartz, a senior official of the American Jewish Joint Distribution Committee, which funneled aid from American Jews to Europe, wrote that *Unzer weg* was received "in the editorial offices in Paris, London, New York, Tel Aviv, Vienna." It was "a mine of information to the news-hungry editors." He said that, "this paper out of the ruins of Munich was proof of vitality and of a faint glimmering of cultural renascence."

Soon the survivors were publishing dozens of Yiddish newspapers, representing a variety of political and cultural slants. In addition to *Unzer weg, Unzer shtime* (Our Voice), *Dos fraye vort* (The Free Word), and *Unzer hofenung* (Our Hope) carried news of the camps out and happenings of the wider world in. There was also an ongoing journal, *Fun letsn khurbn* (Out of Our Most Recent Catastrophe). In the camps, Yiddish culture came back to life as Jews created associations of all sorts. There were Yiddish kindergartens and soccer leagues, yeshivas, and theater troupes. People pulled Yiddish songs from their memories, mounted productions of Sholom Aleichem plays. They also set up governing bodies and businesses, formed clubs, alliances, marriages. A form of "normalcy" also returned when the survivors revived many of the political and religious groups of the prewar years. Once again, Zionists could face off against Bundists; socialists could debate Hasidim. Yiddish talk flowed. The Jews were alive again.

The first peacetime Passover in April 1946, was a milestone. The story told in the traditional Passover seder, of the liberation of the Jews from slavery in Egypt, held special meaning for the survivors. Levi Shalit, editor of *Unzer weg,* wrote in his editorial, "And one wants so much, dear sister and brother Jews who survived the catastrophe, to hear at least today a word of consolation — today, at the first liberated Passover, after six years of bloody Sabbaths and holidays, today, on the happiest day of our people." So he advised his readers, "Don't tell that your children were gassed in chambers. . . . Don't tell how you slaved . . . don't draw a parallel between Hitler and Pharaoh, but instead let us read the ancient Haggadah which always renewed us in the Diaspora. . . . Tell it on the last night of the seder, here, in the European desert, on your way to your liberation."

Throughout the newly freed American Zone, in displaced-persons camps, in hospitals, in public buildings and homes, survivors planned seders of their own. Rabbi Abraham J. Klausner, a U.S. Army chaplain, oversaw a seder for two hundred Jewish survivors who had "graduated" from the camps and were living in Munich, along with a handful of military personnel. Held in the Deutsches Theater Restaurant in Munich, this seder used a *Haggadah*, the book that contains the traditional holiday prayers and stories, that had been put together specially for this event.

Illustrated with haunting woodcuts by the survivor Miklos Adler, the *Haggadah* combines three languages. The introduction was in the English of the American liberators. A formal storytelling section as well as portions of the traditional service followed in Hebrew. Then, at the point at which the leader of the service is directed to explain the story to his son who is too young to even know what questions to ask, the *Haggadah* slips into Yiddish: "For thousands of years the Jewish People have commemorated the day of their Exodus from bondage. Through slavery, force, inquisition, destruction, and troubles, the Jewish People have borne in their hearts a longing for freedom and expressed this longing universally so as not to leave out a single tormented Jewish soul. From parents to children, from generation to generation, the story of the Exodus from Egypt is passed on as a personal memory; it never pales or loses luster."

The Yiddish section then goes on to quote a central portion of the Hebrew service, the part that establishes the link between millennia of Jewish lives: "In each and every generation one should regard oneself as though he had come out of Egypt." The Yiddish then resumes: "There is no higher historical consciouness than this. There is no more complete fusing of the individual and the community to be found on the face of the earth and in the depths of the generations than this."

The ancient story had been retold, the ancient questions asked and answered. The link had been rejoined: Hebrew inside of Yiddish. Yiddish as the vehicle for Hebrew. Perhaps there might be a future after all.

Primo Levi lived to see the end of the war. When his camp was liberated, he and a couple of fellow inmates, not knowing which direction might be safe for Jews to travel, made a long, convoluted journey toward home. On the way, the Yiddish he had learned in the camps continued to serve him well. He described how he and his friends arrived in a small Romanian town.

> A single, minute, archaic tram ran from one end of the city to the other; the ticket collector stood at a terminal; he spoke Yiddish, he was a Jew. With some effort we managed to understand each other . . . the local Jewish community had formed a relief centre. If we had one or two hours to spare, he counselled us to go as a delegation to the centre; we should be given advice and help. In fact, as his tram was about to leave, he told us to climb on, he would put us down at the right stop and would take care of the tickets. . . .
>
> Two old patriarchs, with a scarcely more opulent or flourishing air than ours, received us in a gloomy, dusty office; but they were full of affectionate kindness and good intentions, they made us sit on the only three chairs, overwhelmed us with

attention and precipitately recounted to us, in Yiddish and French, the terrible trials which they and a few others had survived. They were prone to tears and laughter; at the moment of departure, they invited us peremptorily to drink a toast with terrible rectified alcohol, and gave us a basket of grapes to distribute among the Jews on the train. They also emptied all the drawers and their own pockets, and raked together a sum of lei which on the spot seemed to us astronomical; but, later, after we had divided it, and taken into account the inflation, we realized that its value was principally symbolic.

Again and again, the reestablishment of Yiddish-based traditions and rituals helped shattered people reconnect with their old lives and begin to integrate the awful experiences of the war. Jews living in the Displaced Persons Center in Landsberg, Germany, in 1947 put on a *purim-shpil*. This one took advantage of the genre's tendency to turn reality on its head. In this play, the participants reenacted death camp scenes, playing all roles — ss officers, even Hitler. We might call it mastery or role playing — an effort to begin to make some sense of a world in which all sense seemed lost.

The next Purim, survivors belonging to the Bobover sect of Hasidim who had made their way to New York put on a *purim-shpil* they called *Tzayt in farnumen poylan* (Times in Occupied Poland), in which a child is torn from his mother, murdered, and then, miraculously reborn, returned to his mother again. But the author of this *purim-shpil,* Moses Aftergute, later reported that, when the play was performed, the audienced reacted with sobbing and fainting. The subject was much too close to home, the experience too fraught with raw emotion. The Bobover *rebe* himself suggested that the play not be repeated. Although popular *purim-shpiln* are often performed in succeeding years, this one has never been performed again.

As well as moving forward, survivors could not help looking back. They took on as their mission the retrieval and publication of any records that remained. In Warsaw, over the next few years, a few surviving members of Emanuel Ringelblum's *oyneg shabes* group dug through the rubble, searching for the three milk cans in which their precious documents had been buried. Eventually, two of them were retrieved. One of the cans is now displayed at the U.S. Holocaust Memorial Museum in Washington, D.C.

In Vilna, the poet and former *papir brigader* Sutzkever lived through the war as a forest-dwelling partisan. He was one of those who helped liberate the city. But what he found confirmed his worst fears. He wrote to a friend: "For two weeks now I've been wandering through the ruins. I've dug out cultural treasures and visited Ponar [the scene of mass slaughter]. I found no one there. Only — ashes. They had dug up the Vilna Jews and burned them. The human ash is sticky and grey. I poured some of it into a pouch (it could be my child or my mother) and I keep it near me."

The YIVO building had been totally destroyed, along with many of the ghetto hiding places of the *papir brigade*. But one underground bunker remained. Less than two weeks after the liberation, in a city that had been mercilessly bombed, Sutzkever, along with fellow partisan Shmerke Kaczerginski, dug through ruins to retrieve whatever treasures they could find. In the destroyed city, with food, clothing, medicine, and shelter in short supply, they worked to save Vilna's rich Jewish heritage. Transporting their collection in a wheelbarrow, they founded the Museum of Jewish Art and Culture, a nod to the past and a prayer for the future.

Unfortunately, the Soviets, who controlled the area by then known as the Lithuanian Soviet Socialist Republic, had no interest in preserving Jewish culture. When they came upon the remainder of the YIVO/Strashun archive that the Nazis had not destroyed, they began work that would complete the job. They ordered twenty tons of Yiddish books and papers to be trashed.

Kaczerginski later recalled, "That is when we, the group of museum activists, had a bizarre realization — we must save our treasures *again,* and get them out of here. Otherwise, they will perish. In the best of cases they will survive, but will never see the light of day in the Jewish world." Although they managed to send a few packages on to New York, the fledgling museum was liquidated and ransacked by the KGB, the Soviet secret police. Its contents were dumped in the basement of the Lithuanian National Book Chamber. The order went out for its contents to be destroyed.

But at the same time those books were disappearing from sight, others were resurfacing. In occupied Germany, the U.S. Army took control of the spoils the Nazis had sent to Frankfurt from Vilna in the early days of the war. These Yiddish books and treasures had been confiscated for the proposed Nazi museum of an extinct people. Now the Americans packed them up in four hundred crates and sent them to YIVO headquarters in New York. About half of the autobiographical essays that had been so important in establishing support for YIVO were part of this shipment.

Sutzkever, the *papir brigader,* managed to reach Eretz Israel along with his wife and two-year-old daughter. Unlike most of his compatriots, he resisted the pull to Hebrew, and for four decades published a Yiddish journal, *Di goldene keyt* (The Golden Chain), named after a play by Peretz. It was the chain of memory, of connection, of unbreakable hope.

In the aftermath of war, an entirely new Yiddish literary genre was born. *Yizker bikher,* or *yizker* books, took their name from the Jewish memorial service. Some began as jottings on scraps of paper by death camp survivors. Others were ambitious projects, with contributions coordinated from all over Europe, as well as from the Americas, Israel, Australia, and South Africa. At their simplest, the books were lists of people who had been murdered; at their most complex, they attempted to reconstruct, or at least give some lasting form to, the communities that had been obliterated. They retold history and included maps, photographs, and charts.

Over the course of time, some fifteen hundred of these volumes were published. They were organized primarily by *landsmanshaftn,* organizations of townsfolk. They often required great feats of organization, with survivors scattered across the globe. But the hardest work was emotional. Some of the books are rich in remembrances of everyday life. "Every shtetl had its madman," reads an account in the book about Pysek contributed by Khayim Shabakh. "Our town was small, so our *meshugener* was only half-crazy." Mostly, the memoir writers were solemn — aware that they were filling in a yawning blank. The maps, photos, documents, and lists would be all that remained of these hamlets and towns.

In the years to come, some of the Nazi war criminals were brought to trial. Often, Jewish witnesses who were comfortable in more than one language would offer their testimony in Yiddish, the language that was most deeply theirs, the language in which the atrocities had occurred. And as Holocaust survivors met in formal settings as the years stretched on, the Yiddish greeting, the Yiddish song, absorbed and expressed some of the fierce emotion of the group.

Recently, a strange item turned up in the linguistic column of New York's *Forward:* a request for information about a Limoges ashtray. The white china piece had a border of gold Stars of David; at its center a Yiddish phrase written in blue: "*Nekomeh bay di vantsn ven dos hoyz brent,*" revenge by the bedbugs when the house burns. A strange bit of decoration for an ashtray, this saying is a variant of a Yiddish proverb, *it is a revenge on the bedbugs when the house burns.* Of course, to burn down a house solely to get rid of the bedbugs would be the act of a madman. But wasn't that what Hitler, a madman, had come close to doing? The Nazis had almost destroyed Europe. And they had treated the Jews as if they were little better than bugs.

At war's end, many Jews found themselves in Limoges, in southern France. Some had survived the war there. For others, it was one more stop on their long, emotion-drenched journey to Israel. The ashtray shows how, through all the tragedy and the unspeakable horror, the Yiddish sense of humor remained. What a deep joke, a typically Yiddish tour de force. In the ruins of Europe, some Yiddish speaker in whom still flared *a pintele yid,* a spark of Jewishness, had conceived the idea of an ashtray commissioned by the former bugs.

CHAPTER 15

America:
Golden Land, Goyish Land

אַן ייִדישער פּאָעט איז דער וואָס לייענט אָדען אָבער אָדען אים לייענט ניט.

An yidisher poet iz der vos leynt Auden ober Auden
leynt im nit.

A Yiddish poet is someone who reads Auden but Auden
doesn't read him.

Jacob Glatstein

Out of the ruins of Europe, ninety thousand Jewish survivors
made their way to American ports. They were met with open
arms and tears of joy. But the welcome came at a price: New
arrivals were expected to quickly learn a new language and get on
with their lives, sparing their hosts the awful details. If the age-old
centers of European Yiddish civilization had been obliterated, they
were not about to be reborn in the land of endless opportunity and
collective amnesia.

Earlier immigrants often continued to speak, read, and write
Yiddish among themselves, and their children tended to retain
some understanding. For their grandchildren, however, it was a
different story. Yiddish was more likely to be an accent, a flavor, the
vague echo of a foreign tongue. Jews even joked about the diminu-
tion of their language with a kind of pride. The youngsters were so

American, *kayn aynhoreh* (a Hebrew-via-Yiddish reflexive warding off of the evil eye), they didn't understand a word.

This climate increased the pressure on the new postwar arrivals to assimilate, at least in the public sphere. Many institutions that had insulated earlier Yiddish speakers were in decline, or were altogether gone.

Guilt, compassion, fear, and unprecedented opportunity all played a part. The American war record had been blemished at best. When the Nazis had risen to power, the United States, with its own underlying strain of anti-Semitism, had accepted only a handful of refugees. In 1942, when news of the ghettos and concentration camps first leaked out, the reports had been carried primarily by the Yiddish press, which at the time was still read by a third of all American Jews. Mainstream American news outlets consistently underplayed the plight of Europe's Jews, relegating stories to back pages or not reporting on them at all. Especially disappointing was the poor showing by the German-Jewish-owned *New York Times*.

For example, the Yiddish press had given ample coverage to a mass demonstration held in Madison Square Garden in New York on July 21, 1942. Called by a coalition of Jewish organizations to protest massacres of Jews in Eastern Europe, the event packed the hall with twenty thousand people, with more massed outside. The *New York Times* described the event as being a "mass protest against Hitler atrocities." It hardly mentioned Jews as organizers, protesters, or victims.

After the war, American Jews were inclined to be careful about making public demands. Because the United States had suffered comparatively little, and because American Jewish efforts to influence U.S. policy to help save their European cousins had been feeble and ineffective, they also carried an element of guilt. And now, with peace, an extraordinary prosperity beckoned. All the newcomers had to do was to jettison their foreignness — change their names, their accents, their language. Who needed the burdens of dogged memory? Now that so much of European Jewry had been destroyed, Yiddish began to feel like bad luck, an eerie link to the dead.

Many survivors were willing to go along. As they established new families, they had a tendency to speak Yiddish at home to their children, drawing what comfort they could from the sounds and cadence of familiar words. In a foreign land, at least the lilt of *mame loshn* might cloak them in the warmth of a remembered home. They named their children after relatives who had died too young. They passed on the phrases, the songs, the expressions. They wrote *yizker* books and a slew of memoirs. But too often the awful silence of Holocaust sufferers was passed on.

Max Weinreich, who had spent the war years in New York, established YIVO in its new home. There was no going back. When the Soviets took over Lithuania, the city became Vilnius. So the New York YIVO emerged as the epicenter of Yiddish scholarly research, the repository for Yiddish books and literature. YIVO published journals, bulletins, and monographs; sponsored classes, lectures, conferences, summer schools. It established a standardized system of transliteration or romanization, based on its standard alphabet. It also housed a new field — Holocaust studies.

But it was not able to pull off a miracle a second time. Americans did not embrace the institution with the same desperate support that prewar Polish Jews had mustered. American Jews had infinitely more options, and Weinreich was not able to inspire American youth in the deep and dynamic way he had in Vilna. The sad truth was that, with every postwar year, Yiddish was receding farther and farther toward the edges of the American scene. Mainstream institutions opened up to Jews, who then had less need for the comfort of Yiddish. In the postwar era, the delicate us/them balance shifted heavily toward merging the "us" with the "them."

For his part, Weinreich focused on the scholastic. He became the first American professor of Yiddish, at New York's City College. He wrote, in Yiddish, a four-volume history of the language. His son Uriel, who was shaping up as his successor, authored what is still the standard college text, as well as the standard Yiddish-English dictionary. The younger Weinreich also set in motion a vast project — a linguistic and cultural atlas of Yiddish that would locate the origins and variations of the language as its speakers had moved through space and time. The project grew to include six thousand hours of tape recordings and a hundred thousand pages of field notes. But Uriel Weinreich's untimely death at age forty felt like the end of a dynasty, and the atlas went unpublished for decades. It was telling that no dynamic young American arose to finish it. The cultural ferment was elsewhere.

A joke long popular with American Jews introduced an immigrant with a heavy Yiddish accent and the ill-fitting name of Shane Ferguson. When asked how he had acquired such an uncharacteristic moniker he replied that, on the boat coming over, he had practiced saying his new American name. But when on his arrival he was confronted with a frightening English-speaking cop, he could only blurt out the Yiddish phrase *"Sheyn fergessen,"* I forgot. In fact, it was his children and grandchildren who made it their business to forget.

In the politically conservative postwar boom times, Jews, like other hyphenated Americans, were moving out to the suburbs and leaving ethnicity behind. Although the older generations still felt at home in Yiddish — indeed, some immigrants spent decades in America barely learning English at all — postwar children knew Yiddish mainly as the punch lines of jokes they couldn't follow.

When Jews sent their children to modern Hebrew schools, classes were taught in English. Yiddish remained the language of instruction in only the most intransigent Hasidic institutions. Then, with the establishment of the state of Israel in 1948, even the sound of the Hebrew prayers changed. Children learned the new Sephardic pronunciation, a legacy of Ben Yehuda's anti-Yiddish crusade. The holy words no longer slid so easily into daily speech. One more link to Yiddish was gone.

Eventually, the Old Country receded from memory. The shtetls no longer existed. The Old Country itself disappeared. As the Cold War deepened, many of the lands of the former Yiddish speakers were closed off to Americans altogether as Russia, Ukraine, and Poland were isolated behind the Communists' Iron Curtain. All that was left was memory. And in get-ahead America, memory was one of the first things left behind.

The 1950s were largely defined by right-wing McCarthyism, which was more than a touch anti-Semitic. The fact that Yiddish had been closely identified with the political left did not do much for its image. When FBI agents wanted to track leftists, they stationed themselves in the parking lots of Yiddish institutions like Camp Kinderland, noting down parents' license plates. After that, only the most devoted or dogmatic Yiddishists would continue sending their children there; most found other, greener fields.

Popular culture shifted too. The Yiddish movie industry never started up again after the war, so Yiddish words and Jewish themes had to be filtered through mainstream outlets. Ironically, the fact that the Hollywood moguls were by and large Jewish kept professionals anxious about having too Jewish a slant. Neal Gabler, who wrote of the Jews' inventing Hollywood, described it as "a ferocious, even pathological, embrace of America. Something drove them to deny whatever they had been before settling here."

Actors who moved from the Yiddish theater to the Great White Way adopted "American" names. In movies and plays, Yiddishisms only occasionally slipped through. Groucho Marx sang, "Hooray for Captain Spaulding, the African explorer," and then added impishly, "Did someone call me *shnorer*," a word that goes beyond the literal "beggar" to mean something closer to "moocher." Even much later, in the 1974 film *Blazing Saddles,* Mel Brooks showed up as the chief of a tribe of Indians who opened their mouths and spoke a foreign tongue — Yiddish. But fewer and fewer in the audience could understand what those headdressed "natives" were saying, or even recognize the language for what it was.

Yiddish theater limped along for a couple of postwar decades, but its audience was mostly gone. The few Yiddish words and expressions that surfaced in the general culture were a sanitized nod to ethnicity, played for nostalgia. By far the most popular and widespread Jewish-identified emissary into popular culture, Molly Berg, starred in her own radio and, later, TV show. In the early years her character spoke an English weighted down with Yiddishisms: "Yes, Jake. Dun't leff. Maybe I'm a plain peison, and I dun't ridd vhat de high writers is writing, bot by myself I found out de whull secret." But such obvious ethnicity had no place on TV and her show, although successful, was the only one of its kind. Most often the sound of a Yiddish accent signaled that it was time for the audience to laugh.

From its height in the 1930s, Yiddish newspaper circulation declined continuously, and as paper after paper folded, former ideological enemies were forced to write side by side. Always hotbeds of injured pride and stiff-necked partisan disputation, the newspapers' bedfellows became more and more strange. Isaac Bashevis Singer told how his brother, Israel Joshua, reported on the internecine warfare among the *Forward* staff. As the elder Singer described it, the Stalinists "seemed to consider this one newspaper and its writers the only major obstacle to the coming of the revolution." As always, it was impressive that Yiddish speakers felt so passionately responsible for the welfare of the whole world. But the arguments were becoming ever more stylized and removed.

It seemed that history had conspired against Yiddish. In Eastern Europe, its natural home, its speakers had been murdered, its culture destroyed. Yiddish speakers in the Soviet Union were facing their own cultural wars. And in the United States, where with every generation the children and grandchildren of Yiddish speakers could move more freely, a separate language seemed more like a hindrance than a help. For most Jewish baby boomers, Yiddish was the language their parents and grandparents spoke when they didn't want their children to understand. Few among the older generation considered the logical outcome of their linguistic strategy. It meant that when they died, Yiddish would be gone.

As the trauma of the war subsided and a new generation came of age, one fact became numbingly clear: There never would be a Yiddishland. There might be Yiddish coffee klatches, Yiddish jokes, Yiddish sayings, and Yiddish songs, but the postwar history highway had taken another route. The Yiddish enclaves left behind in the aging city centers would lose business, close down their theaters, schools, radio stations, and newspapers. And they would not be replaced.

A new word was even being heard in connection with *mame loshn — toyt,* dead. Unbelievable as it sounded, the rumor persisted: The thousand-year-old language could actually die. The brief Yiddish flowering — only a century had passed since the publishing of Mendele's first Yiddish tales — had been abruptly cut off. New institutions had not had time to take root. And now it was too late — the remaining Yiddish speakers lived increasingly apart.

The United States represented the largest concentration of Jews in the world, and American Jews now identified with Israel, locked in its David-and-Goliath struggle with neighbors who swore they would drive it into the sea. Jewish children in the United States learned Israeli dances, sang Israeli songs. Jewish pride now stemmed from Hebrew, language of the brave muscular men and free vibrant women of the sunbaked, forward-looking kibbutz. By 1960 only 3 percent of American children enrolled in Jewish education learned Yiddish.

The loudest lamentations came from the Yiddish poets, who lived mostly in New York and Tel Aviv. Not only was their personal creative medium dying, but a whole cultural vision was about to be lost. Hitler had murdered their people, but the Jews were allowing their own heritage to die.

So Yiddish poets did what they had always done. They poured out their hearts in Yiddish verse, declaiming their love for their language, their anguish at its decline. The ever diminishing numbers of Yiddish newspapers, books, and journals were full of impassioned odes to the death of the language in which they were written. If the literary quality of their work varied, the intensity of their love for the language never did. It is hard to imagine another tongue that is itself the subject of so many desperate laments. Eliezer Greenberg wrote in "Stammerers in All the Tongues of the World,"

> O stammerers in all the world's tongues:
> In what tongue other than Yiddish
> does Jewish laughter so deliciously ring out?
> In what tongue other than Yiddish
> are Jewish sobs so bitterly torn from the lungs?

In 1969 Cynthia Ozick wrote a short story called "Envy, or Yiddish in America," about a Yiddish writer in New York desperately trying to eke out a living:

> He swallowed scraps. Synagogues, community centers, labor unions underpaid him to suck on the bones of the dead. Smoke. He traveled from borough to borough, suburb to suburb, mourning in English the death of Yiddish. Sometimes he tried to read one or two of his poems. At the first Yiddish word the painted old ladies of the Reform Temples would begin to titter from shame, as at a stand-up television comedian. Orthodox and Conservative men fell instantly asleep. So he reconsidered, and told jokes.

One of his jokes concerns a funeral cortege whose route passed "the newspaper offices of the last Yiddish daily left in the city. There were two editors, one to run the papers off the press and the other to look out the window. The one looking out the window saw the funeral procession passing by and called to his colleague: 'Hey Mottel, print one less!'"

The writer, critic, and Yiddish expert Irving Howe, along with Eliezer Greenberg, gave this death a human face. In 1982 Howe wrote of the Yiddish poet Jacob Glatstein, "Glatstein knew — he had every right to — that he was a distinguished poet who, if he wrote in any other language, would be famous, the recipient of prizes, and the subject of critical studies. It was hard for me to explain . . . the utter indifference of American literary circles to the presence of a vibrant Yiddish culture that could be found, literally and symbolically, a few blocks away."

One writer who never resigned, never accommodated, was Isaac Bashevis Singer. Even as an old man, he continued to turn out tales of *goylems* and *dybbuks,* of haunted girls in timeless shtetls, of insane women in prewar Polish cities, of elderly men still finding the energy to argue with their friends and deceive their wives in post-Holocaust New York. His work still debuted in the *Forward,* but more and more of his audience read his work in translation. (Although Singer lived in the United States for over four decades and had an excellent command of English, he always wrote in Yiddish and relied on translators.)

In the 1970s the *New Yorker* became a regular outlet for him. An American publisher of Singer's memoirs could afford sumptuous illustrations by Raphael Soyer. The irony of it all would have made a great Yiddish joke were it not for the tragedy. A mature Yiddish literature could produce a writer of Singer's stature and, over the course of a long working life, nurture his creative growth. Literary audiences could appreciate the distinct pleasures of a writer deeply rooted in a particular culture.

The only problem was that both the culture and the language were almost gone. Gentile audiences, as well as a new generation of Yiddish-illiterate Jewish baby boomers, discovered Singer in translation. Perhaps these younger Jews who moved with ease in the English-speaking world helped him find a wider readership. But the more at home they felt in America, the less at home they felt in Yiddish.

By this time, however, they began to sense what was being lost. There was a sizable literature of Jewish twenty-somethings with minimal command of Yiddish interviewing, hanging out with, or working for the aged Singer. They saw this curmudgeon as a doting *zeyde,* grandfather; their cherished link to a lost world.

Singer was awarded the Nobel Prize for Literature in 1978. That honor gave a tremendous psychological boost to Yiddish, recognizing one of its own as a writer of the greatest distinction. By extension, the award recognized the language itself.

At the same time, one segment of the American Jewish community took a very different stance indeed. Unlike the majority of American Jews, who made their peace with the blessings of the United States, this group emphatically turned its back on secular society. In creating a world as separate as possible from the culture around them, they created a surprising by-product — the possibility of a real future for Yiddish.

After World War II, a small number of ultra-Orthodox Jews, mostly Hasidim, made their way to New York, where they joined their compatriots who had emigrated before the war. More came in the mid-1950s, when anti-Semitism drove them from Communist Hungary and Poland. They called themselves Haredim, God fearers, a term that is slightly more inclusive than Hasidim, although outsiders would be hard put to tell the two groups apart.

They maintained their devotion to their dynastic *rebes.* They continued to be known by the Yiddish names of their *rebes'* towns — Satmar, Belz, Ger — places that existed no more. The men wore the clothing of eighteenth-century Hasidim. They produced large families — six, eight, even ten children — to begin to try to make up for the millions of murdered Jews. And in another conscious effort to keep themselves apart from the American culture as well as from their assimilated cousins, they made a point of speaking Yiddish. They did it because they had always done it. They did it because the six million, the holy martyrs, had done it. They did it because it insulated them from secular society. They did it because, with all that had happened, Yiddish, that most commonplace ordinary tongue, was assuming an aura of holiness. They compared Yiddish to the *mentele,* the embroidered cover for the Torah. Because the *mentele* enfolds and protects the holy Law, it becomes holy too.

The Haredim continued to teach in Yiddish in their yeshivas. Their *rebes* continued to give their talks in Yiddish, and their followers continued to memorize them. In their schools and their homes, in their social and religious gatherings, Yiddish performed its old functions: It brought the community closer together and protected it from the outside world. No matter that the rules had changed, that their "alien" host country had provided a place where Jews could feel relatively comfortable, or that many of the outsiders were less observant Jews. Yiddish would remain their private language, their particularly hard-line Jewishly mystical way of responding to a Christian, materialist integrationist world. For the Haredim, Yiddish acted much like the men's long coats and fur hats. It provided a layer of insulation. It kept them continually aware that they were different. Outsiders saw it as a sign as strange and foreign as their *peyes* and their long, never-trimmed beards.

But no matter how much the Haredim closed themselves off, creating enclaves in Brooklyn and the Catskills, the wider world impinged. Although their schools continued to teach in Yiddish, translating the Hebrew texts sentence by sentence, as they had for centuries, these pupils were required by law to learn enough English to pass tests in language and math. So they were never entirely ignorant of the language of the land, as had often been the case in Europe. They had to interact daily with other people, including other Jews who, as the years went on, knew less and less Yiddish. Speaking the language required more and more of a conscious effort. By the 1980s even some yeshivas had caved in to the changing reality and begun to teach in English.

In the non-Haredi Yiddish world, the language was growing progressively weaker. In 1983 the *Forward,* one of the few remaining Yiddish papers, reduced its operations from a daily to a weekly. In 1990 it began publishing, in addition to its Yiddish weekly, a version that was entirely in English, with only a couple of columns dedicated to the old *mame loshn.* In time, this English paper even began to use the standarized YIVO system for transcribing Yiddish into the Roman alphabet. It was a sign of a different time.

The Yiddish readership that had once supported dozens of newspapers and had covered the spectrum from the extreme right to the extreme left, from the religious fanatics to the fanatic secularists, was dying. The few Yiddish-speaking children of Holocaust survivors were nowhere enough to repopulate its ranks. Jewish baby boomers had other causes, other ways to get ahead. They had more choices than any previous generation of Jews. The one thing they had little of was Yiddish. Apart from the occasional code word, mock accent, or two-generation-removed nostalgic or demeaning joke, Yiddish had no place in their lives at all.

As the immigrant generation died off, the tattered old books they had *shlepped* with them from the Old Country to the slums to the better class of apartment buildings to the green suburbs were increasingly left behind. Although the Sholom Aleichem and the Workmen's Circle Yiddish schools continued to function in the postwar decades, where they had an influence far beyond their numbers, they never served more than a tiny minority of Jewish families.

Still, the educators were a dedicated lot. One woman remembers a beloved Yiddish teacher, when asked to respond to a question in English, saying, *"A ki git bloyz milkh; oyb men vil fleysh muz men es derhargenen."* A cow gives only milk; if you want meat, you must slaughter it.

The cow was not slaughtered, but neither was it well fed. By the time the baby boomers had children of their own, speaking, reading, or studying Yiddish had become the province of a specialized group of enthusiasts. Although it was still common for Jews to know and use a small number of Yiddish words and phrases, the use of the language as a complete system had become rare.

The beloved volumes of Sholom Aleichem, the well-thumbed collections of Yiddish poetry created by romantic dreamers and sweatshop firebrands, the translations of Tolstoy, Shakespeare, Ibsen, and the Bible, the political harangues, the minutes of the *landsmanshaftn,* the sheet music for the vaudeville songs were shredded, incinerated, buried, or dumped. In some cases the children of the great poets could barely read their parents' words; their grandchildren didn't even know that the old-fashioned books with the strange writing contained poetry at all.

Then, in the 1980s, something strange happened. As the Yiddish proverb says, *the grandson remembers what the son wants to forget:* Americans discovered klezmer music. A new generation of Jews, raised on TV and rock 'n' roll, was ready to listen to something else, something they perhaps had not heard at all — a minor-key, high-spirited wailing that had been hovering, just beyond their perception, throughout all their lives. By this time, a whole generation had passed since the abyss of World War II. American culture could afford to become more ethnically aware, to think about turning down some of the heat of the melting pot. American Jews had become secure enough to cast a glance back to see what they had lost. Even as their parents were throwing out their grandparents' old Yiddish books and canceling their subscriptions to the last Yiddish papers, the youngsters were coming back through sound.

One New York musician, Henry Sapoznik, described his circuitous return. It was the late 1970s. He was making his third pilgrimage to study with a master of Appalachian music when the teacher remarked on the number of Jews who were playing old-time American mountain tunes. "One day he asked me in all candor: 'Hank, don't your people got none of your own music?'"

It turned out they did. Klezmer music had been around for

something like four hundred years. The words *kley zemer* are Hebrew for "instrument of song." But the term had passed into Yiddish, and was used for both the music and the musicians. Its plural was the Europeanized *klezmer* or the Hebrew *klezmorim*.

Primarily tunes that accompanied specific dances that came at set places in wedding celebrations — "Hora mit tsibeles" (Hora and Onions), "Shver un shviger" (Father-in-law and Mother-in-law) — the music that grew out of a folk tradition took full advantage of modern technique and idioms. It was accessible and exotic. It felt both near and tantalizingly far. And all of the words to all of the songs were Yiddish. Like the language itself, the genre had been overlooked as being low status. Now, as the immigrant generation grew silent and America entered a time of roots and world music and fusion, everyone wanted to play it, whether they were Jewish or not. Aspiring *klezmorim* began studying Yiddish, if only to be able to pronounce the words to the newly rediscovered songs.

By this time, in the 1980s, four decades after Max Weinreich had taught his first class in an American university, it was no longer a fluke to find Yiddish in college. Dozens of schools were offering introductory courses. One could also do a semester's worth of Yiddish readings in translation; a handful of schools even offered graduate courses. A full century after Yiddish-speaking Jews began arriving in great numbers, their descendents were extraordinarily well represented throughout the academic world. The long Jewish dedication to learning had translated easily into the secular sphere. The quotas limiting Jews had fallen, and by the 1980s quotas were aimed at inclusion, with multiculturalism the new goal. Just as African Americans studied their history and women searched out the female writers who had been forgotten or ignored, a small but growing number of Jewish students discovered the Yiddish that had been in their background all along.

Once again, the irony would have been delicious if the subject had not been such uncountable loss. The old Yiddish proverb,

Hebrew one studies; Yiddish one knows, had been turned on its head. No longer the jargon that people spoke without thinking, it was becoming a language that people studied and taught. Yiddish turned out to have a history, a grammar, a literature. Now it even had scholars.

CHAPTER 16

Russia:
The Heartthrob Yiddish Poet

"בין פֿרײַ, בין פֿרײַ, בין פֿרײַ!" האָסטו געזאָגט;
ווילד ווי דײַנע פּאָעמעס, האָסטו אויסגעשאָקלט דײַנע ווילדע האָר.

"Bin fray, bin fray, bin fray!" hostu gezogt;
vild vi dayne poemes, hostu oysgeshoklt dayne vilde hor.

"am free, am free, am free!" you said;
wild as your poems, you shook out your wild hair.

Chaim Grade,
Elegy for the Soviet Yiddish Writers

The differences between the United States and the Soviet Union after the war could not have been more striking. To understand the fate of Yiddish in the Soviet lands, we cannot do better than to look to the life of Peretz Markish, a Yiddish poet of great flights of passion and searing good looks. He had thick black hair atop a wide forehead and dark, penetrating, silent screen star eyes. He also had a wife, Esther, who wrote an autobiography/hagiography that gives us a vivid look at an extraodinary time.

We are lucky to have the devoted and tightly tuned Mme. Markish as intermediary. It can be difficult to read the Russian Yiddish poets. Florid and stentorious, they can be tough going in our more cynical age. ("I lie abandoned on the ways, the paths of dawn; / Unknowing if I am at home or in foreign parts — I run!") We can almost see the great man holding forth on the makeshift stage of a warm, wood-floored room filled with people perched on folding chairs, the air dense with cigarette smoke and yearning.

> Your heart is close. I hear its music like a well
> of my own self, but don't know how to reach its rim.
> As in a wood, I go around within you still,
> a wood where I've not ever been. . . .
>
> The day fades. Soon it will sink behind a hill.
> What if it's gone? If night falls, night with not one star?
> As in a wood, I go around within you still,
> and, like the first time, blaze a path to where you are!

When Markish was born in Polonnoye, a small town in tsarist Russia, now Ukraine, in 1895, he seemed poised for some kind of renown. His family was in many ways typical: His father studied Torah while his mother supported the family by selling herring. Little Peretz was attractive and multitalented. At ten he ran away to pursue his first career as a synagogue singer, but he was writing poems in Russian at age fifteen. He fought and was wounded in World War I. By age twenty-two he saw his poems, now in Yiddish, reach publication. Markish had the poet's omnivorous quality:

> With free outstretched arms
> The world I greedily embrace,
> And gaze in mute exultation
> Afar and aloft into the vast before me!

His wife described his working style. Here was the way he collaborated with a colleague who was translating his poems from Yiddish into Russian, which is remarkable considering that Peretz was entirely at home in Russian:

The air would be filled with shouts, in Russian and Yiddish, singing, stamping, and general clamor: Markish was working with the translator — that is, he was tearing the translation to pieces, demonstrating that words were only the receptacle for feelings and that poetry could not be translated by trying to match up words with the original. In an effort to explain the feelings expressed in his verse, Markish would often demonstrate with dramatic gestures. On one occasion, alarmed by a strange thud, I peered through the crack in the door. Markish was prone on the floor, arms spread wide, literally embracing it; the verses in question represented the author embracing the whole world, the entire universe.

While still a young, hungry poet, Markish had traveled widely — to Warsaw, Paris, London, Berlin, even Palestine. When contemporary critics dismissed him and his compatriots as nothing more than a *khalyastre,* a gang, they proudly accepted the label, publishing an anthology under that title. But in 1926, after five years of wandering, Markish returned to the Soviet Union. Many of his most talented contemporaries were making the same choice. In the new workers' paradise, the state was supporting Yiddish schools, theaters, and publishing houses. The future for a Yiddish poet obviously lay there.

Markish soon met Esther, a good-looking sixteen-year-old student with a talent for languages who came from the Jewish version of wealth. Her family warned her against the thirty-three-year-old poet who had a reputation as a womanizer, but there seems to have been no turning back. They married, had two sons, and, in the early days at least, occupied a privileged place in the Yiddish-Soviet literary world, with priority accommodations in special writers' housing as well as domestic help.

Markish worked at the state-supported Yiddish publishing house, Emes (Truth), and continued to write his romantic verse. But by the mid-1930s the purges had begun. Although the Jews' religion had already been dismantled, their attachment to Yiddish still left them open to suspicion of internationalism.

For a while, Peretz Markish retained his favored position. (To show the extent of the purges, Esther Markish's father, brother, and all five of her uncles were arrested, although none of them was a political person.) At the height of the purges, in 1939, while Esther Frumkin was toiling in a labor camp in Siberia, Markish received the Soviet government's Order of Lenin, the highest award conferred on a private citizen. His wife asks the obvious question: "But was Markish in fact happy about the award with which the Soviet regime honored him — in the wake of those terrifying years when that very same regime had put to death or interned dozens, if not hundreds, of people who were close to him? I am convinced that he was. His faith in 'our radiant future' and in Stalin personally had not been destroyed, or even shaken."

If we want to see the party line, we can read this poem by Markish's contemporary, the Yiddish poet Isaac Feffer.

> When I mention Stalin — I mean beauty,
> I mean eternal happiness,
> I mean nevermore to know,
> Nevermore to know of pain.

From this distance, it is impossible to know how much of the literary output of that era was heartfelt, how much for show. Still, given the Jews' always precarious status and the Yiddish penchant for irony, it is hard to take such a statement at face value.

It can be argued that the Yiddish poets had no alternative. They could not leave the Soviet Union. And even if they could have gotten out, they and their families had nowhere to go. They faced the same nonchoices as other European Jews as the world moved closer to war. We must remember that Soviet authorities even denied permission for Eastern European Jews fleeing from Nazi persecution to settle in underpopulated Birobidzhan.

When World War II began, Yiddish writers became even more committed to supporting the Soviet state. When the Hitler-Stalin Pact disintegrated in 1941, Russians were well aware of Nazi anti-Jewish policies, as well as the force with which they were prepared to back them up. As soon as Nazi troops invaded the Soviet Union, they began mass murders of Jews.

In the early days of the war, when Poland was divided between Germany and the Soviet Union, an additional two million Eastern European Jews came under Soviet control. Yiddish writers from what had been Russia and Ukraine met with their counterparts from the great Yiddish centers of Warsaw and Vilna. Records of these meetings are tense with restrained emotion. The Soviets, by this time accustomed to walking a narrow path, made only bland statements in favor of solidarity, but the Polish Jews who reported on these encounters were sure that their Soviet cousins envied them their rich Jewish culture.

In 1941 Stalin found a use for the former "rootless cosmopolitans." He came up with a plan that harnessed the Jews' fears for their future, putting them to use for the Soviet cause. The leading Soviet Yiddish literary figures made a radio broadcast, in Yiddish, to Jews in England and the United States, asking them to support the Soviet effort. As part of the historic transmission, Markish called on "our Jewish brethren the world over" to "join the struggle. . . . We are one people, and now we are become one army."

These Soviet writers became the nucleus of the Jewish Antifascist Committee, which worked throughout the war. They published a Yiddish newspaper that was distributed internationally. In 1943 they organized an extraordinary fund-raising tour to England, Canada, Mexico, and the United States. A group that included Shloyme Mikhoels, the adored actor and director of the Moscow Yiddish State Theater, traveled to New York, where they met everyone from Albert Einstein to Charlie Chaplin. They visited Sholom Aleichem's grave in Brooklyn and held a rally at the Polo Grounds that attracted some fifty thousand people. No less than seven American Jews wrote Yiddish poems in honor of the event.

Meanwhile, Soviet losses were staggering. Markish spent the war heading a shortwave Yiddish broadcast service directed at American Jews. Now that the international character of Yiddish was useful, the status of the language again improved. By this time, though, Markish seems to have understood that Jews were tolerated in the Soviet Union only when it suited the needs of the state. The poet Abraham Sutzkever met him in Moscow at the end of World War II. He gave the sense of a man under great pressure. In a poem that commemorated their good-bye, Sutzkever wrote, "Moscow had too long rained red stars / On us out of her skies."

In the Cold War era, as open hostilities between the United States and the Soviet Union became a real possibility, Stalin, always obsessed with the Jews, began to fret anew about their international allegiances. Once again Yiddish became suspect. Jewish institutions were shut down, and Jews learned to keep quiet about their background.

The establishment of the state of Israel in 1948 complicated the loyalty issue even more. Jews like Markish who had actively worked for the Communist dream, as well as Jews who had simply put up with the Soviet system, were jolted by the existence of a real Jewish state. Now they had a focus for their longing and their discontent.

The Israelis made a brilliant choice by sending, as their first ambassador to the Soviet Union, the Russian-born Golda Meir. When she arrived in Moscow, she made a point of attending services at the one remaining synagogue. Afterward, walking home, she wrote, "I hadn't gone very far when an elderly man brushed up against me in a way that I knew at once was not accidental. 'Don't say anything,' he whispered to me in Yiddish. 'I'll walk on, and you follow me.' When we were near the hotel, he suddenly stopped, turned around to face me, and standing there on that windy Moscow street, he recited the thanksgiving prayer, *Shehehiyanu.*"

The prayer, in Hebrew, is recited when one wants to thank God for bringing the speaker to an auspicious occasion. The contact had been made in Yiddish. Together, the two languages still formed the Jewish bond.

Later, Meir attended Rosh Hashonah services. Despite warnings that circulated among Moscow Jews about the dangers of being seen in a Jewish context in public, fifty thousand people jammed the streets. Meir wrote:

> I felt as though I had been caught up in a torrent of love so strong that it had literally taken my breath away and slowed down my heart. I was on the verge of fainting, I think. . . .
>
> Out of that ocean of people, I can still see two figures clearly: a little man who kept popping up in front of me and saying, *"Goldele, lebn zolst du. Shana Tova!"* (Goldele, a long life to you and a Happy New Year), and a woman who just kept repeating, *"Goldele! Goldele!"* and smiling and blowing kisses at me.

Stuck in a cab unable to make any headway against the crowd, Meir recalled,

> I wanted to say something, anything, to those people, to let them know that I begged their forgiveness for not having wanted to come to Moscow and for not having known the strength of their ties to us. . . . But I couldn't find the words. All I could say, clumsily, and in a voice that didn't even sound like my own, was one sentence in Yiddish. I stuck my head out of the window of the cab and said, *"A dank eich vos irh seit geblieben Yidden"* (Thank you for having remained Jews), and I heard that miserable, inadequate sentence being passed on through the enormous crowd as though it were some wonderful prophetic saying.

As the Cold War deepened, the Jews' international connections that Stalin had exploited shamelessly during the war now spelled their doom. The purges began again, and Jews were targeted first. There were no longer any Jewish religious officials to be hunted down, but Jewish cultural leaders were easy to find. They were the heads of all the Yiddish institutions that the state had supported off and on over the past three decades. Markish and his comrades must have breathed an air fetid with fear.

The Yiddish broadcasting service was the first organization to be closed. Then Mikhoels began receiving death threats. He was so worried about going out alone that when he had to walk his dog at night, he would call Markish to go with him. Sadly, his fears were justified. In January 1948 he was found dead on the street. We now know what was always suspected — that he was killed on the personal orders of Stalin. The next year, his theater was shut down. The Jewish Antifascist Committee was halted as well.

At the end of 1948, the Emes publishing house was closed. Here is Esther Markish's description of the scene:

> The staff had come to work as usual in the little old house on Staropansky Lane. The new linotype machines, which Markish had helped to buy, were humming away. The chief editor Moisei Belenky was in conference with Strongin, the director, when, without a word of warning — as in a movie about Nazi Germany — trucks filled with State Security agents pulled up in front of the house. Soldiers in civilian clothes burst into the printing plant and disconnected the machines. Everything came to a standstill; all was silence.
>
> "Your publishing house is closed down," one of the pogromists bellowed.
>
> They then proceeded to the second floor, sent the editorial staff packing, and gave orders to Strongin and Belenky to prepare an "act of closure."

Markish went home and wrote this grim poem:

> How much time is left
> Until the bitter end,
> How much time is left for grieving!
>
> Fill your glass with wine!
> Let's lift our faces to the stars.
> And may our destiny be done!

It was 1949 when Markish, along with hundreds of other leading Yiddish writers, critics, and scholars, was arrested. The Yiddish literary world was padlocked shut. For six years, Markish's family had no idea if he was alive or dead. Esther writes:

> Shortly after Markish's arrest, the Jewish Section of the Writers' Union was liquidated. A Jew, Alexander Bezymensky, the "komsomol poet," was charged with the formalities. He summoned the Jewish writers who were still at liberty and informed them that enemies of the people and traitors to the motherland had been "unearthed" in the Jewish Section and that it had been decided to close it down!
>
> The spectacle of the extermination of Jewish literature was to be reenacted a few days later in a more solemn setting: at a general meeting of the Moscow Section of the Writers' Union. On this occasion, the inglorious role of hatchet man was given to the Jewish poet A. Kushnirov, who had been a front-line officer and had lost his son during the war.

Esther describes how Kushnirov was supposed to get up in front of his colleagues to announce the end of the Jewish section, which had been the epicenter of Jewish literary and political power. Its closing meant the end of the dream of a home for Yiddish writers in the Soviet Union. "Kushnirov, who knew only too well what was expected of him, was literally dragged onto the podium. Before he could utter a word, however, he burst into tears and was led away."

For a time Esther went to the Lefortovo Prison office faithfully every week and brought the small amount of money she was allowed to pay, ostensibly for better food for her husband. But soon these visits ceased because she, along with her sons and a nephew who happened to be living with them, were sent into "internal exile," sentenced to ten years in a remote region of Kazakhstan, with all their property confiscated. The charge was simply their relation to Markish, "a traitor to the motherland." The police soon came to arrest them and seal off their apartment. As the authorities were sticking the tape to the front door, the boys' Yiddish-named cat, Shifra, darted back in. Esther and the boys pleaded to open the door and let the cat out, but the police would not listen. The cat was entombed in the apartment.

Esther and the boys spent two years in an isolated provincial town. Esther sold her knitting. Her mother sent them packages of food. Eventually they were permitted to return to Moscow, where they were allowed to move back into two of the rooms of their old apartment. All this time, the leading Yiddish writers, editors, and scholars were in government hands, their whereabouts and fates unknown.

We now know that on August 12, 1952, Peretz Markish, along with a dozen other Yiddish literary and cultural figures, was executed in what has come to be called the Night of the Murdered Yiddish Poets. Among the other victims were Dovid Bergelson, Itsik Feffer, Dovid Hofstein, and Leyb Kvitko, the leading Yiddish poets. Also killed on that night were the cultural leaders S. A. Lozovskii, B. A. Shimeliovich, L. Talmi, E. I. Teumin, I. S. Vatenberg, Ch. Vatenber-Ostrovskaia, I. Yuzefovich, and Binyamin Zuskin. Shmuel Persov was arrested with this group and died in prison.

Stalin had evidently been hoping for a show trial, but the defendants, who had confessed to "bourgeois nationalism" under torture, retracted their confessions. Although the true number will probably never be known, a good estimate is that four hundred Yiddish writers, editors, and cultural leaders were killed. The Yiddish infrastructure and the whole range of Yiddish institutions were dismantled as well. The atmosphere of terror was so pervasive that Jews routinely burned their beloved Yiddish books in their ovens. It was dangerous even to own something in that hunted language.

Yiddish literature in the Soviet Union was silenced. There were no more Yiddish schools, theaters, publications, or broadcasts, with the exception of the one tiny newspaper in Birobidzhan. Over the entire Soviet Union, which had been home to five million Yiddish speakers half a century before, there was only one small Yiddish outlet. As the Soviet noose tightened, the Yiddish air supply was choked off. The only place people felt safe speaking Yiddish was among trusted family and friends. Yiddish speakers were well aware of the riches they had lost. This Yiddish saying remained popular in Soviet years: *A word is like a bird. Spoken or written, it can fly away and never be recaptured.*

In the decades to come, some older Jews continued to speak Yiddish among themselves. A few younger ones took it up privately, an act of rebellion. But there was no aboveground outlet. The simple fact of the existence of the international non-Soviet language could prove incriminating. For anyone who had a hope of making a life for himself, the old *mame loshn* was something to be forgotten, or at least hidden away.

With Stalin's death in 1953, the icy grip loosened a bit. Eventually, Markish was "rehabilitated," his death blamed on "enemies of the people." In one grisly housecleaning incident, years after his death, the police phoned his widow and told her to come and collect his gold teeth.

More silent years passed. Even though there were still no publishers who would print Markish's poems, no schools that would teach them, no journals that would comment on them, the family counted it as a major achievement when in 1965 they were able to hold an "evening" at the Central House of Writers in Moscow to commemorate what would have been Markish's seventieth birthday.

As Esther wrote, "What distingushed that evening was not the fact that . . . the house was packed full, nor that hundreds of people were left standing outside the doors of the Writers' Club surrounded by a cordon of police. No, the extraordinary thing about the evening was that every speech reverberated with the cry, 'They murdered him! They murdered him!' Five or ten years earlier, no one would have dared to say that in public."

At the "evening," their son, Simon, made a speech worthy of his father: "Memory is both our torment and our treasure. It is in the nature of man to want to forget — to hide from his memories like a coward, to put on blinders, to block his ears, to pretend to the outside world and to himself that the past did not exist. But it is still more terrible and tormenting when memories recede and grow dim. . . . You have to summon all your strength, all your courage, to resuscitate the past, no matter what the cost!" He invoked his father, "the memory of his beauty, his talent, his stormy and colorful life, his visions and delusions, and his tragic end."

It took almost another decade of ceaseless badgering and privation, but Markish's widow, along with her sons and their wives, were eventually able to leave the Soviet Union for Israel. Their Yiddish heritage, like Shifra, their cat, had been sealed off long before.

CHAPTER 17

Israel: A New Nation, a New Tongue

א שפּראַך איז אַ דיאַלעקט וואָס האָט אַן אַרמיי אַן אַרמיי און אַ פלאָט.

A sprakh iz a dialekt vos hot an armey un a flot.

A language is a dialect that has an army and a navy.

Joshua Fishman

The building of the state of Israel is the great Jewish postwar story. For lovers of Yiddish, however, an undercurrent of loss runs underneath the heartfelt gain. When World War II ended, two-thirds of the European Jews who remained alive made their way to the Holy Land. On arrival, even the nonreligious among them kissed the ground or at least broke into song. The poet Itzak Manger pointed toward the intensity of their feelings when he wrote, "How can I kiss your dust? I am your dust."

Still, their new surroundings were not all milk and honey. Some of the "surviving remnant" were overwhelmed by the guilt of having simply endured. Others were stung by what they felt was a less-than-perfect welcome. Jews already living in Eretz Israel were not above stereotyping the new arrivals as passive ghetto dwellers. Their Yiddish speech only reinforced the cliché.

Luckily, these considerations took a backseat as the new arrivals passed from the most tragic episode of modern Jewish history to its most exhilarating — the creation of a Jewish state. Most of the new settlers were youthful — teenage orphans and young adults. They were the ones who had made it through the hiding, fighting, starvation, diseases, and death camps. With the older generation as well as the old institutions gone, the young had that much more impetus to put the past behind them. If *iberlebung* — survival, experience — had taught them anything, it was that much of their personal and collective agony had stemmed from their lack of a country, the Yiddishland that had never come to be. Israel was their only hope.

Even though Yiddish remained a sentimental link to childhood, family, and home, it was also seen as dead weight; the language of persecution and fear. It was not unheard of for Yiddish-speaking survivors to turn on the language. Some vowed not to speak it again. Many felt it was better to just let the old *mame loshn* die along with the people and places that were already gone. The death of a language seemed a small price to pay for a real chance at life.

The *olim,* the new immigrants, learned *ivrit,* the Hebrew name for modern Hebrew. They were proud of the language, which was so much a part of the Israeli miracle. When Israel was declared a state in 1948, Hebrew became officially what it had been for half a century — the core of the Zionist dream, a central element of nation building. The rebirth of the language was proudly included in the Declaration of Independence as one of the most important achievements of the new state.

Still, the fallout of the latest miracle continued to be a sustained and public debasement of Yiddish. As the poet Yosef Papiernikov wrote in the 1950s, "For more than 30 years, I've lived in poverty, loneliness, and love of the land, and almost alone I wrote songs to Israel in Yiddish. . . . As one impoverished at a wealthy man's celebration, I am in my own land, where after decades I've not yet become a part of it. I remain an outsider with my abashed poem: my Yiddish song of love, praise, and thanks."

The country's first premier, native Yiddish speaker David Ben-

Gurion, set the tone of public humiliation. Listening to a Holocaust survivor's tale, he remarked on how touching it had been, even though it had been recounted in what he called "that unfortunate tongue." On the street, it remained common for strangers to berate people conversing in Yiddish.

Because the new Israeli state was socialist, government financing of major institutions had a huge effect on culture. For example, it controlled the distribution of newsprint, a valuable commodity in a news-hungry society. Although sufficient paper was consistently found for Hebrew dailies, as well as for dailies in other, much less populous immigrant languages, somehow there was not enough paper when the dailies were printed in Yiddish. (Yiddish newspaper publishers got around this hurdle by putting out two different papers — one on Mondays, Wednesdays, and Fridays, a different one on Tuesdays, Thursdays, and Sundays.) For decades, the only radio stations were government controlled. Only half an hour each day was allotted to Yiddish programming even though, as late as 1972, a quarter of all Israeli radio listeners reported that they tuned in to a Yiddish program at least once a week. And because television was likewise state funded, for decades there was no Yiddish at all to be had on TV.

All through this same period, the 1950s, 1960s, and 1970s, Israeli Yiddish radio broadcasts were beamed at the Soviet Union. The acerbic joke circulated that more Yiddish could be heard in Moscow than in Tel Aviv. Although imports of Hebrew books were not taxed, books in Yiddish were. In the new Jewish homeland, where, according to the Law of the Return, anyone with a Jewish mother was welcome, the quintessential Jewish mother's tongue was not welcome at all.

There were holdouts — immigrants who were too old, too tired, too beaten down by the horrors they had suffered, to master the harsh new sounds or remember the strange words. Especially if they lived in communities with other Yiddish speakers, they could, and did, live out their lives in Yiddish. One joke has kibbutz children planning out their "let's play grown-ups" game. They talk about being mommies and daddies, working in the children's house, the fields, and the communal kitchen. "And then we'll get old," one tells another, "and we'll speak Yiddish."

For young people in a young country, Hebrew was not only a point of pride but also an intimate part of their beloved land. Having a single, unifying language was also a practical necessity. Threatened by enemies on all sides, few Israelis had the luxury of fighting for a competing tongue. As Jews arrived from North Africa, from the Middle East, from Ladino-speaking regions, and later from Russia, the besieged country had to leapfrog past two thousand years of exile. These new Israelis had to be quickly knit into one people who could, at minimum, communicate with one another. Languages tend to evolve over hundreds of years, out of the limelight; this nation under siege had neither privacy nor time.

The government set up *ulpans,* total-immersion language communities. In the Israeli army, where conscription was universal for both women and men, Hebrew was taught as part of basic training. In Israeli schools, which had long been the centers of language building, the goal was to have children speaking Hebrew not just in class but on the playgrounds. A standard joke describes two men arguing about the status of Yiddish and Hebrew. To see how far the new language and the new national ethos have come, one of them punches a young boy on the cheek to see if he will cry out in Yiddish and run for his mother, or if he will curse his attacker in Hebrew and fight back.

But even Yiddish speakers who learned Hebrew, especially if they arrived as adults, retained the inflections and accents of their youth. European-born women would greet each other with a singsong "Shalom-shalom" that set them apart from their native Hebrew-speaking children. The latter spoke a Hebrew that sounded strong and self-assured, even if it could veer off toward the aggressive and harsh. Not for them the endless affectionate diminutives of Yiddish, the self-mocking humor, the proverbs that assumed the speaker's modest place in the world. Their greeting was a businesslike, punched-up "Shalom!"

As might be expected in a nation of immigrants, linguistic awareness was high, and jokes often used the unexpected juxtaposition of a Yiddish word or phrase as the punch line. Most often, the Yiddish speaker was the object of automatic derision — the beautiful young girl seen from a distance whose status is downgraded when lowly Yiddish comes out of her mouth. A perhaps apocryphal tale, recounted in an Israeli newspaper in 1956, shows that, even three-quarters of a century after Ben Yehuda's arrival, the "new" Hebrew language was still fighting the old Yiddish shibboleth. The story was told that, in the old days of the pioneers, a man named Shtibel, who was giving soldiers extracurricular boxing lessons, was accused of doing so in Yiddish. He defended the charge by insisting that Hebrew, with only four available words for "blow," "slap," "knock," and "punch," could not convey enough meaning. He then described the Yiddish alternatives:

> A dry blow to the chin that makes your head sing is *zheng*. A regular slap, not too hard: *patch*. But stinging slaps that leave a red mark on the cheek: *flask*. A very quick blow with an open hand that confuses you so you don't know what happened: *vish*. A strong right that at least breaks one rib: *knok*. A blow under the eye that leaves a shiner for at least two months: *shnit*. A blow with the back of the hand that splits your lower lip and occasionally knocks out a tooth: *ris*. A healthy header that knocks the other guy's head into the wall: *zets*. A slow but strong slap in the ear: *flik*. A smeared slap, it is not as strong as it is insulting, that starts at the forehead and pulls the hair over the entire face: *shmir*.

His superior was convinced. The Yiddish boxing continued.

But in the real world, it was Hebrew that won. In the first two decades of the existence of the state of Israel, some ten thousand new vocabulary words were introduced. An entire new literature bloomed. There was no longer a question of "if" or "to what extent." Modern Hebrew had become a language like any other, with product labels, slang, movies and TV, a system of education ranging from preschool to postgraduate.

At the same time, an entirely opposite trend took hold. (*He sits above and stirs the pot below,* meaning that God has nothing better to do than to produce complications in the lives of lowly humans.) Small colonies of ultra-Orthodox, mostly in Jerusalem, continued to live apart from the hurly-burly of modern Israel. And they continued to speak Yiddish, in firm contradiction to all of the trends and policies around them. Descendants of the earlier colonies of pious Jews whose numbers had been increased by the arrival of Hasidic Holocaust survivors, these people refused to speak modern Hebrew, not wanting to profane the sacred language. Some would not even recognize the existence of the secular Israeli state. They were waiting for the coming of the Messiah, and until that time they would close their walls around them, speak Yiddish, and ignore politics whenever they could. When the state was declared, the number of these pious scholars was minuscule, and so they were left to their lives of study, exempt from the draft, the living embodiment of the old tradition. Despite a high birthrate, by 1972, fourteen years after statehood, the children in Yiddish-speaking Haredi schools still accounted for less than 5 percent of school-age youngsters.

To most Israelis, these Yiddish-speaking Haredim, God fearers, seemed as archaic and out of place as the clothing style they shared with their compatriots in the United States and Europe. In Israel, however, the contrast was even greater. The men's long black coats, heavy stockings, and high fur hats were absurdly, touchingly, out of place in the harsh Middle Eastern sun.

The Haredim retained their Yiddish names, yet another trait that set them apart from the less religious new immigrants. It was common to celebrate one's arrival in Israel by adopting a new Hebrew name, which was often a translation of one's Yiddish moniker. The Yiddish man's name Hirsh, because it means "deer," became the Hebrew word for "deer," Tzvi. A family name of Jacobsen would be translated as Ben Jakov, son of Jacob. If one was tapped for a high government post, this name change became mandatory. David Gruen became David Ben-Gurion. Yitzhak Yserntisky turned into Yitzhak Shamir. Goldie Meyerson was renamed, in middle age, Golda Meir. For her, the switch to Hebrew was no easy matter. She had been born in tsarist Russia, had immigrated to the United States as a child, and had vastly enjoyed her first job, teaching Yiddish. "Yiddish, it seemed to me, was one of the strongest links that existed between the Jews, and I loved teaching it. It wasn't what the Milwaukee Normal School was preparing me for, but I found it exceedingly satisfying to be able to introduce some of the Jewish children of the city to the great Yiddish writers I so admired. English was certainly a fine language, but Yiddish was the language of the Jewish street, the natural, warm, intimate language that united a scattered nation." When she moved to Palestine she learned Hebrew, although, she admitted, she never became as proficient in it as she was in Yiddish, her first language and love. So, while many government officials eagerly took on Hebrew names, Meir resisted. When, as foreign minister, she was ordered to "go Hebrew," she refused to change Goldie to the officially recognized Zehavah. She only went as far as becoming Golda Meir.

Somewhere in the middle of all this, a Yiddish literary circle managed to hold on. Poets, journalists, novelists, and critics who ended up in Israel after the war were not always eager, willing, or even able to take on a new language. And because of the nature of their recent lives and their unfathomable loss, it was often difficult for them to focus on their new surroundings. Although some chronicled life in the new state, Yiddish writers more typically took as their subject remembrance, an attempt to make sense of their Yiddish-speaking past. They turned out novels and memoirs of lives that had been lived in Yiddish, a body of work that spanned the spectrum of high art and low schlock. For the best of them, writing came from a source so deep that it had to be expressed in their primary tongue. As Abraham Sutzkever, the partisan-poet who had rescued Yiddish books from destruction in Vilna, wrote: "I didn't just sing. It was a must / To howl the sewer out of me!"

For almost half a century Sutzkever published his Yiddish literary magazine, *Di goldene keyt* (The Golden Chain). Here is his poem called "Yiddish":

> Shall I start from the beginning?
> Shall I, a brother,
> Like Abraham
> Smash all the idols?
> Shall I let myself be translated alive?
> Shall I plant my tongue
> And wait
> Till it transforms
> Into our forefathers'
> Raisins and almonds?
> What kind of joke
> Preaches
> My poetry brother with whiskers,
> That soon, my mother tongue will set forever?
> A hundred years from now, we still may sit here
> On the Jordan, and carry on this argument.
> For a question
> Gnaws and paws at me:
> If he knows exactly in what regions
> Levi Yitzhok's prayer,
> Yehoash's poem,
> Kulbak's song,
> Are straying
> To their sunset —
> Could he please show me

Where the language will go down?
Maybe at the Wailing Wall?
If so, I shall come there, come,
Open my mouth,
And like a lion
Garbed in fiery scarlet,
I shall swallow the language as it sets.
And wake all the generations with my roar!

But for all the force of their writing, Israeli Yiddish writers had precious little impact on their own country. Although after the war visting Yiddish literary lights no longer had to contend with stone-throwing bullies, by and large the public scorn for Yiddish continued. By the 1970s a few government shekls had been pried loose for literary prizes, but Yiddish newspapers and radio broadcasts were seen as a sop to old folks who somehow couldn't or wouldn't make the linguistic grade. In studies conducted between 1916 and 1972, of eight languages included, Yiddish was the only one whose use continued to decline.

Still, despite active discouragement by the Israeli government, Israelis continued to speak Yiddish informally. It was said that in Israel one spoke Yiddish, read English, and wrote Hebrew. And even in spite of the language police, some Yiddish did manage to make its way into Hebrew. One of the more picturesque terms is *vus-vus*. In Yiddish, *vus* simply means "what." Sephardic and Oriental Jews could thus poke fun at their Ashkenazi brethren by calling them *vus-vus*es, because the former Yiddish speakers were always saying, in effect, "What's that? What's that?" The term spread, and a secular Israeli will now call a Haredi a *vus-vus*.

In time, with Hebrew firmly established and Yiddish no longer a threat, the Israeli government could afford to loosen its policy of neglect and disdain. In 1976 it established the World Council for Yiddish and Jewish Culture under the auspices of the Department of Education. Its first conference was run by the former Yiddish teacher Golda Meir. In 1984 the Israeli government awarded its highest honor, the Israel Prize, to Abraham Sutzkever for his work on *Di goldene keyt*. But it was a bittersweet gesture. The chain traveled backward, but its path to the future was anything but strong. The writers, editors, and critics were all growing older and more frail. No one was coming to take their place.

As in the United States, Yiddish established a beachhead in academia. Hebrew University, which in the 1930s had refused the offer of a fully funded chair in Yiddish, finally came around and began teaching Yiddish in 1952. (It offered the chair to Max Weinreich, but he was, by that time, ensconced in New York.)

In terms of speakers and influence, the numbers were small and growing smaller. The newest immigrants, from Soviet and post-Soviet lands, were more likely to speak Russian than Yiddish. Even the noise of the old language battles had weakened. With the exception of the ultra-Orthodox, the sound of Yiddish in Israel was sinking to a whisper. It had little strength, like an old man struggling for a last breath.

PART 5

Present and Future

CHAPTER 18

Europe and Israel: Bulletins from Now

אין די אידישע היסטאַריע, איז די וועג צווישן קראנק זיין און שטארבן,
זעהר לאנג.

In die yidishe historye, iz di veg tzvishen krank zein
un shtarben zehr lang.

In Jewish history, the road between being sick and dying
is a very long one.

Isaac Bashevis Singer

At the beginning of a new millennium — the second for Yiddish — we are looking at both death and change. The vast majority of the world's three million Yiddish speakers are old. Within a few decades, most of them will be gone. In the four corners of the old Yiddish world — Russia, Eastern Europe, Israel, and the United States — radically different paths have led to an outcome that sounds much the same: an eerie stillness in which few words of *mame loshn* are heard.

The United Nations counts Yiddish among its endangered languages, which means that it might be among the half of the world's six thousand tongues that UNESCO says will die over the course of the next century. (In all fairness, most of those threatened languages were never spoken by more than small local populations. Few have the treasures of literature, culture, and advocacy that Yiddish enjoys. Yet that very richness makes the threat to Yiddish all the more poignant.) Could Yiddish die? It is possible. Having learned something of its history and picked up a bit of its take on life, we must be realistic. *All the brides are beautiful, all the dead are pious.* Languages grow and thrive because people need them. A language maintained artificially is nothing but words.

Yet death can also mean transformation. As with a person, after the tears, and after the dreams in which the beloved appears for a moment, strangely alive, survivors can take hold of the life that has passed. They can integrate it in time, possess it as something whole. The loved one, though dead, lives on in the heart.

That said, before we put in our order for a gravestone for Yiddish, we should scan some news reports on the state of the language today.

In Europe, half a century after the end of World War II, there are few Yiddish speakers. Even the number of European Jews — roughly one million in Western Europe and one million in the former Soviet Union — is declining so steadily that there is some concern over its dipping below critical mass. Low birthrate, the move to Israel, high rates of intermarriage and assimilation — the word for "assimilated" in Yiddish is *fargoyisht* — are reasons for the plunge. And if there are few Jews, there is certainly little Yiddish — not much speech or even cultural memory. The literature has not been translated, the plays are not being performed. Very little of the folk or popular art has been saved.

The great exception is klezmer music, which has attracted a following far beyond Jews. In a strange twist (*Vu den?* What else?), one of the most popular venues for the genre is Germany. Perhaps it is a safe way for a new generation of Germans to get to know some small thing about Jews. Perhaps, because klezmer's tempo and outlook tend toward the giddily upbeat, with even its slower tunes soulful, it is more appealing than guilt-inducing Holocaust tales.

A couple of German universities now offer courses and degrees in Yiddish, which should not be surprising, considering the languages' linked histories. (Polish universities also offer a few Yiddish courses. These, like the German ones, are taught by non-Jews.) A German publishing house, in cooperation with YIVO, is finally bringing out the eleven-volume *Language and Culture Atlas of Ashkenazic Jewry,* the project of decades-long scholarship begun by Uriel Weinreich that provides a map of a vanished world. It is hard to know whether to call this joint venture heroic, tragic, or just time marching on.

If you are looking for a Jewish-run academic Yiddish setting in Europe, you must go to Oxford. (The world's oldest English-speaking university taught Hebrew to Christians for five hundred years; Jews were not admitted until the nineteenth century.) Nowadays the thirty-year-old Oxford University Centre for Hebrew and Judaic Studies grants degrees in Yiddish studies, sponsors courses and conferences, and publishes academic works in English and Yiddish.

The search for real, living Yiddish in Europe, however, leads to the Haredi neighborhoods of London, Paris, or Antwerp. Although this population, combined, numbers less than a hundred thousand thanks to a high birthrate and a high rate of retention, it is the one area of European Jewry that is growing. It is possible that its numbers will double every fifteen to twenty years.

Of the three communities, Antwerp's is the strongest. Because of courageous treatment by the Belgian government and people during World War II, Jews there did not meet quite as disastrous a fate. (Their population went from ninety thousand in 1935 to twenty thousand a decade later. The neighboring Netherlands ended the war with 30,000 Jews, but it had begun with 140,000.) Since then, the country's multilingual school system has allowed Yiddish to thrive. Today it is possible to live in Antwerp and speak only Yiddish. True, we are talking about small numbers: only five thousand students attend Yiddish-language schools. But Jews are *a kleyn folk ober a shtark,* a small people but a strong one. Stranger things have happened. These numbers do continue to grow.

In the traditional Yiddish centers of Eastern Europe, however, growth is nowhere to be seen. Although it is difficult to get an accurate accounting, estimates place the number of Jews in Poland between five thousand and twenty-five thousand. The range is large because many Poles of Jewish or mixed ancestry suppressed their Jewishness during the Communist era and are only now going public with their background. But background is, in most cases, all that remains. Few of these newly aware or newly public Jews have much sense of their heritage.

With the end of Communism, American money began to underwrite community-building programs for Polish Jews. These include a few sporadic courses in Yiddish for interested nonacademics, but the cultural atmosphere in Poland is still so fractured that even supporters of this effort expect little in the way of results.

In the wider Polish society, it is still easy to find linguistic reminders, none of them flattering, of the centuries when Jews and Poles lived side by side. A person who is decked out ostentatiously is described as being dressed for a Jewish wedding. A tumultuous din is noisy as a *cheder*. A coward is said to be as brave as a Jew against dogs; a debtor is someone who kisses the Jew's beard.

Most of what passes for Jewish life in Poland these days is the sale of "rabbis" — cheap tourist souvenirs of vaguely Hasidic-looking bearded figures wearing *kapotes,* long coats, and *shtraymls,* large fur-trimmed hats. These are sold to tourists visiting the concentration camps or the sites of the ghettos or shtetls.

Vilna, now known as Vilnius, the capital of Lithuania, continues to play a role in the Jewish tale. In 1988, when Dr. Antanas Ulpis, the director of the Lithuanian National Book Chamber, announced his retirement, the world learned that forty years earlier, he had disobeyed a Soviet order to destroy the Jewish books that had been dumped in his basement. Thousands of volumes, the remains of the great Strashun Library and the YIVO collection, as well as seventy-five thousand periodicals, had sat out the Soviet years on his cellar floor.

The question of what to do with these mildewed survivors has proven deeply unsettling. The Lithuanian government has not wanted to relinquish these treasures. The remaining Jewish population of Vilna, although aging and dwindling, has felt strongly that the heritage of their city should remain. Israeli and American Jews have argued that they can better care for the books and can share them with the Jews who would actually use them.

Recent years have seen some movement toward compromise. Parts of the Vilna collection have been microfilmed, courtesy of war reparations money from Germany. Some material has made its way to YIVO in New York, where it has joined other Vilna books that had been smuggled out both during and after the war.

And finally, Vilna has seen something new. For the past few years a summer program in Yiddish has attracted scholars and an assortment of visitors. For a brief time in the warm weather, Yiddish words can be heard. Yiddish books are read, Yiddish songs are sung. Beyond that, things are fairly quiet. A recent Jewish guidebook advises that, although the names of certain Vilna streets still evoke echoes of the old Jewish quarter, visitors will get more of a sense of Jewish life by visiting the forest in nearby Ponar, site of the massacre of seventy thousand Jews.

In the Soviet Union, Yiddish saw its share of tragedy as well. Less than a year after Stalin ordered the executions on the Night of the Murdered Yiddish Poets in 1952, he himself died. Recently uncovered evidence shows that, had he lived, he might have begun his plan to move all the Jews out of the western Soviet Union into the wastelands of Sibera and the Jewish Autonomous Region of Birobidzhan.

But anti-Yiddishism survived even Stalin. For the decades of the 1960s, 1970s, and 1980s, the only Yiddish publications in the entire Soviet Union were the newspaper the *Birobidzhaner shtern* and one journal, *Sovietish heymland* (Soviet Homeland), said to have been published in response to Western pressure. Occasionally, the state publishing house reprinted a slim volume of stories by Sholom Aleichem, but it included only those tales that poked fun at shtetl life.

Real change came only when the Soviet Union collapsed. In 1989, in the transitional Gorbachev era, the poet Peretz Markish and the other prominent victims of the Stalinist culture wars finally had their names cleared. In the same year a Jewish Cultural Center opened in Moscow, named after the murdered actor and director Mikhoels. At the high-profile opening ceremonies (foreign guest speakers, international coverage), the programs were printed in Russian, Hebrew, and English. In honoring the central figure of Soviet Yiddish theater, its language was not even heard.

Also in 1989, the last Soviet census counted a million and a half Jews, a population more accurately described as potential Jews. For most of the two-generation-long Soviet era it was difficult, if not impossible, for Jews to learn much about who they were. At the same time, their "nationality" had to be stamped on their passports, serving as a bar to good jobs and good schools. Under those circumstances, many who were able to, decided to hide or deny their Jewish background.

With the end of Communism, Jews focused first on the newly opened borders. Cynics might have seen this relaxed emigration policy as just the latest version of the Russian attempt to solve its Jewish Problem, but Jews were more interested in action than analysis. In the 1990s close to a million Jews left the former Soviet Union. Of those, eight hundred thousand moved to Israel. The remainder went primarily to the United States and, surprisingly, to Germany, which, in a move toward setting a new course, offered them citizenship as well as targeted financial and social help.

Before he left the former Soviet Union for Israel in 1993, Velvl Tshernin wrote a Yiddish poem, "The Attraction of Memories." This excerpt shows the deeply ambivalent nature of the centuries-long sojourn of the Jews in Russia.

> The stolen Russian spring
> With buds on strange birch trees

With drunken winds and remnants
Of leftover snow, again reminded
Me that, to sum it up, I am a Jew
That must be longing to return home.

Still, Jewish life did improve for those who stayed behind in what were now Russia, Ukraine, and Belarus. People could actually learn something of their Jewish heritage. And it turned out that a large part of that was Yiddish. Some of the old people remembered it; some, in spite of everything, had continued to speak it privately. There was even a small circle of Jews born after World War II who treasured the subversive position of the language and its culture, creating poems they shared among themselves.

In the first post-Soviet decade, however, progress in reclaiming Yiddish was slow — a concert by a visiting klezmer group, an occasional Yiddish class sponsored by an American organization. One Jewish day school in St. Petersburg built Yiddish into its curriculum for young children. A handful of universities in the former Soviet Union began to offer courses in Yiddish. But, with almost six thousand years of Jewish history to explore and a country to rebuild, Russian Jews have had a lot of cultural catching up to do.

Here is how the American scholar David Roskies described a class for senior citizens he held in Yiddish in Kiev in 1989 (keep in mind that the Passover seder often concludes with a song about Elijah the Prophet, whose appearance on earth announces the coming of the Messiah):

> I am teaching a group of native-born, Yiddish-educated Soviet pensioners, reading Peretz's neo-folktale, "The Conjurer," in the Yiddish original, a story about a magician who comes to town on the eve of Passover. When his true identity is revealed and a seder is literally conjured up at story's end, the students look to me with blank stares. No one has ever heard of *Eliyohu hanovi* (Elijah the Prophet), and only one elderly

woman can explain to her classmates that *novi* has something
to do with the *profet* of the Old Testament.

The Jews' legacy of Soviet rule has been ignorance, embarrassment, and confusion, all mixed with a hunger to reach beyond that
and learn more.

Nikolai Borodulin, born in the Soviet Union in 1961, told how,
in 1989, when a non-Jewish friend wished him a good Rosh
Hashonah, he had no idea what his friend was talking about. Not
only did he not recognize the name of the Jewish New Year, but he
did not know any Yiddish. Just as in many American families, his
parents and grandparents had spoken the language when they did
not want him to understand them.

In post-Soviet times, Jews hoping to understand their origins
have had to learn and reinvent a great deal. Many have approached
this task with the intensity and dedication that has always charac-
terized this group. In the beginning of the twenty-first century, we
can say that there *has* been a real Jewish revival. But catching up on
religion, history, and the skills needed for emigrating have come
first. Most Russians who want to learn a Jewish language are studying Hebrew. The few young Yiddish literati who wrote during
Soviet days have settled in Tel Aviv or New York. (One, Boris
Sandler, now edits the Yiddish edition of the *Forward* in New York.)

In the former Soviet territories, most of the current Jewish
revival has been underwritten by Israelis and Americans, few of
whom see Yiddish as a priority. Americans have, however, sponsored a few Yiddish courses and klezmer concerts. And scattered
throughout the former Pale, prosletyzing sects of Hasidim have
opened a few Yiddish-language *cheders,* where Russian children are
again being taught in Yiddish. These numbers, it must be said, are
minuscule. Perhaps as important as what this minirevival says
about Russian Jews is what it tells us about Jews in the West.

Ashkenazi Jews around the world continue to train their sights
on the former Soviet Union because, in terms of *yerushe,* heritage,

these territories are often ground zero. Secular Jews come to search out the sites of the old shtetls. Ultra-Orthodox visit the graves of famous *rebes*. Every year at Rosh Hashonah, five thousand Hasidic men make a pilgrimage to Uman, in Ukraine, to visit the grave of the eighteenth-century Hasid Nakhman of Bratslav. They sing and dance, and they pray facing upward, remembering Nakhman's admonition to speak directly to God.

In 1992 Western money helped to track down and restore some of the ethnographic treasures that S. An-ski had collected in the days preceding World War I. Some had been lost in the bombings of World War II, but hundreds remained. A selection of the photographs and artifacts, which had not been displayed since 1939, was chosen for an ambitious traveling exhibit. Beginning at the Russian Museum of Ethnography in St. Petersburg, the show traveled to Amsterdam, Cologne, Frankfurt, Jerusalem, and New York. An international audience saw the photographs of people and places, as well as a smattering of the objects — mezuzahs, skullcaps, Torah crowns, Chanukah lamps, sketches for costumes of *purim-shpiln,* folk illustrations used in Haggadahs — that had been carefully collected in the shtetls almost a century before.

Meanwhile half a world away, Birobidzhan, largely isolated and barely developed, slumbered on. By the time the Soviet Union imploded in 1991, only 10,000 of the region's 210,000 inhabitants were Jews. Although they were well aware of the history of their area, most knew little about their Jewish heritage. They did know one thing, however: Finally they had the option of leaving.

Within a decade, almost all of the region's Jews had emigrated — most to Israel, some to the United States. Of the few who remained (something in the range of a few thousand — 1 or 2 percent of the total population), only the very elderly have any sense of what it means to be Jewish.

But younger Jews have new ideas. Jewish holidays have been celebrated publicly for the first time in decades. The first Jewish school in half a century opened in 1992. Taught in Russian, students learn Hebrew and Yiddish. Remarkably, half the students who choose to attend the school are not Jewish. They are Russian, Ukrainian, and Korean residents of Birobidzhan who are interested in the heritage of the area and want to know more about Jews. The common perception among Russians has long been that Jews are intelligent, even though, under Communism, it was unclear just what Jews actually were. This joke has been circulating throughout the former Soviet Union: Question: How does a smart Russian Jew telephone his relatives? Answer: From Tel Aviv.

In Birobidzhan, the Teachers' College has once again begun teaching Yiddish and Jewish literature. Start-ups include a small Jewish community newspaper, a Sunday school, and a kindergarten. A few more young people can now read the street signs that, all along, have been written in Yiddish as well as Russian.

Ironically (and what would Russian-Jewish history be without irony), some of the strongest support for a Jewish presence in Birobidzhan now comes from Moscow, which looks at the Jewish connection as a possible jump start for an economic revival. *Who is to be called mighty? He who suppresseth a wisecrack.*

Nikolai Borodulin, the Birobidzhan native who first learned about what it meant to be a Jew after the fall of the Soviet Union, has moved to the United States. Of sixty family members who lived in Birobidzhan, most have moved to Israel. Only a handful remain. Borodulin tells this joke, referring to the three successive waves of official support for the Jewish presence in Birobidzhan (the initial phase, the post–World War II period, and the present time):

A religious man was warned about an approaching flood. As the water lapped at his ankles and his friends invited him to come with them in their boat, he said, "I am not afraid, my God will save me." When the waters rose and reached his waist, others offered a dry spot, which he again refused. The waters continued to rise, up to his chin. Another offer of help was tendered, another rebuffed. "My God will save me," he affirmed.

After the man drowned and went to heaven, he asked God why
He had not rescued him.

"You idiot!" God answered. "I sent you three boats."

In all, the Soviet story has not made for a pretty tale. This new
interest in the area that is still referred to as the Jewish Autonomous
Region might be the latest piece of a pattern of support and abandonment, the cynical use of the dreams of a people.

Yiddish language and culture were not able to survive the Soviet
Union. In the land where, a century ago, five million people created
a vibrant Yiddish culture, only the faintest of echoes remain.

In Israel, half a century has passed since the founding of the state.
The precarious settlement in a "dead land" has become a pros-
perous nation, its linked achievement, the revival of Hebrew, by
all measures a success. In Jerusalem, Israelis and foreign visitors
crowd the downtown pedestrian mall. They buy Hebrew versions of the essentials of modern life — fresh-brewed coffee, ice
cream with local fruits, T-shirts with clever slogans, *kippot* (skullcaps) with embroidered names. The street where all this happens
is named for that old ascetic, dreamer, and superachiever, Ben
Yehuda.

Now a new generation of Israelis, born into prosperity and a
measure of stability, has the luxury of wondering about their roots.
In the 1970s Israelis began traveling in significant numbers to
Eastern Europe. On Marches of the Living they became aware that
not only had a people and a culture been destroyed but a language
had been too. A few even thought the language would be worth
learning. In 1978, for the very first time, Yiddish was offered in a
couple of Israeli public schools.

Over the next twenty years, Yiddish lost something of its pariah
status. A film about a Yiddish theater troupe won first prize at a
major festival. It was no longer unusual for an Israeli university to
offer an introductory course in Yiddish, and Hebrew University
granted Yiddish Ph.D.'s.

But some victims of the language wars would call this all academic — scraps thrown to the vanquished after the victory has been won. Yiddish as a widespread, casually spoken language was a dead issue. The Yiddishists, that small number of Israelis who were committed to the old tongue, were aging. Sometimes it looked like the only vitality *mame loshn* still possessed lay in the long litany of skirmishes and dead ends.

In 1996 the Israeli government created two new national authorities: one overseeing Ladino, the Spanish-Jewish language, and one overseeing Yiddish. The Ladino organization got immediate funding and staffing; the Yiddish group had to wait for over a year. Then, a combination of Yiddishist infighting and government intransigence combined to cancel the Yiddish authority's first large project, a yearlong celebration with the theme of "Yiddish lives!" (Whatever happened to the Yiddish proverb, *better kindness than piety?*)

Still, even now a few Yiddish literati survive in Tel Aviv. A handful of books is published every year. The occasional Yiddish play is performed, most often with simultaneous Hebrew and Russian translation. And a new idea is being heard. There is a growing sense that Yiddish should have a special place in the world's only Jewish nation. One hears the argument that in Eretz Israel, Yiddish — the language of the six million, the tongue of the early Zionists — deserves some protection.

In the meantime, however, Yiddish, that guttersnipe of a language, has found ways to survive without special handling. *If you can't go over, you go under.* Despite all the years of language policing, in what may be one of its most delicious legacies, Yiddish has managed to infiltrate modern Hebrew. Because the newer, carefully contrived and protected tongue began as a high-status language (its uses were formal, public, polite), it did not have a vocabulary for the intimacies of life. When Ben Yehuda was inventing new words, endearments did not seem essential; outbursts of emotion were not on his list. Or perhaps these kinds of expressions cannot be mandated but must evolve, like language itself, from a place of deep human need.

After more than a century of modern Hebrew, when Israelis curse, shout, fondle their babies, murmur words of love, many of the words they use came originally from Yiddish. (Curse words are also often of Arabic or Russian derivation. At least there is some equal opportunity here.) Babies' names pick up the *-ele* Yiddish ending, an affectionate diminutive. Sometimes the Yiddish background of a word is just a matter of pronunciation. The Hebrew word *mishpacha,* accent on the last syllable, means "family," as in the formal sense of the families of the earth, or the family of man. When given its Yiddish *tam,* taste, however, the word becomes *mishpukhe,* with accent on the middle syllable. The Yiddish-inflected word is intimate and has a slightly different meaning. It is family, but in the sense of one's own beloved, imperfect, close-knit group. Several of the same Yiddish words that have made their way into mainstream English have also become common in Hebrew: words like *ganef,* thief, and *mentsh.*

But the real news about Yiddish in Israel comes from the Haredim. Although they all understand *ivrit,* modern Hebrew, if for no other reason than its link with *loshn koydesh,* the holy language, they make a point of speaking Yiddish among themselves. In the last decade or two, they have become more outspoken and aggressive. With their high birthrates and overarching desire to distance themselves from secular culture, they represent the one area of Yiddish growth.

For the Haredim, who account for 3 or 4 percent of Jews worldwide, Yiddish is yet another intimate daily link with their beloved past. It is the language spoken by generations of revered *rebes,* the language of the "pure" Hasidic life. It is the tongue of the pious European Jews who journeyed back to Eretz Israel over the centuries, the language of the holy martyrs of the Holocaust.

So, in Yiddish's newest *ironye,* irony, the Yiddish language itself is assuming something of an aura of holiness. *If you live long enough, you see everything.* One Haredi woman teacher put it this way: "Everything taught in Yiddish goes straight to the soul."

Haredim explain their devotion to Yiddish in terms of the time the Israelites lived in slavery in Egypt. They say that those ancient Jews maintained their Jewish identity precisely because they kept their Jewish language and their Jewish names. So now they give their children Yiddish names, to remember those who were lost. Little Moishes and Frumes help to recall the Holocaust dead.

The Haredim have a complicated relationship to Yiddish. *So what else is new?* Continuing the Ashkenazi tradition, students in the best yeshivas study Hebrew texts by discussing them in Yiddish. These yeshivas are so respected that they even attract the Ladino-speaking Sephardim.

The situation is more complex for Haredi women. Because they do most of the functioning in the outside world, they are more likely than the men to be comfortable in modern Hebrew. But because of the new Yiddish consciousness, even women who may not speak it easily try to use it with their children. But fundamentalism is on the increase, so the youngest generation is likely to be more fluent than their parents, a neat reversal of language use.

Haredi schools, however, are inconsistent in their use of Yiddish. Practices vary greatly from one sect to the next, and even between schools that belong to the same sect. (Remember that the sects are still named for the old Yiddish towns their leaders came from — Ger, Satmar, Belz.) In some Haredi schools, more Yiddish is used in the primary grades; in others, more is used as the children grow older. Schools for girls often have different policies than schools for boys.

Some sects, particularly the Lubavitchers, do not use much Yiddish because they are interested in bringing assimilated Jews back into the fold. This means that their ranks are swelled by non–Yiddish speakers. So not all Haredim speak Yiddish, and those who do, use it to varying degrees.

One more example of the strange-but-true: Although Israeli Haredim can be aggressive about what they consider proper standards of dress and behavior, they make no attempt to impose Yiddish on non-Haredim. If anything, they are wont to keep it to themselves. A secular linguistic researcher noticed that, when she began to dress in a way that let her blend in with the Haredim, she heard much more Yiddish spoken casually around her in the Jerusalem street.

For all their linguistic awareness, Haredim do not look at language in the same way that more secular speakers do. They do not take an interest in language per se. They take Yiddish as it comes, freely mixing it with *ivrit* if they live in Israel, or English if they live in New York. They have no use for the YIVO system of standardized spelling and do not study spelling, grammar, or linguistics at all. Likewise for literature, which they consider a distraction from important spiritual concerns.

Although most of their lives are structured and defined by their religion, there is some mundane Yiddish literature, although that term should be understood in a broad sense. Yiddish newspapers aimed at the Haredi audience are thriving. A handful of weeklies is published in New York and shipped around the world. There are some Yiddish genre books and a few children's books, but they are of low quality and occupy a place of low status. (Low status! Isn't this where we came in? *For every new song you can find an old tune.*)

Much of what the Haredim do these days sounds much like what Yiddish has always done — create a safe space for the in-group and keep the outsiders at bay. Yiddish acts as an insulator, except that now the Haredim use it to distance themselves from other Jews. An even larger difference may be that, where Yiddish culture traditionally embraced the Jewish world and the human foibles of its people, the Haredim take a narrower view. They do not glory in the range of human nature. Their culture does not include poetry or science; it has little use for art high or low. Although many run thriving businesses, worldly success is not an end in itself. There is some punning, but in general it has little regard for language.

No one can tell what the future of Yiddish will sound like, but there is one safe bet: It will likely sound a lot louder as the Haredi community grows more populous. Estimates place the turn-of-the-century Haredi population at five hundred thousand to seven hundred thousand worldwide. (The 1997 estimate of worldwide Jewry of all persuasions is thirteen million.) Of the roughly half million Haredim, about three hundred thousand live in Israel. Two-thirds of these are children. At current rates of increase, the number of Haredim will soon reach into the millions.

Logically, anyone would say that the future of Yiddish lies with these ultra-Orthodox. But logic has not been the starring player in the historical drama we have laid out thus far, and nobody sees any reason for it to get more than a cameo appearance now. Still, it is quite possible that Yiddish will again coalesce into a widespread, useful language that helps to reinforce a culture.

Indeed, some say that it already has.

CHAPTER 19

America: Preserving Tomorrow's Song

א איד קען ניט לעבן אהן ניסים.

A yid ken nit lebn ohn nisim.

A Jew can't live without miracles.

At the beginning of the twenty-first century, it is still possible to hear Yiddish spoken in the United States. But unless you move in Haredi circles, you will not hear a lot. A century and a quarter after Jews began leaving the Yiddish heartland, few of their descendants in America and beyond have much *mame loshn* left. If Jews sprinkle a few mispronounced or half-understood Yiddish words into their speech, like sugar over dry cereal, they are likely used as code: Yes, I am Jewish, or at least cool.

Yet the American landscape is dotted with pockets of extraordinary creativity and vibrant growth. An interactive Web site is making the totality of Yiddish theater accessible. The National Center for Jewish Film distributes dozens of restored and subtitled Yiddish videos. YIVO, in brand-new headquarters, boasts over three hundred thousand volumes and twenty million documents. It offers Yiddish classes, an address for scholars, as well as a broad array of informal help.

In New York at least one Yiddish play, with simultaneous translation in English and Russian, is performed each year. In Toronto a biannual weeklong event that bills itself as a festival of new Yiddish culture attracts seventy thousand participants. Nationwide, the Yiddish calendar is full of conferences, festivals, and musical performances. Women's groups continue to rediscover and reclaim a language that has always had female associations. Gay and lesbian Jews have found a kindred culture in the outsider stance of Yiddish, while for intermarried families, incorporating a bit of Yiddish or *yidishkayt* can be less threatening than tackling the charged issue of religion.

There are some, however, for whom Yiddish is much more than a diversion.

Aaron Lansky, who was born in Massachusetts in 1955, remembers when his Hebrew school teachers — native Yiddish speakers — were replaced by younger Israelis with their Sephardic pronunciation of Hebrew and their anti-Yiddish bent. Lansky did not have much Yiddish himself. Although it had been his American-born mother's first language, the family's use of it had receded to almost nothing by the time he was growing up. But when he studied Jewish history in college he realized that, if he really wanted to understand the last thousand years, he would have to learn *mame loshn*.

In the late 1970s, about the same time the klezmer maven-to-be Henry Sapoznik was rethinking his trips to South Carolina, Lansky became a graduate student in Yiddish at McGill University in Montreal. But he soon found that precious few books were available. Hardly any Yiddish texts were in print, and students were reduced to going from door to door in Jewish neighborhoods searching for old, unwanted copies of classic Yiddish works. In one generation Yiddish books had gone from being ubiquitous to becoming almost extinct.

Lansky took a leave from school, planning to spend two years collecting whatever books remained. Jewish experts, who warned him against wasting his time on this unrewarding quest, guessed that he would find seventy-five thousand volumes representing an unknown number of titles.

Too ignorant or idealistic to take their advice, Lansky began collecting, first from the back of a motorbike, then graduating to a used truck. He sat in kitchens where old folks insisted on feeding him food and stories about how important their Yiddish books had been in their lives.

Lansky rescued not only the books but the concept of *zamlers,* collectors, that had been used by both Dubnow and Weinreich before him. Soon a small army of energetic elderly Yiddishists and idealistic young folks was scouring North America while Lansky was renting ever more warehouse space. His graduate studies were eclipsed by his mission. He founded the National Yiddish Book Center in Amherst, Massachusetts, and within a decade had amassed a million books. When the rented and borrowed buildings were full, their floors sagging, he passed duplicate volumes on to the four-hundred-odd libraries in twenty-six countries that were by this time assembling Yiddish collections.

By the beginning of the new century, the National Yiddish Book Center had moved into a state-of-the-art building whose architecture recalled the vanished wooden synagogues of Eastern Europe. With a membership of thirty thousand, it began a project of incredible imagination and scope, digitizing thirty-five thousand different Yiddish titles — virtually the entire corpus of Yiddish literature. The language thus leapfrogged from the trash bins of history to the forefront of technology. Throughout, Lansky's task has been ingathering. The material he found has made it possible to build an easily traveled road to a world that came perilously close to being lost.

Because the Yiddish that once was, is no more. That death of a culture, and the near-death status of its language, must be acknowledged and mourned. No matter how many signs we see of deep cultural stirrings, all the conferences and concerts and collections in the world are not indications of a living language. Even though a few committed Yiddishists teach their children to speak *mame loshn,* brilliant and brave and brash as they are, they cannot be considered more than the outriders of a special-interest group.

Incredibly, even with this is-there-a-pulse-here state of affairs, one regularly hears talk of a Yiddish revival. A reporter finds a festival, notices the college courses, maybe even straps on a pair of headphones and attends a Yiddish play, collecting fodder for a colorful newspaper piece. But renaissance it's not. With the exception of the klezmer concerts, the audiences tend to be graying or academic or both. The festivals that attract broader audiences may have Yiddish at their center, but the actual activities and "explorations" expand in a wide arc. Content is often "Yiddish-influenced" or "Yiddish-style" — a storyteller recounting a version of a Hasidic tale, an artist giving a workshop on Jewish paper cutting. As Ruth Wisse, the Y. L. Peretz Professor of Yiddish at Harvard, wrote, "If this constitutes a revival, how would you describe a linguistic decline?"

We might do better to think in terms of shift. The descendants of Yiddish speakers are using Yiddish as a matrix of meaning. They are placing Yiddish in a historical context, beginning to appreciate what has been, and what might yet be.

Yiddish is now taught routinely at U.S. colleges, although the numbers of courses and students are down since the high point of the 1970s. (The study of language in general is off; the ethnic revival has come and gone.) These offerings are unstable; one knowledgeable estimate places the number of schools that offer the language in the middle two digits. And only a handful offer anything beyond the introductory year.

Sometimes a course on Jewish literature or history will include a few Yiddish texts in translation, but the Yiddish canon is almost never integrated into a broader curriculum. Sholom Aleichem will not be taught as part of European literature; Glatstein will not be found in a course on American poetry. In the United States a graduate degree in Yiddish must be cobbled together from other departments. Harvard has the only endowed Yiddish chair. So yes, Yiddish can be found in academe. But the course list is so slim, the qualifications of the faculty so spotty, that one professor called his field "a quiet disaster."

Still, students come. They are looking for a visceral link to their immediate past. They want to hear the sounds, meet the souls, root out the origins of the songs and the *shtik*. (*Shtik*'s literal meaning is "piece"; a secondary meaning is "prank." In English it has grown specialized, referring to the verbal habits of comics who are a generation or two removed from the mother tongue. The word, like its speakers, has migrated from its Yiddish origin.) But the resonance is there. As Matthew Goodman recently described his experience of learning Yiddish as an adult, "Yiddish still retained something that could cause a person like me — assimilated, deeply conflicted about my Judaism, raised in an entirely English-speaking household — to fall in love with it. . . . the work always had a certain quality not of learning, necessarily, but rather of remembering."

A growth area is Yiddish summer programs. Beyond learning the *alef beys,* the *abc*'s in the classroom, these vacations-with-credit offer singing, dancing, and shmoozing. (The word, which has come to mean a relaxed, intimate sort of chatting, comes from the Yiddish *shmues,* conversation, yet another example of how cultural connotations attach themselves to the language.) One can now shmooze for a month each summer in New York, Oxford, Paris, Vilna, or Kiev.

About one hundred or so books are still printed in the language each year. Some of the books are closer to pamphlets, some are new editions of old works, and some are children's tales, so the output is not exactly huge. About half of all new Yiddish publications are aimed at Haredi audiences. Yiddish speakers tend to concentrate at the extremes of the political and religious spectrum, with the left wing and right wing eyeing each other across the middle ground of the descendants of Holocaust survivors.

The Haredim divide Yiddish literature into traditional and modern. But for them, "traditional" means worldly, the outlook that was considered modern until World War II. They define "modern" as being like them. These ultra-Orthodox turn out religious tracts as well as what might be called schlock religious novels. (*Shlok,* which primarily means "bad" in Yiddish, has assumed a narrower English meaning of "shoddy.") The output of secular, or at least non-Haredi, Yiddishists tends toward the scholarly and the literary, or the frankly nostalgic.

Of work that has been produced, a minute amount is available to English speakers. Lansky estimates that just 0.5 percent of Yiddish literature has been translated into English. That means that although most major works have been translated, the works of many significant Yiddish poets, lyricists, and essayists is virtually unknown. Even taking into account the enormous contemporary popularity of klezmer music, the only time a tune crossed over was fifty years ago, when the Andrews Sisters recorded a version of "Bei mir bist du shein" (To Me You're Beautiful). The only Yiddish song that made its way into the American folk idiom was Joan Baez's softly poeticized 1960s version of "Dona, Dona." Although the last verse was rendered as:

> Calves are easily bound and slaughtered
> Never knowing the reason why
> But whoever treasures freedom
> Like the swallow, has learned to fly

the literal translation as well as the Yiddish sounds are more direct and harsh:

> Poor wretched calves are bound
> And they are dragged and they are killed,
> Who has wings, flies upward,
> Is by no one made a slave

> Bidne kelber tut men bindn
> Un men shlept zey un men shekht,
> Ver s'hot fligl, flit aroyftsu,
> Iz bay kynen nit keyn knekht.

But a certain *tam*, taste, of Yiddish has spread. Yiddish cadence and inflection can be felt in the work of American writers like Philip Roth and Bernard Malamud. Here is a snippet from Grace Paley's story "In This Country, but in Another Language, My Aunt Refuses to Marry the Men Everyone Wants Her To":

> My aunt was making the bed. Look, your grandmother, she doesn't sweat. Nothing has to be washed — her stockings, her underwear, the sheets. From this you wouldn't believe what a life she had. It wasn't life. It was torture.
> Doesn't she love us? I asked.
> Love you? my aunt said. What else is worth it? You children. Your cousin in Connecticut.

As well as coloring literary language, Yiddish has enriched everyday English speech. The current edition of the *Oxford English Dictionary* contains 144 words of Yiddish origin. Several, like *shlep, nosh,* or *chutzpah,* have spread so far into the American hinterlands that speakers are probably not aware of their origin. (The story here is that, as Jews know less and less Yiddish, millions of non-Jews know a little bit more.) Other words, typically referring to holidays or cultural practices, our old friend the *purim-shpil,* for example, have remained in the Jewish community. Then there are the Yiddish proverbs that, translated, suffuse American Jewish speech: *If my grandmother had wheels, she'd be a trolley* (and other, less family-friendly versions). *The apple doesn't fall far from the tree. If you lie down with dogs, you get up with fleas.*

There are also structural borrowings. Expressions like *enjoy!, don't ask, better you should, go know, I should care,* are literal translations of Yiddish usage. The type of reasoning that follows logic to its illogical conclusion has a source in the Talmudic disputation that was the hallmark of Yiddish education. *I need it like I need a hole in the head.* Answering a question with a question *(You're asking me?)* has been described as a tactic for concealing identity, a must for Yiddish speakers who wandered homeless across an unwelcoming world.

Today, Yiddish speakers and Yiddish enthusiasts can find each other on the Internet, or *internets. Shtrosers,* surfers, turn on their *kompyuters* and shmooze across time zones and continents, at sites like the Virtual Shtetl, an apt name for a "non-place" community. On the Web Yiddish is, for the most part, written in Roman letters, which breaks the old Hebrew link but brings in a wider audience. There is some drift, in Internet-land, toward the use of standardized YIVO transliteration or romanization, but the system is so little known that spelling is still an informal affair.

Mendele, a fairly intellectual site that includes scholarly papers, heated discussions, and bulletin-board-like announcements and requests, has subscribers on every continent except Antarctica. Sometimes its discourse is about mourning: arguments, in Yiddish and English, over whether or not Yiddish is dead. They go like this: The language is not dead, it was murdered. The fact that a few Yiddish words and phrases have found their way into American speech means nothing. It is like the American bagel — large, doughy, and lacking in taste.

Meanwhile, a new undertaking, Project Onkelos, largely volunteer, is making Yiddish more accessible to those who don't speak it at all. Named after the first-century C.E. scholar who translated the Torah into Aramaic, this massive project is beginning, by baby steps, to provide side-by-side Yiddish-English translations of important texts. As one *Mendelyener,* Mendele correspondent, wrote, "What a great way to begin *moshiakhs tsayt!"* — the era of the Messiah.

But so much has been lost. Chagall's painting *The Birthday,* with its floating man hovering in the air above his beloved, his face touching hers, is justifiably well known. But few realize that this painting, like many of Chagall's works, illustrates a Yiddish phrase. To cause someone to fall madly in love is *fardreyen im dem kop,* to twist his head around; just what has happened to the besotted young man.

We must also remember that language, which changes what we see, is itself always in flux. Even as Yiddish declines precipitously in most of the world, it is being renewed by the Haredim. And their world is changing too.

In the years after World War II, the ultra-Orthodox in the United States made some accommodations to the secular world around them. They sent their daughters to public schools; they made compromises with modern styles of dress. In the past two decades, however, like fundamentalists in other religions, they have gone on the offensive. Their schools are becoming more strict, their observance of religious law more insistent, their separation from the mainstream more resolute. Like their compatriots around the world, they are using Yiddish more.

American Haredim who may speak halting Yiddish themselves are struggling to make it once again the language of the home. A community member described the way that parents "will break their teeth to speak Yiddish to the children." Tens of thousands of Haredi children in the United States now learn Yiddish first and English second. There are even a few young adult men who live so totally within the Haredi community that, although born and raised in the United States, they know virtually no English.

A story is told about an American Haredi man who kept asking his friend a question in Yiddish. The question concerned the friend's wife. But because in his sect it was not considered proper to refer to the woman directly, the questioner tried several forms of circumlocution. When his friend pretended to not follow his drift and answered his questions literally, the first man finally blurted out his question directly — but could only bring himself to do so by switching to English.

In the United States, as in Europe and Israel, literature for children and, to a lesser extent, popular fiction represent growing fields. But even though many sects now strongly encourage Yiddish, language is seen as a means, not an end.

New York is the world center for Haredi newspapers. Several of its weeklies, among them *Der yid* (The Jew) and the *Algemeyner zhurnal* (General Journal), are sold internationally. They focus on political and local news of interest to the community. Their language is hybrid, with lots of English in the American publications, just as their Israeli equivalents contain lots of *ivrit*. An ad in a New York Yiddish paper advertises, in Yiddish letters, *"bus servis,"* while another one is looking for *"drivers mit ķars oder on ķars,"* drivers with or without cars.

Among both secular and Haredi Yiddish speakers, regional accents have blurred, thanks to the vast geographical upheavals of the last century. To some extent these distinctions have been replaced among the secular by Standard Yiddish, especially as more Yiddish speakers learn the language as adults, in an academic setting. In the Haredi world, accents are more likely to reflect their speakers' abode — New York, Jerusalem, Johannesburg, or Melbourne.

The ultra-Orthodox have also been creating what might be called a new dialect of their own. Reflecting the way that the men, in particular, liberally mix Hebrew and Yiddish into their English, linguists have labeled their speech Yeshivish. Three-quarters of this vocabuluary comes from Yiddish. This is far from being a complete language, but it does reflect social separation. For example, some Haredim will refer to a *tish,* which is the Yiddish word for "table," in a way that differs from its literal use. Derived from the informal talk a *rebe* might have given around the table after a meal, it now describes a ritual that is the high point of the Sabbath or festival. The *rebe,* surrounded by hundreds or even thousands of his followers, sitting at a table covered by a white linen cloth, eats his largely symbolic meal and then offers his followers both literal leftovers as well as prayers, lectures, and songs.

One man who functions in both worlds is Abraham Heschel. A Hasid from Borough Park, Brooklyn, he wears not just the beard and the *peyes* but also, in the New York summer heat, the long black coat and the black hat. Now working on a research project for yivo, he is aware of his anomolous status. He says that, in the old days, when the Bundists ran the organization, they would never have hired him.

The belief is common on both sides of the facial hair divide that the other party has hijacked Yiddish. Even as some assimilated Yiddish speakers or Yiddish enthusiasts can recognize in Haredi life some of the qualities of the old shtetl world they admire, others point out its chilling lock-the-gates quality. They object to the way that some Haredim assume a fanatical high ground.

But Haredim see hijacking and fanaticism as well. Until two hundred years ago, Heschel says, there was no such thing as a secular Jew. All Jews lived in communities that looked and sounded much like his own, integrating the sacred and the mundane. Just as his Borough Park neighbors ignore Sholom Aleichem and Singer, he faults worldly Yiddish speakers for making the same error, focusing only on writers whose outlook reinforces their own.

Heschel complains that today's Yiddishists "act as if Peretz and Sholom Aleichem were the beginning and the end. What about the *Tsenerene?*" — the women's Bible, with its holy texts, interpretations, and tales, that has been in print for four hundred years. "What about the *tekhines,* the women's prayers?"

He has a point. But even in the "good old days," the Hasidim never made up more than half the population, and they lived, like it or not, cheek by jowl with less pious Jews. Like much in our modern world, Yiddish can be viewed as a string of special-interest groups.

It is quite possible that one of them, the Haredim, will define its future. Indeed, there are those who say that the future of all of Judaism lies with them, as less committed Jews yield to assimilation. The only certainty is that no one can predict the future. Truth to tell, we are looking at tea leaves, searching for signs.

Isaac Bashevis Singer invoked the future to answer the oft-repeated question of why he wrote in a dying language. Bringing up the example of the rebirth of Hebrew, Singer said, "With the Jews, resurrection is not a miracle, but a habit."

In the meantime, Jews of all persuasions look to feed the eternal flame. Zelik Akselrod wrote in his poem "They Tell Me": "Now I know the meaning of it all. . . . But I cannot say it plainly. Sometimes rain does not fall from heaven. Yet deep within me, I have surely preserved tomorrow's song for your sake." The poem was written as the Nazis were shutting down Jewish life in Vilna. Akselrod urged writers to protest the closing of the last Yiddish newspaper, *Vilner emes* (Vilna Truth). He was arrested and murdered for his pains. His poem remains.

Lansky urges us to save and make available those cultural remnants, and he places Yiddish literature squarely in the continuum of Jewish creativity, life, and thought. He asks us to see the language and its culture in terms of other great legal and literary periods that, although finite, Jews still study and cite after thousands of years. Yiddish literature, he explains, asks the question, "How do we live our lives as Jews in a modern world?" Then he goes on: "In authentically Jewish fashion, Yiddish offers no absolute answer. But it gives us a profound way to ask the question, and I think that's exactly what we need."

It is tempting to imagine what might have happened if only, if only . . . What if things had been different? What would the great centers of Vilna and Warsaw be like today? Let's give ourselves, for a moment, permission to dream. *If you're going to eat pork, let the fat drip down your beard.*

Given the ambivalence of the interwar period, it is possible to picture very different outcomes for Yiddish. By now, its vibrance might have naturally diminished. It might have shrunk into a corner of ethnic nostalgia, little more than a tourist attraction in a Europe bent on smoothing over old divides.

Quite the opposite is possible as well. The Yiddish business, professional, political, and artistic communities might have drawn strength from each other and from the deep traditional well. Polish Jews could have continued to create a rich and vibrant culture in Yiddish. Instead of being a unique case, Lucy Dawidowicz might have been the first of a wave of young Americans who traveled to Eastern Europe to take part in a dynamic cultural renaissance. And if Yiddish had thrived in Europe, it would have been that much easier for later generations of Americans to reclaim their roots.

We must also remember this unsettling fact: The unbearable tragedy of the Holocaust played an important role in the court of world opinion, making it that much more possible for Jews to create a modern state. With Jewish life decimated in Europe, survivors who went to Israel found Yiddish phobia the price of nation building. So we are left with paradox.

It is unlikely that Yiddish will ever revive as a widely spoken language. But Yiddish can be remembered. It can still connect Jews to each other and to their past. It can link Jews and non-Jews alike to one of the great expressive traditions of the world.

Sometimes in memory it is possible to know a person, or a culture, with a clarity and a wholeness that was not possible in the confusion of living. Goodman, the adult Yiddish learner, described how he came to terms with learning a language that was dying before his eyes. He saw death as not necessarily signifiying the end of life: "'Here,' we will say, handing our children a photograph, 'you never knew her, but she was beautiful, and we loved her very much.'" The job of the coming years will be to reclaim the past, and to integrate Yiddish into Jewish, and human, history.

Sometimes, sitting in a Yiddish conference, festival, or class, it is possible to think that the language and its world still exist. Conference-goers tend to be extravagantly enthusiastic. In the intensity of the Q&As, their faces project the relief and excitement of hearing a publicly spoken *yidish vort*, Yiddish word. In our impersonal, homogeneous existence, Yiddish can look like a shortcut to paradise lost. It is the mother baking *challah*, the special Sabbath bread. It is the shoemaker putting down his tools for an hour of study with his fellow cobblers. We learn from Yiddish that there is no perfection in this world; that it is possible to live a full life in the margins. Yiddish teaches us how to make something from nothing; how to richly define and inhabit our own life.

These days, if you walk in Meah Shearim or Borough Park, the ultra-Orthodox neighborhoods of Jersualem or New York on a *shabes,* you will sense the glad quiet. Families shuttle between *shul* and home. Warm dinners are waiting; slow-cooking *cholent,* crusty *challah,* sweet ritual wine. The Jews are in charge of their own piece of the world and, as the children chatter away in Yiddish, life is good. *For every new song you can find an old tune.* If the secularists argue that the Haredim turn their backs resolutely on modernity and mainstream culture, the argument can be made that the genius of Yiddish was its creation of a parallel universe.

Perhaps Yiddish has attained mythic status because, for so much of its life, it had to fill such large shoes. Let it be said one more time: The Yiddish language had to take the place of all those things a nation provides — official centers of learning, judicial and legislative systems, economic stability, armed forces. Because it had to furnish so much, the language can still conjure up images of a whole vanished world, the Yiddishland that never came to be. This may be why people so often say that Yiddish can't be translated. (This is most often heard from those who do not use it as a complete, expressive linguistic system.) Although no language can hope to translate its idioms, obsessions, and idiosyncrasies, what cannot be conveyed from Yiddish is the sense of an entire world that is gone.

This poem by Sutzkever gives a sense of how we humans still manage to infer much from little:

> If you remain
> I will still be alive
>
> As the pit of the plum
> Contains in itself the tree
>
> The nest and the bird
> And all else besides.

The few remaining commonly used words of Yiddish are the plum pits for contemporary Jews. From these words, phrases, expressions, and proverbs, they have managed to imaginatively re-create an entire past. Today Jews in the United States and Western Europe no longer need the warmth and safety of the outcasts' separate brilliant tongue. If not always influential and powerful, they at least generally welcome members of the cultures in which they dwell.

Still, Yiddish retains a particular place in the Jewish as well as the non-Jewish heart. It did what mothers have always done for their children: made them feel safe; mediated between them and the great, wide world. Its role is no different today. As the essence of a mother remains in her offspring long after she dies, the worldview of Yiddish has shaped who we all are. The language and culture have played a key role in producing modern Jews, and through them have influenced non-Jewish culture as well.

The sense that no part of the human condition is off bounds, the acknowledgment of the lowliest of human needs while encouraging and providing for the loftiest possibilites: That's Yiddish. "Let's talk *mame loshn*" doesn't mean literally "let's speak in Yiddish vocabulary." It means "let's be honest with each other, tell it like it really is." *Neither wisdom nor prayer will help when the cards aren't running.* The great question is whether or not the cards are running for Yiddish right now. It certainly has a history of unheralded, under-appreciated winning hands. It grew from a sacred tongue but never left it behind. It kept it in "warm storage," protected but accessible. It remained open to neighboring languages without ever losing its sense of itself. It nourished a far-flung homeless people. And even in "dying," it allowed the Jewish nation to be reborn.

When a beloved family member dies, Jews pray, "May their life be remembered as a blessing. May they be bound up in the bond of life." These days, the Yiddish festivals, conferences, and Web sites are re-creating and strengthening those bonds. The Haredim, from their separate stance, are creating new ones as well.

Yiddish had a fate both exalted and tragic — exalted because of its millennium of centrality to a culture; tragic because of the intense compression of its flowering and the equally compacted course of its swift decline. Even though the great strength of the Yiddish language and worldview has been its ability to pluck confidence, courage, and hope from the depths of tragedy and despair, my hope for the language would be that utterly Yiddish blessing — *may we meet only on happy occasions.*

For a subject that has been so close to so many people's hearts, the number of books on the language itself is quite small; most are jokey-cozy or scholarly. They are likely to end with some prognostication about the future. Reading old volumes, with old views of what is to come, their relentless optimism is unsettling. Books written through the post–World War II period duly note the aging and decline of the Yiddish-speaking population but expect an imminent turnaround. And really, who could blame them?

Despite the anguished history of European Jews, who could have imagined the blows inflicted on Yiddish? No one in his right mind could possibly have foretold the destruction of the Holocaust, or foreseen the Stalinist purges. Who could have predicted the rapidity and enthusiasm with which Yiddish-speaking Americans dropped their beloved tongue?

To go back even farther, say, a thousand years, no one looking at that scrappy little dialect would have envisioned such a long, full, and wealthy life. So yes, things are looking pretty poorly for Yiddish as a mainstream tongue right now. And what the outcome will be with the Haredim remains to be seen. But as the great fictional sage Tevye the dairyman said in Yiddish, mangling one more reference to Hebrew liturgical text, "As we say on Yom Kippur, the Lord decides who will ride on horseback and who will crawl on foot. The main thing is — hope! A Jew must always hope, must never lose hope."

Hope was a mighty force in Singer's 1978 Nobel Prize acceptance speech, which he gave in both Yiddish and English:

The high honor bestowed upon me by the Swedish Academy is also a recognition of the Yiddish language — a language of exile, without a land, without frontiers, not supported by any government, a language which possesses no words for weapons, ammunition, military exercises, war tactics; a language that was despised by both gentiles and emancipated Jews. The truth is that what the great religions preached, the Yiddish-speaking people of the ghettos practiced day in and day out. They were the people of the Book in the truest sense of the word. . . .

To me the Yiddish language and the conduct of those who spoke it are identical. One can find in the Yiddish tongue and in the Yiddish style expressions of pious joy, lust for life, longing for the Messiah, patience, and deep appreciation of human individuality. There is a quiet humor in Yiddish and a gratitude for every day of life, every crumb of success, every encounter of love. The Yiddish mentality is not haughty. It does not take victory for granted. It does not demand and command but it muddles through, sneaks by, smuggles itself amid the powers of destruction, knowing somewhere that God's plan for Creation is still at the very beginning. . . .

Yiddish has not yet said its last word. It contains treasures that have not been revealed to the eyes of the world. It was the tongue of martyrs and saints, of dreamers and Kabbalists — rich in humor and in memories that mankind may never forget. In a figurative way, Yiddish is the wise and humble language of us all, the idiom of frightened and hopeful humanity.

Glossary

abba father (Hebew)
af, auf in, near
ale every
alef beys alphabet (literally, a, b)
alter old
Am Israel the people of Israel
arbeter worker
asher yotser who has fashioned (Hebrew)
Ashkenaz German (Hebrew)
Avrom aveynu Abraham our ancestor
balebuste housewife
bank-kasir teller
bank-konte bank account
bentshn after-meal prayers
beser better
bez lilac
bibliotek library
blintz cheese-filled pancake
broit bread
bube grandmother
bubele term of endearment (literally, little grandmother)
bube meyse old wives' tale
bukh book
bulbe potato
bund bond, alliance
cantor singer in religious services
challah ritual bread
Chanukah holiday celebrating the victory of the ancient Jews over the Syrians

Chasid *see* Hasid
chaver friend
cheder elementary school (literally, room)
cholent meat and bean stew
chutzpah nerve
classiker classic
Days of Awe period of introspection at Jewish new year
der, di the
derech way
dienstik Tuesday
doikeyt hereness
donershtik Thursday
driter third
eder rather than
efer ashes (Hebrew)
emes truth
Eretz Israel land of Israel
erev preceding night (Jewish holidays begin at sundown)
ershter first
esn eat
faigele little bird
fargoyisht assmilated
farvus why
feltrosh felt
fenster window
ferdelekh little horse
firzogerin interpreter
folkshul people's school
forverts forward
fotografye photograph

frayheit freedom
fraynd friend
Gan Eden Garden of Eden
ganef thief
ganz whole
gas street
gast guest
gazolin gasoline
glezele small glass
goldene medine golden land
golus exile
gottenyu dear God
goy non-Jew
goyish non-Jewish
griener greenhorn, newcomer
gymnasium elevated high
school
Haggadah the book read during Passover seder
Haredim God fearers
harts heart
hartsik caring
Hasid pious person; pl.
Hasidim or Hasids
Haskalah Enlightenment
heder *see* cheder
heym home
heymish homespun
hot has
hoyzfraynd household friend
iberlebung survival
internets Internet
ivriim Hebrews (Hebrew)
ivrit Hebrew (Hebrew)
ivri-teutsh Hebrew German
judeln Jewish German dialect
judenteutsh Jewish German

kadimah forward, eastward
(Hebrew)
kashe buckwheat
kavod honor (Hebrew)
kehile community
keyt chain
khalyastre gang
khumesh sacred books
khurbn destruction
kibbitz joke or kid
kind child
klezmer music, musician
kniehoysen knee stockings
kohl mit vaser cabbage with
water
kol mevaser a voice proclaiming (Hebrew)
Kol Nidre solemn service at
Yom Kippur
kompyuter computer
koved honor
kulturjuden cultural Jews
kumzitz get-together
(Hebrew)
lager camp
landsman fellow countryman
landsmanshaft organization of
people from one area
latke pancake
legaler yontev legal or secular
holiday
lernen learn
licht light
loshn ashkenaz language of
Ashkenaz
loshn koydesh holy language
mahzor festival prayerbook

mame loshn mother tongue
margeritke daisy
maskil enlightener; pl. maskilim
megile literally, scroll; more often, the story of the events of the holiday of Purim
mekhae joy
mentele Torah cover
mentsh decent person (literally, man)
mer carrot; also multiply
meshugener crazy
metukan improved
milikher dairyman (literally, milky one)
milon dictionary (Hebrew)
minkhe afternoon prayer
mishegas craziness
mishpukhe family
mit with
mitvoch Wednesday
mitzve good deed, commandment
moehl ritual circumciser
montik Monday
morgen morning
motosikel motorcycle
nikhter sober
nister hidden one
nosh eat a small amount
ober but
on without
oneg shabbat, oyneg shabes delight in the Sabbath
Ostjuden eastern Jews
ovent evening
oyrech guest

papir paper
peyes earlocks
pilpul dialectic learning
pintele yid spark of Jewishness
Poylin Poland
pripetshik fireplace
Purim literally, lots; more often, a holiday celebrating the saving of the Jewish people in ancient Persia
purim-shpil play that is put on at Purim
rebe Hasidic leader
rebetsin rabbi's wife
roiz rose
Rosh Hashonah Jewish new year
rugelach horn-shaped pastries
seder ritual Passover meal
shabes Sabbath
shalachmones gifts given at Purim
shiker drunk
shlemiel awkward misfit
shlep drag
shlepper bum
shlimazl unlucky person
shmuk prick
shnapps whiskey
shnuk jerk
shnorer beggar
shofar ram's horn blown at the new year
shpil play or talk
shpilmener tale tellers
shtern star
shtetl small town

shtik piece, prank
shtikl small piece
shtoser surfer
shtot city
shvue oath
Simchas Torah holiday celebrating the Torah
soldatske soldiers'
sufit ceiling
svetshop sweatshop
tageblat daily sheet
take so
tam taste
tayer darling
tekhine women's prayer
telefon telephone
telegraf telegraph
tey tea
tizmoret orchestra (Hebrew)
tog day
toyt dead
tsadik saintly person
tsatskele term of endearment
  (literally, little toy)
tsayt times
Tsenerene women's book of
  Bible commentary
tsu to
tsveyter second
un and
unsere, unzer our
varheit truth
vaybertaytsh Yiddish typeface

velt world
veltlech small world
vi like
vort word
vu den? what else?
vus makhst? what's doing?
yaldi my child (Hebrew)
yeder each
yenta busybody
yerushe heritage
yeshiva, yeshive religious secondary school
yeshive bukher Yeshiva student
yid Jew
yidene Jewish woman
yidish, yidishe Jewish
yidishkayt Yiddishism; literally,
  Jewishness
yidishtaytsh Judeo-German
yizker prayer for the dead
yizker bukh book commemo-
  rating lost communities
yor year
yunge youngster
zaft juice
zaftik juicy, buxom
zamer sing (Hebrew)
zamler collector
zayn his
zeyde grandfather
zhargon jargon
zuntik Sunday

Sources

Web sites

The Web is changing the nature of the Yiddish community. The following Web sites will give you a sense of the current cultural interest in Yiddish and can point you toward more specialized information.

Der Bay www.derbay.org

Mendele http://shakti.trincoll.edu/~mendele

National Center for Jewish Film www.jewishfilm.org

National Yiddish Book Center www.yiddishbooks.com

The Spoken Yiddish Language Project at Columbia University
  www.columbia.edu/cu/cria/Current-projects/Yiddish/yiddish.html

Virtual Shtetl www.ibiblio.org/yiddish/shtetl.html

Yiddish Theater Digital Archive Project at New York University
  www.yap.cat.nyu.edu

YIVO www.yivoinstitute.org

Zemerl, a database of Jewish songs www.princeton.edu:80/zemerl

Archives

There are two centers for Yiddish in the United States. YIVO, in New York City, is a library and research institution that is open to the general public. It sponsors exhibits, classes, and lectures.

YIVO
15 West 16th Street
New York, NY 10011-6301
(212) 246-6080

The National Yiddish Book Center, in Amherst, Massachusetts, is primarily a book depository and clearinghouse. It also includes a permanent exhibit, as well as rotating exhibitions, lectures, and activities. There is a gift and book shop.

National Yiddish Book Center
1021 West Street
Amherst, MA 01002-3375
(413) 256-4900

Books

I have included an extremely long list of some of the books that I have consulted. If you just want to dip into a couple, depending on your interests, I would suggest the following:

The Shtetl Book, compiled by Diane K. Roskies and David Roskies, is a wonderful compendium of various aspects of shtetl life. The most memorable and humbling book I encountered was *There Once Was a World,* by Yaffa Eliach. This is a labor of scholarship, devotion, and love by a Holocaust survivor whose town exists now only in the pages of this book, as well as in an exhibit at the Holocaust Museum in Washington, D.C.

Covering that same period, Lucy Dawidowicz's *From That Place and Time* gives a fascinating personal account of a year in Vilna. Zvi Gitelman's *A Century of Ambivalence* offers an excellent overview of the last century of Russian-Jewish relations. *A Survivors' Haggadah,* edited by Saul Touster, is a touching book with strong illustrations.

Anyone interested in the American experience should read *World of Our Fathers,* by Irving Howe. Eleanor Mlotek and Joseph Mlotek have compiled three enjoyable books of Yiddish songs with English translation. The first is called *Mir trogen a gezang!*

If you want to learn a bit of *mame loshn, The Complete Idiot's Guide to Learning Yiddish* by Benjamin Blech is very user-friendly. And you can never go wrong by reading Isaac Bashevis Singer.

Aaron, Frieda W. *Bearing the Unbearable.* Albany: State University of New York Press, 1990.

Actions Committee of the Zionist Organization. *The Struggle for the Hebrew Language in Palestine.* New York: ACZO, 1914.

Aleichem, Sholom. *Favorite Tales of Sholom Aleichem.* Trans. Julius Butwin and Frances Butwin. New York: Crown, 1983.

———. *From the Fair.* Trans. Curt Leviant. New York: Viking Books, 1985.

———. *Stories and Satires.* Trans. Curt Leviant. New York: Yoseloff, 1959.

————. *Tevye the Dairyman and The Railroad Stories.* New York: Schocken Books, 1987.

Alter, Robert. *Hebrew and Modernity.* Bloomington: University of Indiana Press, 1994.

Ansky, S. *The Dybbuk.* New York: Schocken Books, 1992.

Antler, Joyce. *The Journey Home.* New York: Free Press, 1997.

————. *Talking Back.* Hanover, N.H.: Brandeis University Press, University Press of New England, 1998.

Bar-Adon, Aaron. *The Rise and Decline of a Dialect.* The Hague: Mouton, 1975.

Baron, Salo W. *The Russian Jew Under Tsars and Soviets.* New York: Macmillan, 1964.

Belcomve-Shaun, Janet. *New World Hasidim.* Albany: State University of New York Press, 1995.

Ben-Avi, Itamar. *Avi* (My Father). Jerusalem: Ben-Yehuda Press, 1927.

Ben Yehuda, Eliezer. *A Dream Come True.* Boulder, Colo.: Westview Press, 1993.

Blech, Benjamin. *The Complete Idiot's Guide to Learning Yiddish.* Indianapolis, Ind.: Alpha Books, 2000.

Brenner, Michael. *After the Holocaust.* Princeton, N.J.: Princeton University Press, 1997.

Cahan, Abraham. *The Rise of David Levinsky.* New York: Harper and Brothers, 1917.

Cala, Alin. *The Image of the Jew in Polish Folk Culture.* Jerusalem: Magnes Press, Hebrew University, 1995.

Cantor, Norman. *The Sacred Chain.* New York: HarperCollins, 1994.

Chazan, Robert. *Medieval Jewish Life.* New York: Ktav, 1976.

Chomsky, William. *Hebrew: The Eternal Language.* Philadelphia: Jewish Publication Society of America, 1969.

Cohn, Michael. *Jewish Bridges: East to West.* Westport, Conn.: Praeger Press, 1996.

Dawidowicz, Lucy. *From That Place and Time.* New York: Norton, 1989.

————. *The Golden Tradition.* Northvale, N.J.: Aronson, 1989.

————. *The Jewish Presence.* New York: Holt, Rinehart, and Winston, 1960.

Deutscher, Isaac. *The Non-Jewish Jew.* Oxford: Oxford University Press, 1968.

————. *The Prophet Armed: Trotsky, 1879–1921.* Oxford: Oxford University Press, 1954.

Dobroszycki, Lucjan, and Barbara Kirshenblatt-Gimblett. *Image Before My Eyes.* New York: Schocken Books, 1977.

Eisenberg, Robert. *Boychiks in the Hood.* San Francisco: Harper-SanFrancisco, 1995.

Eliach, Yaffa. *There Once Was a World.* Boston: Little, Brown, 1998.

Estraikh, Gennady. *Soviet Yiddish.* Oxford: Oxford University Press, 1999.

Faitelson, Aleks. *Heroism and Bravery in Lithuania, 1941–1945.* Trans. Ethel Broido. New York: Gefen Books, 1996.

Falk, Avner. *Herzl, King of the Jews.* Lanham, Md.: University Press of America, 1993.

Fellman, Jack. *The Revival of a Classical Tongue.* The Hague: Mouton, 1973.

Feinsilver, Lillian Mermin. *The Taste of Yiddish.* South Brunswick, N.J.: Yoseloff, 1970.

Fishman, David E. *Embers Plucked from the Fire.* New York: YIVO, 1996.

Fishman, Joshua A. *Ideology, Society, and Language: The Odyssey of Nathan Birnbaum.* Ann Arbor, Mich.: Karoma, 1987.

————. *Never Say Die!* The Hague: Mouton, 1981.

————. *Reversing Language Shift.* Bristol, Pa.: Multilingual Matters, 1991.

————. *Yiddish in America.* Bloomington: Indiana University Press, 1965.

————. *Yiddish: Turning to Life.* Philadelphia: Benjamins, 1991.

Flam, Gila. *Singing for Survival.* Urbana: University of Illinois Press, 1992.

Forman, Frieda, et al. *Found Treasures.* Toronto: Second Story Press, 1994.

Frieden, Ken. *Classic Yiddish Fiction.* Albany: State University of New York Press, 1955.

Gabler, Neal. *An Empire of Their Own.* New York: Crown, 1988.

Geipel, John. *Mame loshn: The Making of Yiddish.* London: Journeyman Press, 1982.

Gilboa, Yehoshua. *The Black Years of Soviet Jewry.* Boston: Little, Brown, 1971.

Gitelman, Zvi. *A Century of Ambivalence: The Jews of Russia and the Soviet Union.* New York: Schocken Books, 1988.

Gittleman, Sol. *From Shtetl to Suburbia.* Boston: Beacon Press, 1978.

————. *Sholom Aleichem.* The Hague: Mouton, 1974.

Glinert, Lewis. *Hebrew in Ashkenaz.* Oxford: Oxford University Press, 1993.

Gluckel of Hameln. *Memoirs of Gluckel of Hameln.* Trans. Marvin Lowenthal. New York: Schocken Books, 1977.

Goldsmith, Emanuel S. *Architects of Yiddishism at the Beginning of the Twentieth Century.* Rutherford, N.J.: Fairleigh Dickinson University Press, 1976.

————. *Modern Yiddish Culture: The Story of the Yiddish Language Movement.* New York: Fordham University Press, 1997.

Gosudartvennyi Muzei Ethnografii Narodov SSSR. *Tracing An-sky: Jewish Collections from the State Ethnographic Museum in St. Petersburg.* Zwolle: Waaders; St. Petersburg: State Ethnografic Museum; Amsterdam: Joods Historisch Museum, 1992.

Greenspoon, Leonard Jay, ed. *Yiddish Language and Culture Then and Now.* Omaha, Neb.: Creighton University Press, 1998.

Gutman, Yisrael, et al. *The Jews of Poland Between Two World Wars.* Hanover, N.H.: University Press of New England, 1989.

Harduf, David Mendel, and Eleanor Harduf. *Harduf's Transliterated English-Yiddish Yiddish-English Dictionary.* Brookline, Mass.: Israel Book Shop, 1997.

Harshav, Benjamin. *Language in Time of Revolution.* Berkeley and Los Angeles: University of California Press, 1993.

————. *The Meaning of Yiddish.* Berkeley and Los Angeles: University of California Press, 1990.

Heinze, Andrew R. *Adapting to Abundance.* New York: Columbia University Press, 1990.

Heller, Celia S. *On the Edge of Destruction.* New York: Columbia University Press, 1977.

Henry, Sondra, and Emily Taitz. *Written Out of History.* New York: Biblio Press, 1990.

Hoffman, Eva. *Shtetl: The Life and Death of a Small Town and the World of Polish Jews.* Boston: Houghton Mifflin, 1997.

Howe, Irving, with the assistance of Kenneth Libo. *World of Our Fathers.* New York: Harcourt Brace, 1976.

Howe, Irving, and Eliezer Greenberg. *Ashes Out of Hope: Fiction by Soviet-Yiddish Writers.* New York: Schocken Books, 1977.

————. *A Treasury of Yiddish Poetry.* New York: Holt, Reinhart, and Winston, 1969.

————. *A Treasury of Yiddish Stories.* New York: Meridian Books, 1958.

————. *Voices from the Yiddish.* Ann Arbor: University of Michigan Press, 1972.

Howe, Irving, Ruth R. Wisse, and Khone Shmeruk. *The Penguin Book of Modern Yiddish Verse.* New York: Viking Penguin, 1987.

Johnson, Paul. *A History of the Jews.* New York: HarperPerennial, 1987.

Joselit, Jenna Weissman. *The Wonders of America: Reinventing Jewish Culture, 1880–1950.* New York: Hill and Wang, 1994.

Kahn, Yitzhak. *Portraits of Yiddish Writers.* New York: Vantage Press, 1979.

Kerler, Dov-Ber. *The Politics of Yiddish.* Walnut Creek, Calif.: Altamira Press, 1998.

Korey, William. *The Soviet Cage: Anti-Semitism in Russia.* New York: Viking Press, 1973.

Kramer, Aaron, editor and translator. *A Century of Yiddish Poetry.* New York: Cornwall Books, 1989.

Kugelmass, Jack, and Jonathan Boyarin. *From a Ruined Garden.* New York: Schocken Books, 1983. (A newer, enlarged edition now exists.)

Kumove, Shirley. *Words Like Arrows: A Collection of Yiddish Folk Sayings.* New York: Schocken Books, 1985.

Kurlansky, Mark. *A Chosen Few: The Resurrection of European Jewry.* Reading, Mass.: Addison-Wesley, 1995.

Landau, David. *Piety and Power: The World of Jewish Fundamentalism.* New York: Hill and Wang, 1993.

Laqueur, Walter. *A History of Zionism.* New York: Schocken Books, 1989.

Leftwich, Joseph. *Abraham Sutzkever: Partisan Poet.* New York: Yoseloff, 1971.

———. *The Golden Peacock.* Cambridge, Mass.: Sci-Art, 1939.

Lelchuk, Alan. *Brooklyn Boy.* New York: McGraw-Hill, 1990.

Levi, Primo. *The Drowned and the Saved.* Trans. Raymond Rosenthal. New York: Summit Books, 1986.

———. *Survival in Auschwitz.* Trans. Stuart Woolf. New York: Summit Books, 1958.

Levin, Dov. *Fighting Back: Lithuanian Jewry's Armed Resistance to the Nazis, 1941–1945.* New York: Holmes and Meier, 1985.

Marcus, Jacob. *The Jew in the Medieval World.* Reprint. New York: Meridian Books, 1960.

Markish, Esther. *The Long Return.* New York: Random House, 1978.

Marovitz, Sanford E. *Abraham Cahan.* New York: Twayne, 1996.

Marshall, David. *Language Planning.* Philadelphia: Benjamins, 1991.

Matisoff, James. *Blessings, Curses, Hopes, and Fears: Psycho-ostensive Expressions in Yiddish.* Philadelphia: Institute for the Study of Human Issues, 1979.

Meir, Golda. *My Life.* New York: Putnam, 1975.

Metzger, Therese. *Jewish Life in the Middle Ages.* New York: Alpine Fine Arts Collection, 1982.

Miron, Dan. *A Traveller Disguised: A Study in the Rise of Modern Yiddish Fiction in the Nineteenth Century.* New York: Schocken Books, 1973.

Mlotek, Eleanor Gorden. *Mir trogen a gezang!* New York: Workmen's Circle, 1987.

Mlotek, Eleanor Gordon, and Joseph Mlotek. *Pearls of Yiddish Song.* New York: Workmen's Circle, 1988.

Muller, Filip. *Auschwitz Inferno: The Testimony of a Sonderkommando.* London: Routledge and Kegan Paul, 1979.

Nedava, Joseph. *Trotsky and the Jews.* Philadelphia: Jewish Publication Society of America, 1972.

Nettle, Daniel, and Suzanne Romaine. *Vanishing Voices.* Oxford: Oxford University Press, 2000.

Nevo, David, and Mira Berger. *We Remember.* New York: Shengold, 1994.

Omer, Dvorah. *Rebirth: The Story of Eliezar Ben Yehuda and the Hebrew Language.* Trans. Ruth Rasnic. Philadelphia: Jewish Publication Society of America, 1972.

Oring, Elliott. *Israeli Humor.* Albany: State University of New York Press, 1981.

Ozick, Cynthia. *A Cynthia Ozick Reader.* Bloomington: Indiana University Press, 1996.

Passow, David. *The Prime of Yiddish.* Jerusalem: Gefen, 1996.

Pat, Jacob. *Ashes and Fire.* Trans. Leo Steinberg. New York: International Universities Press, 1947.

Pawel, Ernst. *The Nightmare of Reason: A Life of Franz Kafka.* New York: Farrar, Straus, and Giroux, 1984.

Payne, Robert. *Life and Death of Trotsky.* New York: McGraw-Hill, 1977.

Peltz, Rakhmiel. *From Immigrant to Ethnic Culture.* Stanford, Calif.: Stanford University Press, 1998.

Peretz, I. L. *Selected Stories.* New York: Schocken Books, 1973.

Pinker, Steven. *The Language Instinct.* New York: Harper, 1994.

Pogonowski, Iwo Cyprian. *Jews in Poland: A Documentary History.* New York: Hippocrene Books, 1993.

Rabinowitz, Dorothy. *New Lives: Survivors of the Holocaust Living in America.* New York: Knopf, 1977.

Rapoport, Louis. *Stalin's War Against the Jews.* New York: Free Press, 1990.

Rich, Jacob C. *The Jewish Daily Forward: An Achievement of Dedicated Idealists: The Extraordinary Story of a Unique Newspaper and Its Publisher, the Forward Association.* New York: Knight, 1967.

Ringelblum, Emanuel. *Notes from the Warsaw Ghetto.* Edited and translated by Jacob Sloan. New York: McGraw-Hill, 1958.

Roskies, David. *Against the Apocalypse: Responses to Catastrophe in Modern Jewish Culture.* Cambridge, Mass.: Harvard University Press, 1984.

———. *The Jewish Search for a Usable Past.* Bloomington: Indiana University Press, 1999.

Roskies, Diane K., and David G. Roskies, comps. *The Shtetl Book.* New York: Ktav, 1975.

Rosten, Leo. *The Joys of Yiddish.* New York: McGraw-Hill, 1968.

Rubin, Barry. *Assimilation and Its Discontents.* New York: Random House, 1995.

Rubenstein, Joshua. *Tangled Loyalties.* New York: Basic Books, 1996.

St. John, Robert. *Tongue of the Prophets.* Garden City, N.Y.: Doubleday, 1952.

Salisbury, Harrison. *American in Russia.* New York: Harper, 1955.

Samuel, Maurice. *Harvest in the Desert.* Philadelphia: Jewish Publication Society of America, 1948.

———. *In Praise of Yiddish.* New York: Cowles, 1971.

Sanders, Ronald. *The Downtown Jews.* New York: Harper and Row, 1969.

Sapoznik, Henry. *The Compleat Klezmer.* Cedarhurst, N.Y.: Tara, 1987.

Schwartz, Howard and Anthony Rudolf. *Voices Within the Ark: The Modern Jewish Poets*. New York: Avon Books, 1980.

Shepherd, Naomi. *A Price Below Rubies*. Cambridge, Mass.: Harvard University Press, 1993.

Shereshevsky, Esra. *Rashi: The Man and His World*. New York: Sepher-Hermon Press, 1982.

Sinclair, Clive. *The Brothers Singer*. London: Allison and Busby, 1983.

Singer, Isaac Bashevis. *In My Father's Court*. Trans. Channah Kleinerman-Goldstein, Elaine Gottlieb, and Joseph Singer. New York: Farrar, Straus, and Giroux, 1966.

———. *Lost in America*. Garden City, N.Y.: Doubleday, 1981.

———. *Nobel Lecture*. New York: Farrar, Straus, and Giroux, 1979.

Singer, Isaac Bashevis, and Richard Burgin. *Conversations with Isaac Bashevis Singer*. Garden City, N.Y.: Doubleday, 1985.

Singer, Israel Joshua. *Of a World That Is No More*. Trans. Joseph Singer. New York: Vanguard Press, 1970.

Spiegel, Shalom. *Hebrew Reborn*. Cleveland: World, 1962.

Steinlauf, Michael. *Bondage to the Dead*. Syracuse, N.Y.: Syracuse University Press, 1977.

Steinmetz, Sol. *Yiddish and English: A Century of Yiddish in America*. University, Ala.: University of Alabama Press, 1986.

Sutzkever, Aaron. *A. Sutzkever*. Trans. Barbara Harshav and Benjamin Harshav. Berkeley and Los Angeles: University of California Press, 1991.

Telushkin, Dvorah. *A Master of Dreams*. New York: Morrow, 1997.

Tigay, Alan, ed. *The Jewish Traveler*. Northvale, N.J.: Aronson, 1994.

Touster, Saul. *A Survivors' Haggadah*. New York: American Jewish Historical Society, 1998.

Troen, S. Ilan, ed. *Jewish Centers and Peripheries*. New Brunswick, N.J.: Transaction, 1999.

Waife-Goldberg, Marie. *My Father, Sholom Aleichem.* New York: Simon and Schuster, 1968.

Wasserstein, Bernard. *Vanishing Diaspora.* Cambridge, Mass.: Harvard University Press, 1996.

Webber, Jonathan, ed. *Jewish Identities in the New Europe.* London: Oxford Centre for Postgraduate Hebrew Studies; Washington, D.C.: Littman Library of Jewish Civilization, 1994.

Weinberg, Robert. *Stalin's Forgotten Zion.* Berkeley and Los Angeles: University of California Press, 1998.

Weinreich, Max. *History of the Yiddish Language.* Trans. Shlomo Noble with the assistance of Joshua A. Fishman. Chicago: University of Chicago Press/YIVO Institute for Jewish Research, 1980.

Weinreich, Uriel. *Modern English-Yiddish Yiddish-English Dictionary.* New York: McGraw-Hill, 1968.

Weizmann, Chaim. *Trial and Error.* New York: Harper/East and West Library, 1950.

Yarmolinsky, Avrahm. *The Jews and Other Minor Nationalities Under the Soviets.* New York: Vanguard Press, 1928.

Zborowski, Mark, and Elizabeth Herzog. *Life Is with People: The Culture of the Shtetl.* New York: Schocken Books, 1952.

Zilberman, Shimon. *The Compact Up-to-Date English-Hebrew Dictionary.* Jerusalem: Zilberman, 1997.

Zucker, Sheva. *Yiddish: An Introduction to the Language, Literature, and Culture.* New York: Workmen's Circle, 1994.

Acknowledgments

A major thank-you to my writing mafia: to Sally Brady, agent extraordinaire, and Betsy Seifter, great writer, editor, and friend; and to my two writing groups: Jeanne Guillemin, Karen McQuillan, and Patricia Welbourn; and Angela Geist, Dan Jacobs, Glenn Morrow, Sherry Nadworny, and Mike Scott.

It has really been a pleasure to work with the folks at Steerforth. All the way through, they have cared about the project and worked to ensure its success. My editor, Alan Lelchuk, and publisher, Chip Fleisher, have been extraordinary. I must also thank Kristin Camp, Stephanie Carter, Robin Dutcher, and Helga Schmidt for all their ideas and hard work.

For Yiddish guidance, special thanks to Rabbi Myron Geller, who helped particularly with jokes and proverbs, and who has always been a ready source with a staggering breadth of knowledge. Aaron Lansky was encouraging and generous at an early stage when this must have seemed like a project with slim chance of success; likewise Dr. Mordkhe Schaechter. The Mendele network has been a worldwide safety net.

Although I could conceivably have written this book without YIVO, I would hate to think about how much more difficult it would have been. YIVO staff who helped include the late Dina Abramowicz, Aviva Astrinsky, Erica Blankstein, Nikolai Borodulin, Paul Glasser, Abraham J. Heschel, Batya Kaplan, Herbert Lazarus, Yeshaya Metal, and Yankl Salant.

Addition thank-yous go to Sidney Belman, Arthur Z. Berg, Irwin Block, Evy Blum, David Braun, Camp Kinderland, Charles Cutter, Joshua Fishman, Ronnie Freidland, Lewis Glinert, Barry Goldstein, Susannah Greenberg, Marjorie Schonhaut Hirshan, Miriam Isaacs, Janos Kobanyai, Fishl Kutner, Curt Leviant, Stephen C. Levinson, Eric Menoyo, Deborah Dash Moore, Bogna Pawlisz, Rakhmiel Peltz, Harriet Reisen, Robert Rothstein, Joshua Rubenstein, Boris Sandler, Betty Silberman, Jessica Singer, Anna

Smulowitz, Mark Southern, Kobi Weitzner, Selma Williams, Gershon Winer, and Seth I. Wolitz. Thanks also to Mimi Krant and Sharon Pucker Rivo at the National Center for Jewish Film, and to the Yiddish group at the Woodbridge Assisted Living Community.

A big thank-you to my grown-up kids, Mirka Feinstein and Eli Feinstein. And the biggest thank-you of all to my husband, Peter Feinstein.

Index

Numbers in italics indicate figures

Josh Reynolds

About the Author

MIRIAM WEINSTEIN grew up in the Bronx following World War II, a time and place where Yiddish
was standard fare. Once a documentary film-
maker, she is now a freelance journalist whose fea-
tures have won several awards from the New
England Press Association. She lives in Manchester, Massachusetts, with her husband, and has
two grown children. This is her first book.

Printed in the United States
by Baker & Taylor Publisher Services